Rowan Bishop's Vegetarian Kitchen

Text © Rowan Bishop, 2011
Typographical design © David Bateman Ltd, 2011
Illustrations © Mark Taylor, 2011

First published in 2011 by David Bateman Ltd,
30 Tarndale Grove, Albany, Auckland, New Zealand

www.batemanpublishing.co.nz

ISBN 978-1-86953-794-4

This book is copyright. Except for the purpose of fair review, no part may be stored or transmitted in any form or by any means, electronic or mechanical, including recording or storage in any information retrieval systems, without permission in writing from the publisher. No reproduction may be made, whether by photocopying or by any other means, unless a licence has been obtained from the publisher or its agent.

Book design: Alice Bell
Printed in China by Everbest Printing Co. Ltd

Rowan Bishop's Vegetarian Kitchen

author of the New Zealand classic
The Vegetarian Adventure Cook Book

David Bateman

To Russell and everyone else in my wonderful family for their unconditional support, optimism and endurance.

ACKNOWLEDGEMENTS
To Mark Taylor for the fabulous illustrations, hard work, patience and insights.

To friends and family who contributed with advice, recipe testing and taste trials, my heartfelt thanks.

To Fairfax Media, and especially *Waikato Times*, for permission to use previously published recipes. Also thanks to ABA Books.

contents

introduction	6
starters	7
soups, sauces & dressings	28
mains	51
salads/sides	94
sweets	120
baking	144
preserves	158
glossary	181
index	186

introduction

Working with and writing about food for so many years has been a fascination that has never diminished and I'm always drawn back. It's been a journey of learning, but like most such journeys, the essence of it can be pared back to just three primary observations:

The quality of the food we eat is our best health insurance;
Taking pleasure from what we eat is fundamental to a balanced life;
Learning to cook well is intensely satisfying on a host of complex levels.

Like many New Zealanders of my generation, I grew up on a farm. Among the important lessons I took from the example of my grandparents and parents was that food should never be taken for granted. As a consequence I've always grown what I can, and to the amusement of all who know me, am always on the lookout for anything in the wild that can remotely be regarded as edible. I also learnt that if the land is looked after, it reciprocates in the quality and quantity of what it produces. I learned how to preserve any abundance to provide variety and nutritive value throughout the year, how to 'stretch' a meal to cater for the many visitors our family were delighted to see, and how important the sharing of, or gift of, food is.

In those days meat was a focal point of our table. It wasn't until I travelled as a young adult that I was introduced to a whole new perspective on food, and developed a curiosity about other cuisines. I embraced the use of herbs, spices and condiments I'd never seen or heard of before and quickly came to understand that an emphasis on meat wasn't a prerequisite for either health or enjoyment. In addition, flavour didn't have to come from fats and sugars; using fresh herbs and spices and reducing cooking times, especially in the case of vegetables, was both a revelation and a joy.

Meat gradually became less and less relevant to our meals, coinciding with the financially challenging years of feeding a family of four children. We grew what we could, and I spent months each year bottling fruit and pickles, making sauces, chutneys and relishes. The satisfaction of producing great tasting, innovative meals from our limited resources was heady stuff, and cooking provided a creative outlet for me.

I began writing food columns, along with other freelance work, and produced a first vegetarian cookbook, *The Vegetarian Adventure*, with friend Sue Carruthers. This was at a time when vegetarian food was denounced as 'fanatical' and 'fringe', as opposed to the popularity and acceptance it enjoys today. Of course, now there is a much wider range of products, condiments and produce to choose from, and the popularity of farmers' markets and promotion of fresh, local and increasingly organic produce is really heartening to see.

Eating vegetarian has always been a preference rather than a moral or philosophical stance for me. It makes sense in terms of good health, looking after our environment, and sharing the world's resources as well as promoting a love of great tasting food.

Enjoy the recipes in this book and I wish you the best of health and good eating.

Rowan Bishop

starters

Warm spinach & artichoke dip 8
Avocado hummus & jalapeno dip 9
Tomatillo salsa/dip 10
Melitzanosalata: Greek eggplant dip 11
Last-minute tomato salsa/dip 12
Mint & almond pesto 12
Black bean salsa/dip 13
Olive & prune tapenade 14
Coriander, mint & cashew pesto 14
Beetroot & fennel pesto 15
White bean pâté with smoked paprika & garlic topping 16
Rocket pesto 17
Roast pepitas 18
Cheese & olive sticks 19
Rice paper salad rolls with satay dipping sauce 20
Cocktail mushrooms 21
Green pea guacamole 22
Party muffins 22
Feta & rosemary baked figs 23
Herbed haloumi 23
Labna 24
Roast capsicum & tomato dip 25
Real peanut butter 26
Fresh beetroot relish 27

Warm spinach & artichoke dip

This is an appetiser to win hearts — delicious, elegant (in a hearty kind of way) and really versatile. Served hot, it is a talking point and always finds favour. Irresistible!

■ **Not recommended for freezing.**

200 g fresh spinach or 100 g frozen spinach
1 cup marinated artichoke hearts, drained and diced
1 red chilli, seeded and minced
1 spring onion, finely chopped
½ cup sour cream
125 g cream cheese
½ cup grated mozzarella
½ cup grated tasty Cheddar
½ tsp salt or to taste
freshly ground black pepper
4 Tbsp finely grated Parmesan for topping (optional)
finely chopped parsley

Wash then wilt the spinach (blanch or microwave), refresh immediately under cold water and squeeze dry. If using frozen spinach, defrost and squeeze dry.
Chop the spinach finely and set aside with the prepared artichokes, chilli and spring onion.
Place the sour cream, cream cheese, mozzarella and Cheddar in a food processor and blend until smooth. Transfer to a bowl, stir in the prepared spinach, artichokes, chilli, spring onion, salt and pepper, then spoon into a heat-proof dish.
Refrigerate, covered, until ready to heat.
Preheat the oven to 180°C. Sprinkle Parmesan on top, if using. Bake the dip, uncovered, for 20 minutes until the cheeses are melted; or heat until bubbling, covered, in a microwave (about 3 minutes on high).
Garnish with parsley and serve accompanied by oven-crisped pita triangles, baguette slices, melba toasts, tortilla chips*, cracker biscuits or any combination of these.

*Brush one side of a tortilla with a neutral oil, cut into dipping-sized wedges and bake at 180°C for 5–8 minutes or until lightly coloured and crisped. Cool on a baking rack.

Avocado hummus & jalapeno dip

It's surprising how different this dip tastes from either guacamole or hummus, and how delicious it is in its own right.

Try it as a dip with tortilla or nacho chips, a spread for crostini or wraps, or as an accompaniment with fritters.

■ **Recipe doubles easily. Not suitable for freezing.**

½ cup cooked chickpeas
1 avocado, ripe but firm
1 tsp tahini (sesame paste)
¼–½ tsp jalapeno chilli*
generous ½ tsp salt or to taste
1–2 Tbsp finely chopped fresh mint
3 Tbsp lemon or lime juice
2 Tbsp extra virgin olive oil

Place the chickpeas in a food processor and grind to breadcrumb consistency.
Peel the avocado, remove the stone and chop the flesh roughly. Add to the chickpeas with the remaining ingredients and process until smooth.
Cover with cling wrap and refrigerate until required. Will keep for up to 4 days, but is at its best freshly made as its colour fades.

*Sliced pickled jalapeno chillies work well with this dip — their flavour is great, and they don't discolour the dip as chilli powder does, but use them judiciously as they can be very hot. An alternative is finely chopped fresh green chilli.

Tomatillo salsa/dip

Combined with chilli, fresh coriander, cumin, garlic and lime or lemon, tomatillos make a Mexican salsa so good it could be addictive. Serve with corn chips as a dip, or as a sauce to include in wraps or to serve with almost anything from tacos to frittatas.

Tomatillos are easy to grow, and self-seeding. Unhusked tomatillos can be stored in a paper bag in a refrigerator for up to 2 weeks.

■ **Freeze or bottle the base salsa as detailed below.**

---

1 kg tomatillos
2 onions, peeled and chopped
1 tsp ground cumin
4–5 large cloves garlic, peeled and sliced
1½ tsp salt or to taste
¾ tsp sugar
2–3 red chillies, seeded and finely chopped
1½–2 Tbsp lime juice or lemon juice for each cup of base mixture
¼ cup finely chopped fresh coriander for each cup of base mixture

Remove the husks, and wash the tomatillos in warm water to remove the sticky coating.
If microwaving, stir the onion and whole tomatillos together in a microwave-safe bowl. Cover and microwave on high for 5–6 minutes. Gently stir, then microwave again for another 5 minutes. Drain off half a cup of liquid at this point and discard.
OR
Place the onion and whole tomatillos in a large shallow frying pan with 1 cup of water and simmer, turning constantly over a low heat, until the tomatillos turn ochre in colour and are soft to the touch without actually splitting. Drain most of the water off.
Stir the cumin, garlic, salt and sugar into the cooked tomatillos.
Place tomatillo mixture in a food processor and pulse to chop.
Stir in the red chillies.
At this point the base mixture can either be frozen as is or transferred to a saucepan and brought to simmer point before being bottled in the normal way.
When required, ensure the base mixture is at room temperature. Stir in the lime or lemon juice along with the coriander. Taste and adjust the salt, sugar, chilli, lime/lemon juice to suit.

Melitzanosalata: Greek eggplant dip

Full of flavour, this is a very popular dip/spread. The inclusion of tahini (sesame paste) gives a pleasant nutty taste, but is not strictly necessary.

■ **Not recommended for freezing.**

400–500 g eggplant
oil
2 cloves garlic, peeled
¼ cup plain unsweetened yoghurt
½ tsp ground cumin
juice of 1½ large lemons (4–5 Tbsp)
1 Tbsp tomato paste
2 tsp tahini (sesame paste), optional
1 tsp salt or to taste
2 Tbsp finely chopped fresh coriander or basil (optional)

Preheat the oven to 190°C.
Slice the eggplant into rounds 4 mm thick. Place sufficient oil in a bowl to dip the eggplant slices into, wiping gently on the lip of the bowl to remove excess oil.
Place the prepared eggplant slices on a baking tray in a single layer.
Bake at 190°C for 25 minutes, turning once, or until both sides are golden.
Remove from the oven and allow to cool.
Chop the eggplant coarsely and place in a food processor with the garlic, yoghurt, cumin, lemon juice, tomato paste, tahini and salt.
Purée, then transfer to a serving dish. Stir in the coriander (or basil) if using.
Cover and refrigerate for up to 5 days.

Last-minute tomato salsa/dip

Whip this up in minutes, adding diced avocado flesh with a little extra lime or lemon juice if you wish.

*400 g fresh peeled tomatoes
   or 400-g tin peeled whole tomatoes, drained
2 Tbsp finely chopped fresh coriander
1 Tbsp lime or lemon juice
1 Tbsp finely chopped red onion
1 red chilli, seeded and very finely chopped
1 garlic clove, peeled and finely chopped or crushed
1 tsp ground cumin
ground rock salt to taste
freshly ground black pepper*

Remove cores and seeds from tomatoes and dice the flesh.
Gently combine all ingredients and serve at room temperature accompanied by corn chips.

Mint & almond pesto

An easy to prepare pesto for an appetiser spread, or try it stirred into hot green beans or a mix of cooked and drained French beans with peas. It's also good tossed into hot new potatoes with a squeeze of lemon and extra chopped mint.

■ **May be frozen.**

*¼ cup chopped fresh mint
2 cloves garlic
½ cup tightly packed Italian (flat-leaf) or curly parsley, chopped
½ cup blanched almonds
½ tsp salt or to taste
freshly ground black pepper
⅓ cup extra virgin olive oil*

Put all the ingredients except the oil in a food processor and process until smooth. Then pour the oil through the feed tube with the motor running. Cover and refrigerate until needed. Will keep for 4 to 5 days.

Black bean salsa/dip

Scoop up this salsa with tortilla or nacho chips and enjoy before everyone else finds out how good it is! Stuff it into wraps with falafels, or use as a colourful and full of flavour salsa for just about anything.

Adding diced avocado is a delicious way to extend this salsa — just adjust the seasonings and the lime or lemon juice to accommodate the avocado.

■ **Not suitable to freeze.**

1 cup cooked black turtle beans*
3–4 medium-sized tomatoes
*   or 3–4 tinned whole tomatoes, drained*
1 small spring onion, finely chopped
1 green chilli, seeded and finely chopped
⅛–¼ tsp chilli powder
1 clove garlic, peeled and finely chopped
juice of two limes
*   or 4 Tbsp lemon juice*
¼ cup finely chopped fresh coriander
½ tsp ground cumin
salt to taste

Ensure the cooked black beans are washed and drained.
Seed the tomatoes and dice the flesh into small pieces.
Combine all the ingredients in a serving bowl and stand for 10 minutes. Taste, adding extra salt if needed.

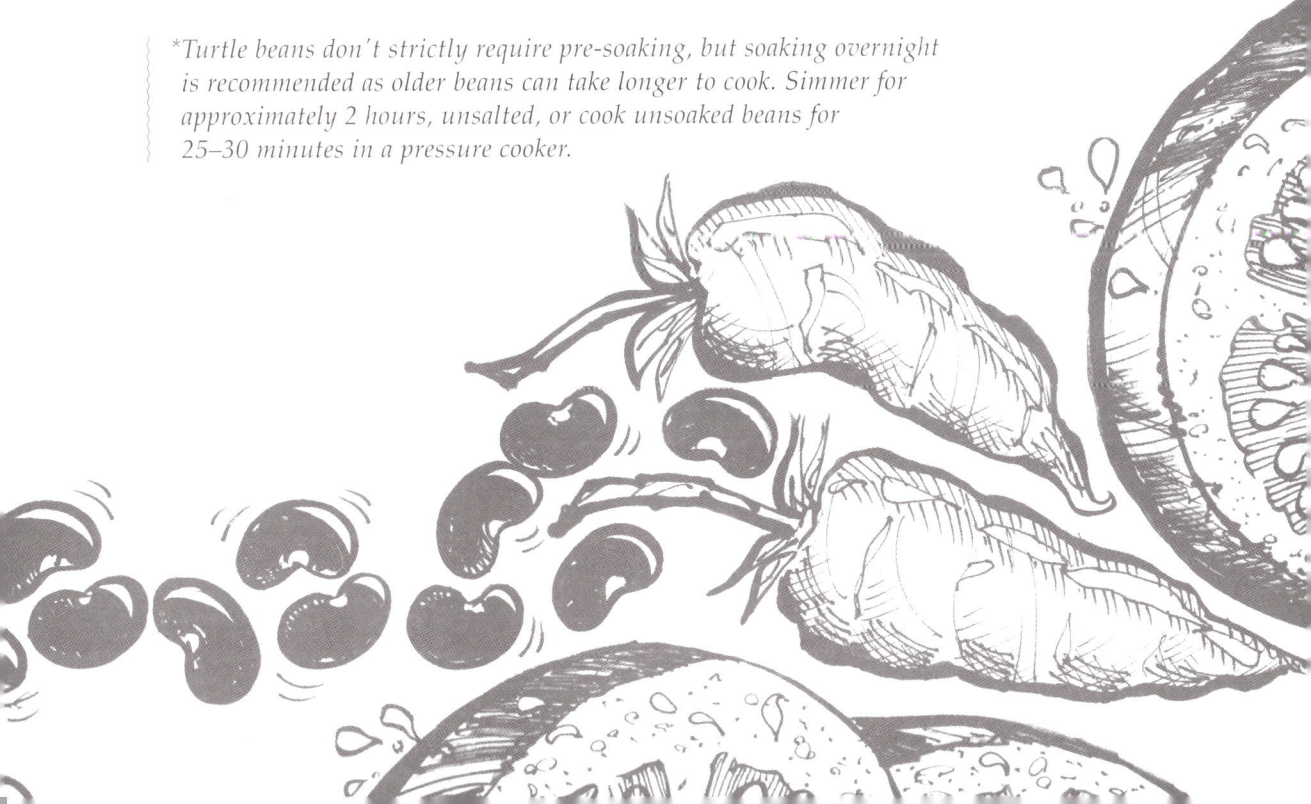

*Turtle beans don't strictly require pre-soaking, but soaking overnight is recommended as older beans can take longer to cook. Simmer for approximately 2 hours, unsalted, or cook unsoaked beans for 25–30 minutes in a pressure cooker.

Olive & prune tapenade

Always useful to have in the refrigerator, this tapenade is a great spread for crostini or bruschetta, or for tossing into pasta with a little extra olive oil.

Prunes combine really well with olives here to create a great combo. Use good quality olives such as Kalamata, rather than the cheaper Spanish olives.

1 cup black olives, pitted
1 clove garlic, peeled
2 Tbsp chopped prunes
1 Tbsp balsamic vinegar
3–4 Tbsp extra virgin olive oil

Place all ingredients in a food processor except 1 tablespoon of the olive oil. Pulse to chop roughly, then decide if the last tablespoon of oil is required in terms of the balance and spreadability.
Cover and refrigerate. Keeps for up to two months.

Coriander, mint & cashew pesto

Coriander pesto is delicious spooned onto crackers as an appetiser, stirred into soups, teamed with fritters, or served as a spread on toast or bread with tomatoes. It's also nice loosened with extra oil and lemon juice for a potato salad dressing.

■ **Recipe doubles easily. May be frozen.**

½ cup roasted, salted cashews or almonds
2 cloves garlic, peeled
⅓ cup finely chopped fresh coriander
¼ cup finely chopped fresh mint
½ cup finely chopped Italian (flat-leaf) parsley
⅓ cup extra virgin olive oil
½ tsp salt or to taste
squeeze of lime or lemon juice

Chop the nuts, garlic, coriander, mint and parsley in a food processor, then add the oil and salt. Process into a purée.
Transfer to a serving bowl, cover and refrigerate until required. Before serving, mix in a squeeze of lemon juice if you wish — it will 'fade' the green of the herbs if added earlier.

Beetroot & fennel pesto

This pesto has that gorgeous beetroot colour and is really popular spooned onto bite-sized crostini (use ficelles for these if you can get them, they're slimmer and bite-sized, as opposed to the larger baguettes). Top with an artfully arranged slice of feta for a great combination.

2 medium-sized beetroot, peeled*
2 cloves garlic
½ tsp fennel seeds
3 Tbsp olive oil
2 Tbsp balsamic vinegar (first measure)
2 Tbsp brown sugar
¼ cup water
½ tsp salt or to taste
freshly ground black pepper
1 Tbsp extra virgin olive oil
1 Tbsp balsamic vinegar (second measure)
3 Tbsp fresh finely chopped fennel leaves or spring onion tops

Preheat the oven to 180°C.
Top and tail the beetroot, peel, then halve each one and slice each half into 6 or 7 segments. Peel the garlic cloves and slice in half lengthwise. Place the prepared beetroot, garlic and fennel seeds on a shallow oven tray and toss in the oil, first measure of balsamic vinegar and sugar to coat lightly. Spread evenly into a single layer. Place in the preheated oven, and roast for approximately 1 hour, tossing regularly. Transfer to a food processor and add the water, salt, pepper, extra virgin olive oil and second measure of balsamic vinegar. Blend to a smooth purée.
Transfer the pesto to a bowl and mix in the prepared fennel leaves or spring onion. Cover and refrigerate until needed. Keeps well for up to 5 days.

*Disposable latex gloves are handy when preparing beetroot because the stain on skin and nails can be quite persistent.

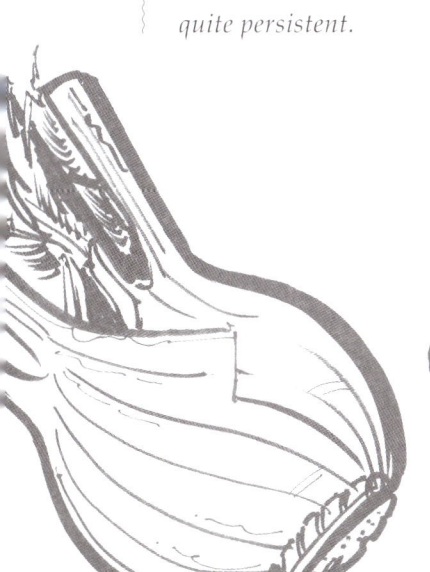

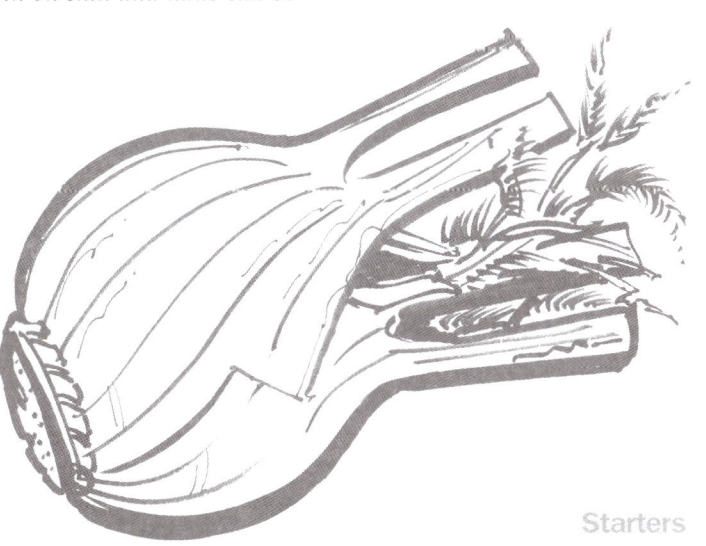

White bean pâté with smoked paprika & garlic topping

It's surprising how popular this simple pâté is, given its humble ingredients. The pâté itself is similar to hummus made with chickpeas, but cannellini beans introduce a softer, sweeter note, allowing the smoky, garlic-infused olive oil topping to provide the perfect complement. Roasting peeled and thinly sliced garlic in olive oil and sweet (dulce) Spanish smoked paprika results in a lovely red, garlicky oil topping.

This pâté is wonderful for scooping onto crackers or spreading in wraps.

Pâté
400-g tin cannellini beans
¼ cup tahini (sesame paste)
juice of 1½ lemons
⅓ cup olive oil
4 cloves garlic, peeled
salt to taste
freshly ground black pepper
4 Tbsp finely chopped Italian (flat-leaf) parsley

Rinse and drain the beans. Place in a food processor with the other ingredients except for the parsley. Process to a purée, taste and adjust lemon and salt to taste.
Stir in the parsley and transfer to two smallish serving bowls or one large.
Distribute the topping evenly over the pâté and serve at room temperature.

Topping
¼ cup olive oil
⅓ tsp sweet (dulce) Spanish smoked paprika
6 cloves garlic, peeled and finely sliced
salt to taste

Preheat the oven to 180°C.
Place the topping ingredients, except the salt, in an ovenproof dish.
Roast, uncovered, at 180°C for 7–10 minutes, or until the garlic is softened and the oil is red/gold.
Add the salt and cool before spooning over the white bean pâté.

Rocket pesto

Stir rocket pesto through cooked spaghetti with a squeeze of lemon juice, some extra finely grated Parmesan and olive oil for a delicious but oh-so-simple dinner (add a hot crusty roll and a salad if you're really hungry).

Alternatively, use as a spread for crostini, a dip for crudités or taco chips, or add to salad dressings.

Rocket pesto is as good as that made from basil, but is even more versatile in that rocket has a much longer growing season, and perennial rocket grows year-round outside.

■ **May be frozen.**

1 cup rocket leaves
1 cup Italian (flat-leaf) parsley
2 large cloves garlic, peeled
4 Tbsp ground or slivered almonds
½ cup freshly grated Parmesan
¾ tsp salt or to taste
½ cup extra virgin olive oil

Pluck the washed rocket and parsley from their stems and measure separately. Pour boiling water over the rocket leaves to cover, especially if using the perennial (wild) rocket or older leaves. Leave for 30 seconds then drain and squeeze dry — blanching will 'fix' the colour as well as smooth any slight bite from the taste. Drain, refresh in cold water, then gently squeeze dry.
Place all the ingredients except the oil in a food processor and process until chopped fine. Pour in the oil slowly through the feed tube.
Transfer to a small bowl and cover with cling wrap.
Refrigerate until needed, or freeze. If not frozen, will keep up to 5 days.

Roast pepitas

Pepitas are the Mexican name for roast pumpkin seeds, a nutritious, popular snack with all ages and a tasty garnish for salads and vegetable dishes. They can be cooked in a frying pan, but a more consistent and manageable result is achieved from oven roasting.

Garlic/chilli pepitas
1 cup pumpkin seeds
1 tsp olive oil
½ tsp garlic salt
½ tsp chilli powder or to taste

Soy sauce pepitas
1 cup pumpkin seeds
1 tsp olive oil
2 tsp soy sauce

Preheat the oven to 190°C.
Combine the pumpkin seeds with the oil and your choice of flavourings above (garlic/chilli or soy sauce).
Line a baking tray with baking paper and spread the pumpkin seeds evenly over the baking tray.
Roast at 190°C for 12–15 minutes, until well browned and popping hot.

Alternatively, if you don't want to use oil:
Roast the pumpkin seeds at 190°C for 12–15 minutes. Remove from the oven and toss in 1 tablespoon soy sauce with no added oil.
Or:
Roast the pumpkin seeds on their own in a dry frying pan over a medium heat until most have 'popped', tossing or stirring continuously. Remove from the heat immediately and toss in 1 tablespoon soy sauce with no added oil.

Transfer the cooked pepitas to a bowl to cool, defending them from all would-be 'grazers' who swing past the kitchen. Store in an airtight jar.

Cheese & olive sticks

These cheese and olive sticks are hard to resist, either just as they are or nibbled at with dips and/or spreads. They're also very welcome as something light but a little different to accompany almost any soup.

1 cup plain flour
½ cup wholemeal flour
125 g cold butter
150 g tasty Cheddar, grated
½ tsp salt or to taste
⅓ tsp chilli powder
½ cup green pimiento-stuffed olives, drained and chopped
6 Tbsp water or milk
1 egg yolk, lightly beaten
freshly ground black pepper

Preheat the oven to 220°C.
Place the flours and butter in a food processor and process until the mixture resembles breadcrumbs. Transfer to a bowl and mix in the cheese, salt, chilli powder and olives.
Mix in the water or milk — a flat-bladed knife is ideal for this. Add another tablespoon of liquid if you think the mixture is too dry — the ideal consistency is when the mixture sticks together when pinched in your fingers. Gather the dough into a ball, wrap in cling wrap and refrigerate for 30 minutes if there is time.
Roll out on a lightly floured bench to 4 mm thick and brush lightly with the beaten egg yolk. Sprinkle lightly with pepper.
Cut into strips 1 cm wide x 8 cm long.
Transfer the sticks to an oven tray lined with baking paper, leaving a narrow space between each.
Bake at 220°C for 10–12 minutes or until lightly golden, but check after 8 minutes. Remove from the oven and leave for a minute or two before transferring to a rack to cool.
Store in an airtight container for up to 3 days.

Rice paper salad rolls with satay dipping sauce

These refreshing appetisers are made with round rice paper sheets. The balance of taste and texture, although simple, is memorable — soft rice 'noodle' pasta enclosing crisp vegetables and dipped in a spiky satay dipping sauce (see recipe on page 47).

■ **Makes 16 bite-sized pieces.**

Salad rolls
8 x 22-cm rice paper rounds
2–2½ cups mesclun salad leaves or finely sliced lettuce
3 Tbsp sweet chilli sauce
½ cup chopped fresh coriander leaves and stalks
3 Tbsp finely chopped fresh Vietnamese or traditional mint
1½ medium-sized red or yellow capsicums, seeded and sliced into thin strips
1½ cups seeded, julienned Lebanese or thin-skinned cucumber
2 spring onions, finely sliced (including the green tops)
½ cup peeled, julienned carrots or daikon or mung bean sprouts

Spread a clean, damp tea towel on your workbench.
Select a dish wide enough for the rice paper sheets to lie in without bending, and half-fill the dish with hot water. As the water cools, replace with more hot water.
Work with four sheets at a time for economy. Lay each sheet in the hot water for 5 seconds only, then place on the damp tea towel to soften further.
Lay 3–4 tablespoons of the mesclun salad leaves in a 3-cm strip along one end of each softened sheet. The fine stalks in the mesclun can be included as they provide some texture.
Sprinkle a generous teaspoon of the sweet chilli sauce over the mesclun, a generous sprinkle of the prepared coriander and mint, then equal portions of the remaining vegetables.
Roll up firmly, folding in the ends as you roll. Place seam-side down on a plate. Repeat the procedure with another four rice paper rounds. Cover with the damp tea towel and refrigerate before bringing to room temperature to serve.
Slice each roll diagonally in half and serve on a platter accompanied by the dipping sauce.

*Prepare all the ingredients on separate plates before you start, then fill and roll in confidence. The cucumber may be replaced with lightly steamed green beans if wished.

Cocktail mushrooms

These 'cocktail' mushrooms are so simple to prepare, and are great for an antipasto platter or nibble selection.

250 g smallish firm button mushrooms
3 Tbsp lemon juice
⅓ cup olive oil
¼ tsp sweet (dulce) Spanish smoked paprika
⅛ tsp chilli powder
¾ tsp salt or to taste
freshly ground black pepper
1 Tbsp kecap manis*
3 Vietnamese mint leaves, finely chopped
  or 2 Tbsp finely chopped traditional mint leaves
3 Tbsp finely chopped Italian (flat-leaf) parsley

Trim and halve the mushrooms, then place in a non-metallic bowl.
Whisk the remaining ingredients together until well combined.
Pour the marinade ingredients over the mushrooms and combine gently but thoroughly.
Marinate 2–2½ hours, turning every hour, or cover and place in a refrigerator for up to 12 hours, turning occasionally.
Bring to room temperature and drain before serving.

*A thick, sweet Indonesian soy sauce.

Green pea guacamole

So simple but so fresh and tasty! Serve as a dip with nacho chips, savoury wafer biscuits, as a crostini topping or as a spread in wraps. Add a little jalapeno pepper or finely chopped fresh coriander if desired.

2 cups frozen peas, thawed
1 avocado, peeled and roughly chopped
3 cloves garlic, peeled
4 Tbsp lime or lemon juice
3 Tbsp olive oil
1 tsp salt or to taste
½ tsp freshly ground black pepper

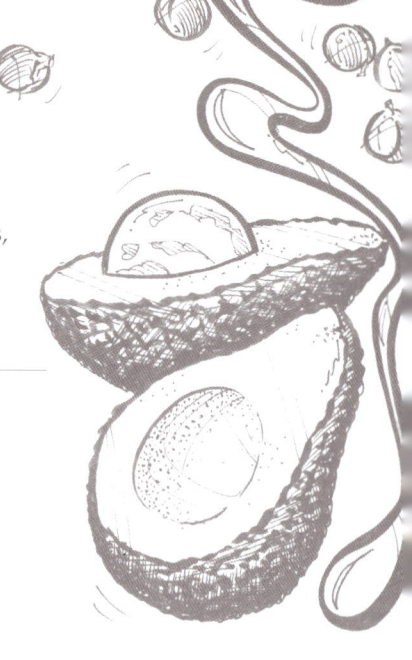

Place all ingredients in a food processor and pulse to roughly purée. Transfer to a serving bowl, cover and refrigerate. Bring to room temperature before serving.

Party muffins

These are the ideal finger food — not messy or likely to drop on the carpet, but very, very tasty. Change the look and taste by varying the vegetables — you can even use grated or thinly sliced cabbage and carrot, pumpkin and kumara. If you don't have feta on hand, increase the tasty grated Cheddar to 1 cup.

■ **Makes 36. Freezes well.**

⅔ cup finely chopped spring onions (or 1 onion, peeled and finely chopped)
425 g zucchini, grated
4 eggs
pinch chilli powder
1 tsp salt or to taste
freshly ground black pepper
1 tsp cumin seeds
1 cup self-raising flour, sifted
90 g feta, grated or crumbled
½ cup grated tasty Cheddar
1 small firm tomato, seeded and diced small (or 3 Tbsp diced red capsicum)

Preheat the oven to 200°C. Lightly grease mini-muffin tins or spray with oil.
Combine the spring onions and zucchini in a medium to large bowl.
Whisk the eggs with the chilli, salt, pepper and cumin seeds and stir into the zucchini mix. Then fold in the flour, cheeses and tomato. Spoon into the mini-muffin tins, filling almost to the rim.
Bake at 200°C for 15 minutes or until golden brown. Transfer to a rack to cool.
Refrigerate (or freeze); when ready to eat, reheat in the oven.

Feta & rosemary baked figs

Fresh figs are so different from dried figs it's difficult to appreciate that they are the same fruit. Each, however, has unique qualities, and these figs baked with feta and rosemary make a simple but impressive appetiser straight from the oven, on crostini or as part of an antipasto platter.

several plump, ripe figs*
2 tsp port or Cointreau per fig
2 x 2-cm pieces mild, creamy feta per fig
freshly ground black pepper
finely chopped fresh rosemary (about ½ tsp per fig, or to taste)

Preheat the oven to 190°C.
Slice the figs in half lengthwise, and make 2–3 slashes on the cut surface of each half with a small, sharp knife. Drizzle 1 teaspoon of the port or Cointreau over each half. Lightly squash a cube of feta into the middle of each half fig.
Grind over some black pepper and sprinkle with ¼–½ teaspoon of the finely chopped rosemary.
Place in a single layer on a baking tray and bake for 10–15 minutes at 190°C or until the figs are heated through and the feta is soft/melted.

*If the figs are large, slice lengthwise into quarters to serve as 'finger food' appetisers, or leave as halves if serving as part of a main course.

Herbed haloumi

Dice the haloumi, then shallow-fry in olive oil with freshly ground black pepper, sea salt and some finely chopped herbs such as basil, thyme or rosemary, or sprinkle it with sumac after it is cooked.
Fry for about 1 minute on each side, until lightly golden. Drain the cooked haloumi on paper towels and try not to eat it all before it gets to the table!
It's a great nibble on its own or combined with halved and pitted black olives, as part of an antipasto (or strewn on almost any salad).

Labna

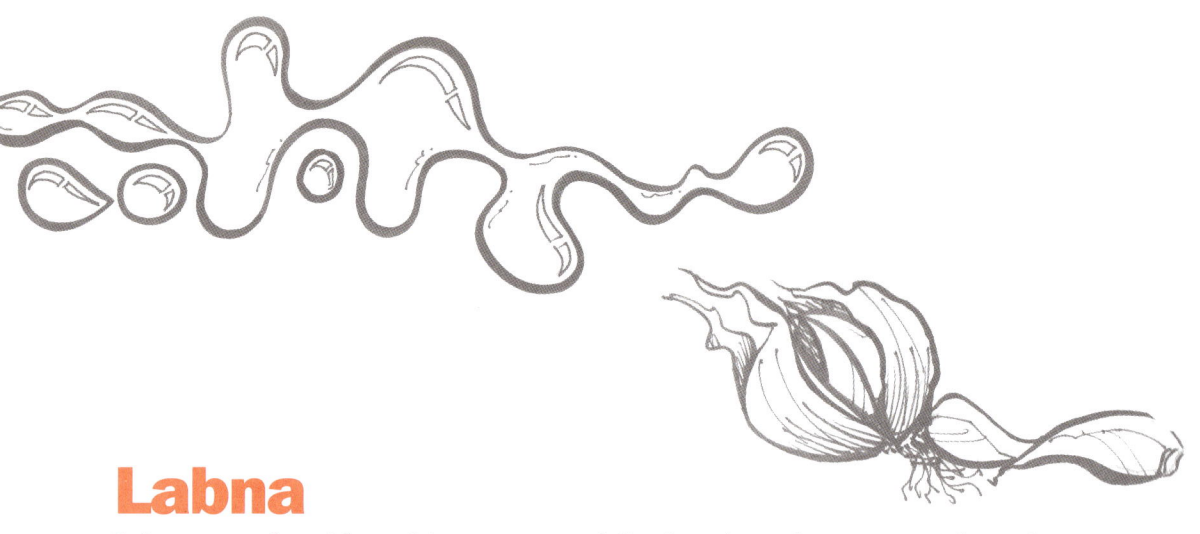

Labna, or yoghurt 'cheese', is unsweetened Greek-style yoghurt strained through muslin for at least 36 hours. It keeps for up to a month rolled into egg-sized balls, covered with extra virgin olive oil and refrigerated. Add dried chillies, bay leaves, peppercorns, coriander seeds or other flavourings to the oil, which can be reused. Or incorporate flavourings into the balls before covering with oil — then spoon out and serve as part of a 'cheese' board.

Spread labna on wraps, pizzas and crackers, or use it as a base for a variety of dips.

Fresh, unflavoured labna that has not been stored in oil can be substituted for cream cheese or sour cream in cheesecakes and smoothies, or rolled into egg-sized balls and served with barbecued fruits, fresh summer berries or fruits, dried fruit compotes or dessert cakes.

Garlic and dill labna is a personal favourite, but other herbs and spices work too. Try finely chopped preserved lime or lemon, for example, with basil or thyme.

Garlic & dill labna

500 g unsweetened Greek-style yoghurt*
¾ tsp flaky or crushed sea salt or to taste
4 cloves garlic, peeled and crushed
¼ cup finely chopped fresh dill leaves
freshly ground black pepper
extra virgin olive oil to cover

Place the yoghurt into a muslin 'bag' and suspend it over a tall jug or bowl (chopsticks pushed through the top of the bag work well to support it as it hangs over the bowl). Refrigerate and leave for at least 36 hours or 2 days. Discard the liquid that drains off. Combine the drained labna with the salt, garlic, dill and pepper and roll into egg-sized balls. Place in a container with a lid and cover with extra virgin olive oil. Keep refrigerated.

*500 g of unsweetened Greek-style yoghurt will produce just a little more than 300 g of labna, or yoghurt cheese.
For a great fast dip, simply use the flavouring quantities above combined with approximately 1 cup of unsweetened Greek-style yoghurt.

Roast capsicum & tomato dip

This fresh, tasty dip is great with tortilla or nacho chips, or served as a side sauce with pies, quiches or tacos. Add a little fresh seeded and finely chopped chilli if you want to spice it up.

■ **Makes about ¾ cup, but doubles easily. May be frozen.**

2 red capsicums
3 tomatoes
2 cloves garlic, peeled
5 sun-dried tomatoes in oil, drained and chopped
¼–½ tsp salt or to taste
freshly ground black pepper
3 Tbsp chopped fresh coriander or basil
3 Tbsp chopped Italian (flat-leaf) parsley

Preheat the oven to 190°C.
Roast the capsicums and tomatoes together at 190°C for about 25 minutes, until the skins are blistered and separating from the flesh.
Peel and discard cores and seeds. Chop the flesh and transfer to a food processor with the garlic, sun-dried tomatoes, salt and pepper. Process to a smooth purée.
Add the coriander (or basil) and parsley and pulse very briefly, just to combine.
Cover and store in the refrigerator for up to 5 days.

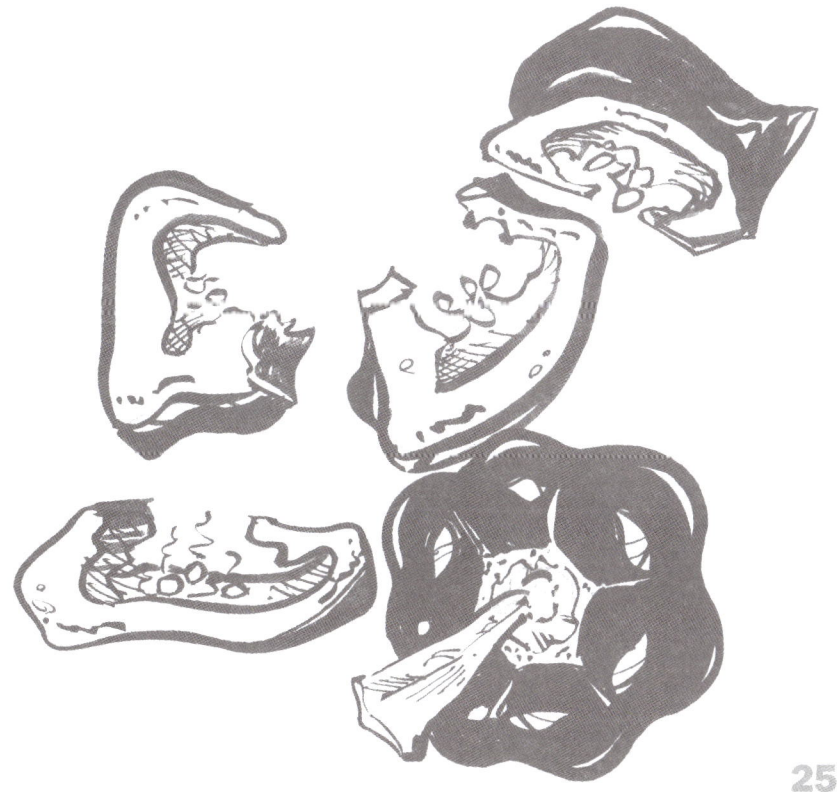

Real peanut butter

Fresh home-made peanut butter is the easiest thing imaginable to make. It tastes fantastic, is not homogenised or emulsified and contains no additives or preservatives. Once you've tried this you'll never buy store-bought again.

Don't use pre-roasted nuts — this peanut butter has a much fresher taste and has extra nutritional content because unblanched (i.e. skin on) nuts are used, and the nuts are roasted longer than usual, resulting in an attractive dark colour and a more intense flavour.

---

500 g raw unblanched peanuts (i.e. skin on)
2 Tbsp olive/peanut oil or rice bran oil
1½ tsp salt or to taste

Preheat the oven 180°C.
Place the peanuts in a roasting pan or ovenproof dish about 30 cm x 30 cm and toss in the oil and salt.
Roast, tossing or turning regularly, for 20–30 minutes, or until the nuts have turned quite a dark brown without scorching. Cool.
Transfer the roasted nuts, including any residual oil and salt, to a food processor and process to a rough texture.
If a crunchy style is required, remove about half a cup of the mixture at this stage and set aside. Continue to process the mixture until it becomes an easily spreadable paste. If not processed sufficiently the mix may appear a little dry — the secret is to process until the nuts release their oil. Stir in the rough-textured mix if crunchy peanut butter is desired, and combine.
Transfer to a sterilised jar with a lid. Keeps indefinitely!

*It's not possible to get this mix
as smooth as commercially made
'smooth' peanut butter.

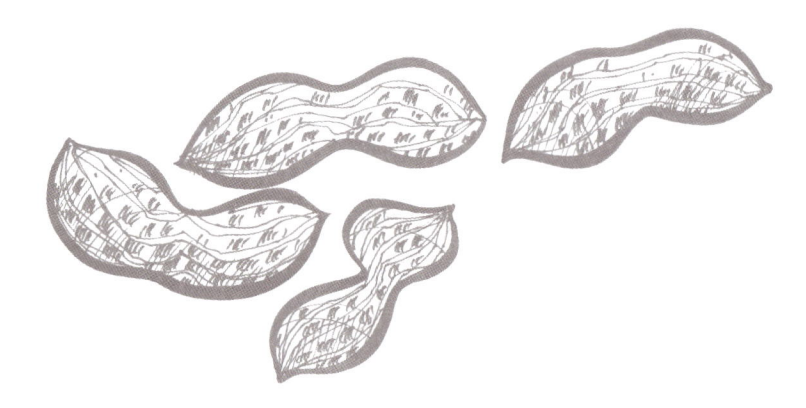

Fresh beetroot relish

This fresh, full-bodied relish partners well with cream cheese on crackers, or can be served alongside pastries.

250 g fresh, trimmed beetroot
3 Tbsp olive oil
1 tsp mustard seeds
1 large red onion, peeled and sliced thinly
3 Tbsp Black Raspberry Vinegar* (page 179)
1 Tbsp brown sugar
½ tsp salt or to taste
freshly ground black pepper (lots)
¼ cup finely chopped fresh mint

Trim (top 'n' tail) the beetroot before weighing. Peel then grate the beetroot into a bowl — you may like to wear latex gloves to prevent staining your hands.
Heat the oil in a medium-sized, heavy-based frying pan and cook the mustard seeds, shaking regularly until they sizzle and start to 'pop'.
Turn the heat down and slowly sauté the onions in the pan, stirring regularly, for about 20 minutes — until very soft and lightly caramelised.
Stir in the grated beetroot, vinegar, sugar and seasoning. Cook on low, stirring regularly, for about 15 minutes. Cover for the last 5 minutes if the liquid is disappearing too fast. The beetroot should be cooked and all the liquid absorbed at this stage.
Cool, then stir in the fresh chopped mint. Cover and refrigerate for up to 5 days.

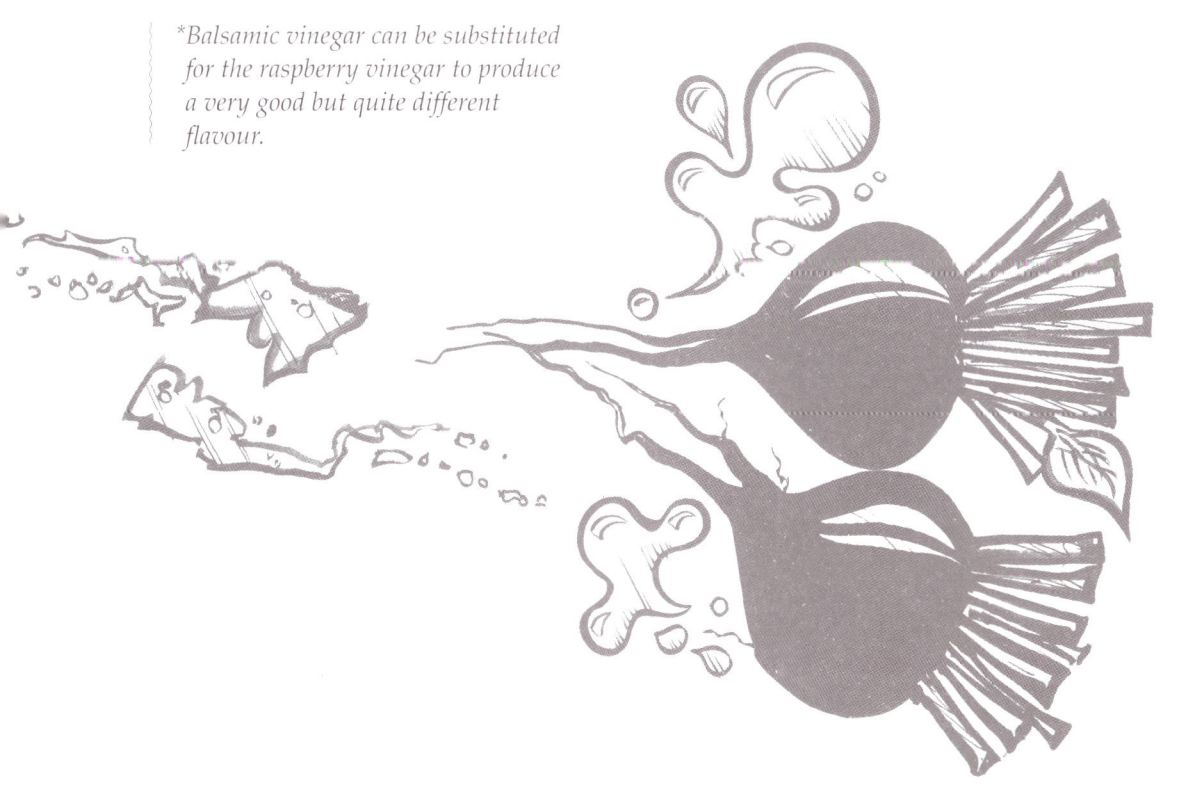

> **Balsamic vinegar can be substituted for the raspberry vinegar to produce a very good but quite different flavour.*

soups, sauces & dressings

Home-made vegetable stock 29
Thai pumpkin soup 29
Mushroom crème soup 30
Moroccan tomato soup with
    Ras el Hanout 31
Leek 'n' lentil soup 32
Mexican chowder 33
Tomato tamarind dhal soup 34
Brazen beetroot soup 35
Spanish black bean soup 36
Borscht with kumara & fennel 37
Pumpkin & chestnut soup 38
Parsnip soup with saffron
    & spice 39
Jerusalem artichoke soup 40
Pumpkin & lentil soup 41
Roast capsicum soup 42
Green sauce 43
Black raspberry vinaigrette 43

Honey cider vinaigrette 44
Aïoli 44
Caramelised balsamic vinegar 45
Summer mayo 45
Herb mayo 46
Chermoula 46
Satay sauce 47
Tamarind mint sambal 48
Tomato pasta sauce 48
Paul's tropical dressing 49
Yoghurt sauce/dressing 49
Roast capsicum & almond
    sauce 50

Home-made vegetable stock

Making your own stock must be one of the most satisfying things a cook can do; it requires very little time, but makes a world of difference to the flavour (not to mention the nutritional content) of dishes, especially soups and sauces.

Use roughly chopped vegetables and well washed peelings, such as carrots, pumpkin and onion, celery (including leaves), parsley stalks, mushroom stalks, potatoes, etc. Broccoli and cauliflower can turn bitter with long cooking, so use other vegetables instead.

Add some bay leaves and fresh thyme if you have some, and some peppercorns.
Barely cover with water and simmer, covered, for one hour.
Cool, strain and refrigerate, covered, for up to 4 days or freeze.

■ **Suitable to freeze.**

Thai pumpkin soup

This tasty soup can be served as a one-dish meal with breads, followed by fruit and cheeses. Lightly spiced with Thai flavours to enhance the natural richness of the pumpkin, this soup is a delicious take on an old favourite.

■ **Serves 4–6.**

1 kg pumpkin (peeled weight)
2 Tbsp oil
1 Tbsp Thai red curry paste
1 tsp finely chopped or minced ginger
2 cups water or stock
2 tsp brown sugar
2 tsp tomato paste
400-ml tin coconut cream or coconut milk
1½ tsp salt or to taste
freshly ground black pepper
¼ cup finely chopped fresh coriander

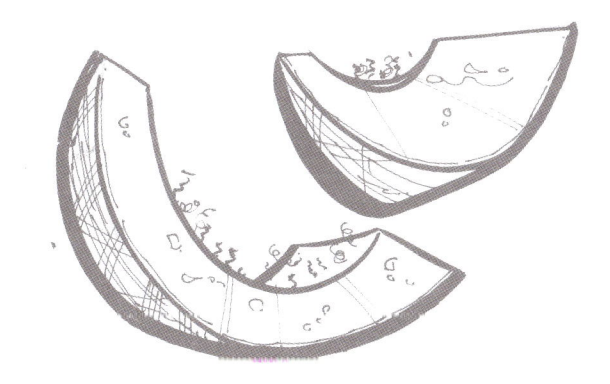

Scoop out the seeds and peel about half a large crown pumpkin and weigh the flesh. Chop into 4-cm chunks.
Heat the oil in a large saucepan, add the curry paste and the ginger and sauté over a low heat until fragrant.
Add the prepared pumpkin, stir briefly, then pour in the water or stock, the brown sugar and the tomato paste. Place a lid on the saucepan and simmer until the pumpkin is soft, about 20 minutes.
Transfer to a food processor and process until smooth. Return the pumpkin mixture to the saucepan. Pour in the coconut cream or milk and season with salt and pepper. Bring back to simmer point, stirring.
Serve in bowls garnished with fresh coriander. A swirl of yoghurt is optional.

Mushroom crème soup

A bowl of creamy mushroom soup is comfort food; a sensual — and sensory — delight to those of us who wax lyrical about such things. This soup is one of those truly delicious creations. The creaminess is largely provided by the inclusion of sweet kumara, with milk and a little cream cheese.

Serve accompanied by breads and cheeses as a main course. As an entrée, serve with crisp toasted bread.

■ **Serves 4–6. Not recommended for freezing.**

Step 1
30 g butter
2 Tbsp oil
1 medium to large onion, peeled and chopped small
2 large cloves garlic, peeled and finely sliced
2 medium-sized kumara, about 370 g
½ cup white wine
2 cups unsalted stock or water
4 bay leaves
2 whole stalks parsley
2 cups milk
¼ cup cream cheese
2 tsp salt or to taste
freshly ground black pepper

Melt the butter and oil in a large, heavy-based saucepan over a low heat.
Sauté the prepared onion and garlic until the onion softens.
Peel the kumara and cut into 1-cm dice. Add to the onion/garlic mixture and sauté about 5 minutes.
Raise the heat and stir in the white wine. Simmer for a few minutes then add the unsalted stock or water and the bay leaves and parsley. Cover, then lower the heat and simmer for 15–20 minutes, until the kumara is cooked.
Discard the parsley stalks and bay leaves. Add the milk, cream cheese and salt and pepper, then purée until very smooth. Transfer back to the original saucepan.

Step 2
50 g butter
3 Tbsp oil
500 g flat (Portobello) mushrooms
1 Tbsp fresh thyme leaves or ¾ tsp dried thyme
grated Parmesan
chopped fresh fennel leaves or parsley

Melt the butter and oil together in a frying pan, over a low–medium heat.
Slice the mushrooms thinly.
Sauté the mushrooms and thyme in the butter/oil mixture gently for 15–20 minutes, until well cooked. Set some mushroom slices aside for garnish.
Purée until very smooth, adding a little of the kumara purée if it's too thick. Transfer the puréed mushrooms to the kumara mixture and combine the two mixtures.
Bring to simmer point (don't let it boil).
Check the seasoning, and serve immediately in heated soup bowls garnished with reserved cooked mushroom slices, Parmesan and fennel or parsley.

Moroccan tomato soup with Ras el Hanout

The inclusion of Ras el Hanout, a traditional Moroccan spice mix (see Glossary, page 184), adds a whole new dimension to tomatoes, and both the spice mix and the soup take only a few minutes to prepare. If you happen to have any roasted red capsicums on hand, they make a delicious addition to this soup, added at the end of cooking time and blitzed with the tomatoes.

■ **Serves 4–6. Freezes well.**

3 Tbsp oil
1 medium-sized onion, peeled and sliced
1 Tbsp Ras el Hanout
3 x 400-g tins, peeled and chopped tomatoes with juice
    or 1.2 kg fresh tomatoes, peeled and chopped
1½ cups water
1½ tsp salt or to taste
1 tsp freshly ground black pepper
1 Tbsp sugar
½ cup unsweetened yoghurt to garnish (optional)
¼ cup fresh, finely chopped coriander to garnish (optional)

Heat the oil in a large, heavy-based saucepan over a gentle heat.
Sauté the onion in the oil until softened, then stir in the Ras el Hanout and sauté for 1 minute. Stir in the tomatoes, water, salt, pepper and sugar and simmer, uncovered, for 15–20 minutes, stirring occasionally. Transfer to a food processor and purée. Return the soup to the saucepan to reheat before serving.
Ladle into warmed soup bowls and garnish with a swirl of yoghurt if desired and a sprinkle of fresh coriander.

Leek 'n' lentil soup

Leeks and lentils may not sound particularly inspiring, but this soup is delicious and literally takes minutes to assemble — great for a quick, healthy, light meal when time is short.

Red lentils are included because they cook in the same time as the potato, adding nutritional value although they make little discernible difference to the taste or texture.

■ **Serves 4 as a lunch or casual meal with breads, cheeses and fresh fruit. May be frozen. Extends well.**

---

350 g trimmed leeks, white part only
50 g butter
⅓ cup red lentils, washed and drained
1 small to medium-sized potato (about 150 g), peeled and diced
2 garlic cloves, peeled and crushed
1 Tbsp ground coriander
375 ml vegetable stock
1½ cups water
1 tsp salt or to taste
½ tsp freshly ground black pepper
½ cup cream
2 spring onions, finely chopped (optional)
½ cup finely chopped Italian (flat-leaf) parsley

Slice the leeks in half lengthwise, then into thin slices across (about 4 mm). Wash thoroughly and drain.

Melt the butter in a large, heavy-based saucepan and sauté the prepared leeks for 3 minutes, stirring. Stir in the lentils, potato, garlic and coriander and continue to sauté until the leeks soften.

Stir in the stock and water, salt and pepper. Cover and simmer over a low–medium heat for 15–20 minutes.

Transfer the cooked leek mixture to a food processor and purée with the cream, spring onions if using and parsley, reserving 2 tablespoons of the parsley for garnish. The spring onions embolden the flavour of the soup but are not strictly necessary.

Return the soup to the saucepan and reheat to simmer point. Add a little more water if the mixture is too thick, and check the seasoning.

Ladle into heated bowls and garnish with a swirl of extra cream if desired, and the reserved parsley. Serve immediately.

Mexican chowder

This soup is an all-time favourite that captures attention and lingers in memory. The chilli should make its presence felt but not be overwhelming.

Works well as a main course accompanied by wholemeal bread or hot crusty rolls, cheeses and fresh fruits.

■ **Serves 6. May be frozen.**

4 Tbsp oil
3 medium-sized onions, peeled and finely chopped
2–2½ Tbsp minced fresh green chillies, with seeds*
4 cloves garlic, crushed
1 Tbsp ground cumin
4 cups diced potatoes (if thin-skinned, don't peel)
2 cups peeled and diced kumara or pumpkin
3 cups water
3 Tbsp chopped fresh basil or 1 tsp dried basil
1 tsp salt or to taste
1 large red capsicum, seeded and diced
2 medium-sized tomatoes, diced
1 cup whole-kernel corn; frozen, fresh or tinned (drained)
4 Tbsp cream cheese
½ cup milk
1 cup grated tasty cheese
finely chopped coriander or parsley for garnish

Heat the oil in a large, heavy-based saucepan over a low–medium heat. Sauté the onions, chillies, garlic and cumin until the onions soften. Add the diced potatoes and kumara (or pumpkin) to the sautéed onions with the water, basil and salt. Cover and simmer for 10 minutes. Add the capsicum, tomatoes and corn. Simmer, covered, for a further 15 minutes or until the vegetables are tender.
Transfer 4 cups of the mixture to a food processor and add the cream cheese and the milk. Process until smooth then return to the saucepan with the grated cheese. Stir to combine and check the seasoning balance.
Reheat gently and garnish with coriander or parsley before serving in heated bowls.

**Discard some or all of the seeds if your chillies are small and especially fiery, but keep in mind that this soup should have a bit of a 'bite'.*

Tomato tamarind dhal soup

Tomato Tamarind Dhal Soup is for serious soup lovers. It's a jaunty combination of colour and flavour that has grunt as well as grace. It's not at all time consuming to prepare and makes a balanced meal served with freshly warmed chapati, or hot crusty breads such as ciabatta or toasted wholemeal breads. The flavours create a lovely balance and the seed/lemon juice garnish adds the final perfect touch. Crumbled feta with a raw seed mix topping is an excellent alternative, or toasted slivered almonds with a squeeze of lemon for each bowl.

■ **Serves 4–6. Freezes well.**

4 Tbsp oil (first measure)
1 large onion, peeled and diced
6 cloves garlic, peeled and finely chopped
2 Tbsp finely chopped fresh ginger
1 tsp turmeric
½–¾ tsp lightly crushed chilli flakes (or chilli powder)
1 cup red lentils, rinsed and drained
4 cups unsalted vegetable stock or water
2 Tbsp tamarind paste (page 185)
2 x 400-g tins of chopped peeled tomatoes
    in thick juice or 800 g fresh tomatoes, peeled
2 tsp salt or to taste
freshly ground black pepper
2 Tbsp brown sugar
¼ cup finely chopped coriander leaves and stalks
2 Tbsp oil (second measure)
1 tsp each of mustard seeds and fenugreek seeds
1 tsp each of fennel seeds and cumin seeds
2 Tbsp lemon juice

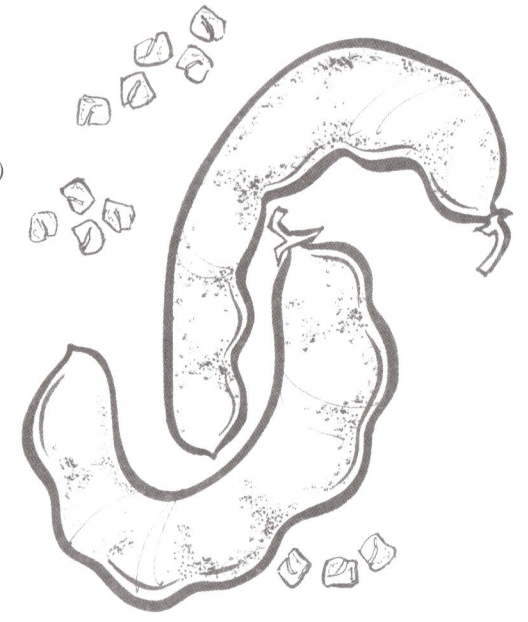

Heat oil in a large saucepan and sauté the onion over a low heat until softened. Stir in the garlic and ginger and sauté for at least 5 minutes before adding the turmeric and chilli flakes. Stir in the red lentils followed by the stock or water, cover and simmer for 15 minutes, then stir in the tamarind paste, the tomatoes in juice, salt, pepper and brown sugar. Simmer for a further 10 minutes.

Transfer to a food processor and purée in two batches. Add half the fresh coriander to each batch and pulse to combine. Return the puréed soup to the original saucepan. Heat the second measure of oil in a small pan and sauté the mustard and fenugreek seeds over a medium heat. When the mustard seeds begin to pop, remove the pan from the heat and stir in the fennel and cumin seeds. There should be enough heat already in the pan to cook these, and it's important not to scorch any of the seeds.

Lastly, stir in the lemon juice and transfer to a small bowl. Set aside.

Reheat the soup to serve. Ladle into warmed bowls with a teaspoon or more of the seed mixture drizzled on top.

Brazen beetroot soup

Visually, this soup is flamboyant, voluptuous and brazen, a great beginning to a meal and always a conversation starter. The flavour is a tease, too — much more vigorous than borscht with the inclusion of garlic, ginger and chilli, but these add rather than detract from the beetroot base.

This soup is intended to be served hot, though it is also delicious served at room temperature or chilled. Note that although the chilli is not overwhelming, it is more noticeable when the soup is heated.

■ **Serves 4–6. Freezes well.**

850 g beetroot (700 g trimmed and peeled)
2 Tbsp olive oil
30 g butter
4 cloves garlic, peeled and chopped
2 tsp finely chopped fresh ginger
½ tsp chilli powder
3 cups unsalted vegetable stock
2 Tbsp red wine vinegar
1 Tbsp sugar
1½ tsp salt or to taste
400-g tin peeled, chopped tomatoes
   (or 400 g fresh peeled tomatoes, chopped)
cream or sour cream and fresh fennel leaves
   to garnish

Chop the trimmed and peeled beetroot into large dice and set aside.
Heat the oil and butter together in a large saucepan over a gentle heat, and sauté the garlic, ginger and chilli powder until fragrant. Stir in the prepared beetroot and sauté for 1 minute before adding the stock, vinegar, sugar and salt.
Cover, turn the heat to medium and bring to simmer point. Simmer gently for 25 minutes or until the beetroot is tender.
Stir in the tomatoes and transfer to a food processor to purée until smooth. You may need to do this in two batches.
Return the soup to the original saucepan and reheat. Adjust seasoning if required. Serve in heated bowls, garnished with a swirl of cream or sour cream thinned with a little lemon juice and fresh fennel leaves.

Spanish black bean soup

This is a nutritious and hearty soup, quickly assembled and economical, producing a delicious one-dish meal. Avocado or sour cream and a squeeze of lime enhance the flavour of this soup, and dry pan-fried tortillas instead of bread makes a refreshing change in keeping with its Spanish links.

This soup contains a relatively small amount of chilli; chilli lovers may want to add more as a garnish or as the soup cooks. Eggplant may be substituted for the mushrooms.

■ **Serves 6 or more. Suitable to freeze.**

2 cups black turtle beans
2 onions, peeled and diced
6 large cloves garlic, peeled and finely chopped
3 cups unsalted stock or water
2 x 400-g tins peeled, chopped tomatoes in juice
2 large red capsicums, seeded and diced
250 g chopped mushrooms or eggplant
2 tsp sweet (dulce) Spanish smoked paprika
1½ tsp chilli powder
2 tsp sugar
4 Tbsp tomato paste
1 tsp freshly ground black pepper
2–3 tsp salt or to taste
avocado, peeled and diced or sliced (or sour cream)
finely chopped fresh coriander
lime segments
tortillas

Drain and rinse the black beans, cover with a generous amount of cold water and leave to soak overnight.
Place all the ingredients, except the salt, garnishes and the tortillas, in a large, heavy-based saucepan. Bring to simmer point and cook slowly, stirring regularly, for about 2½ hours, or until the beans are tender. Stir in the salt at this point — if added earlier it can cause the beans to toughen.
Ladle into bowls and garnish with the avocado (or sour cream) and the coriander and accompany with lime segments.
Serve with tortillas heated in a dry pan.

Borscht with kumara & fennel

Borscht can be eaten hot, at room temperature or chilled, and is traditionally served with sour cream. It tastes very good and is a beautiful rich, vibrant colour. This version contains a hint of anise (fennel) to add interest and lift the flavour, while kumara injects sweetness and smooths the texture.

It's been interesting to see beetroot enjoying a comeback — roast beetroot is everywhere, the young leaves are an integral part of mesclun salads, and beetroot dips and spreads are popular. In the 1970s borscht was a fashionable soup to produce at dinner parties, but otherwise some method of pickling was the most usual treatment.

■ **Serves 4–6.**

---

4 Tbsp oil
2 red onions, peeled and chopped
2 tsp fennel seeds
2 cloves garlic, crushed
2 tsp peeled and finely chopped fresh ginger
1 kg beetroot, peeled and cut into 2-cm dice*
2 bay leaves
1 small to medium-sized carrot, peeled and chopped
600 g kumara, peeled and chopped
6 cups vegetable stock
3 Tbsp balsamic vinegar
freshly ground black pepper
salt to taste
¼ cup sour cream or yoghurt
sprigs of fresh fennel leaves to garnish (or mint or coriander)

Heat the oil in a medium to large saucepan over a low heat. Sauté the onions, fennel seeds, garlic and ginger very slowly, for about 10 minutes.
Add the prepared beetroot, bay leaves, carrot, kumara and stock, then bring to a boil. Reduce the heat and simmer, covered, for 35–40 minutes, until the beetroot are soft. Remove the bay leaves.
Transfer the soup to a food processor or blender and purée in batches if necessary. Return to the saucepan and reheat, adding the balsamic vinegar, pepper and salt to taste.
If the borscht is to be served hot, pour into heated bowls and serve, adding a spoonful of sour cream or yoghurt to each bowl and sprinkling with chopped fresh fennel, mint or coriander. Thin the sour cream or yoghurt with a little lemon juice if you wish.

*Use gloves when preparing beetroot, unless you don't mind stained fingers!

Pumpkin & chestnut soup

Pumpkins and chestnuts are made for each other in this soup, where the chestnuts enhance but don't overpower. Crown pumpkins are preferred for soups as they have such flavoursome, dense flesh.

■ **Serves 6. Suitable to freeze.**

300 g chestnuts (about 15 large)
1 kg seeded but unpeeled pumpkin
2 Tbsp olive oil
30 g butter
3 shallots or 1 medium-sized onion, peeled and sliced
2 cloves garlic
2 bay leaves
½ cup orange juice*
5 cups vegetable stock
1 tsp salt or to taste
freshly ground black pepper
¾ tsp freshly grated nutmeg (preferably), or ground nutmeg
1 parsley stalk
½ cup cream
cream and chopped parsley for garnish

Prepare and peel the chestnuts as detailed on page 181.
Peel the pumpkin and cut into 3-cm pieces. Set aside. Peel and slice the shallots (or onion).
Heat the oil and butter together in a large saucepan over a medium heat and sauté the shallots, garlic and bay leaves until the shallots are well softened.
Stir in the prepared chestnuts and pumpkin, orange juice, stock, salt, pepper, nutmeg and parsley. Cover and simmer for 15–20 minutes or until the pumpkin is soft.
Discard the parsley stalk and bay leaves.
Transfer the soup to a food processor and purée until smooth. This will probably require processing in two lots. Return the soup to the original saucepan, stir in the cream and reheat before serving but don't boil.
Serve garnished with a swirl of cream and a sprinkle of chopped parsley.

*Use fresh orange juice, or store-bought with no additives or preservatives.

Parsnip soup with saffron & spice

Saffron and spices impart a little Eastern allure to produce an elegant soup full of subtle nuance — still familiar but far from pedestrian.

■ **Serves 4–6. Freezes well.**

1 kg parsnips (800 g trimmed and peeled)
generous pinch (½ tsp) of saffron threads*, crushed
1 Tbsp coriander seeds, crushed
3 Tbsp olive oil
30 g butter
3 cloves garlic, peeled and chopped
2 tsp ground cumin
2 cups vegetable stock
2½ cups milk
1 tsp salt or to taste
freshly ground black pepper
cream for garnish (optional)
Italian (flat-leaf) parsley, chopped

Chop the prepared parsnips into large dice.
Crush the saffron threads in a mortar and pestle and soak in 2 tablespoons warm water for 5 minutes.
Crush the coriander seeds and set aside.
Gently melt the oil and butter in a large, heavy-based saucepan and sauté the garlic until fragrant.
Stir in the crushed coriander seeds and cumin and sauté 1 minute before adding the soaked saffron and the prepared parsnips. Stir to combine, then pour in the stock. Cover and simmer for 15 minutes or until the parsnips are tender.
Transfer to a food processor and purée with the milk and salt until smooth — you may have to do this in two lots.
Return the soup to the saucepan to reheat. Add a little more milk if too thick, and check the seasoning.
Pour into heated bowls to serve, garnished with a swirl of cream if you like, some parsley and a grind or two of black pepper.

*1 tsp turmeric may be substituted for the saffron if saffron is not available. This will give the soup a little more colour and a good, but different, flavour.

Jerusalem artichoke soup

'Jerusalem' artichokes are a misnomer. The Italian name for them, girasole, has been corrupted to 'Jerusalem', and the tubers are not, in fact, related to globe artichokes at all but are members of the sunflower family, also known as sunchokes.

Although their knobbly bits and nondescript colour are not particularly endearing, Jerusalem artichokes have a subtle nutty/oyster flavour that can be quite addictive. Add raw to salads, or mash, sauté, roast or add to casseroles. Roast artichokes with baby beetroot make an impressive flavour combination.

■ **Serves 4. Recipe is easily doubled. May be frozen.**

1 large leek or onion
2 Tbsp oil
30 g margarine or butter
2 cloves garlic, peeled and chopped small
700 g Jerusalem artichokes
1 medium-sized parsnip or potato
1 litre vegetable stock (or water)
100 ml 'lite' cream
1–1½ tsp salt or to taste
freshly ground black pepper
croutons
3 Tbsp finely chopped parsley
extra virgin olive oil

Discard the green leek leaves and finely slice the white stem, wash well and drain (or peel and finely chop the onion). Heat the oil and butter in a large saucepan over a gentle heat. Sauté the prepared leek and garlic slowly, until softened.
Meanwhile, scrub the Jerusalem artichokes. Don't peel, but discard any particularly gnarly pieces or dark skin. Peel the parsnip (or potato), then dice both the artichokes and the parsnip and stir into the leek mixture. Cover and sweat for 5 minutes, stirring or shaking regularly.
Stir in the vegetable stock. Cover and simmer for 25 minutes, or until the vegetables are tender. Transfer the mixture to a food processor and purée, then return to the original saucepan (or use a wand/whizz stick). Stir in the cream with the salt and pepper. Heat but don't boil. Serve in warmed bowls, garnished with croutons, parsley and/or a drizzle of oil if you wish.

For a really special soup, substitute 300 g chestnuts, boiled and peeled (page 181), for the parsnip or potato. Increase the cream to 150 ml and stir in ½ tsp freshly grated or ground nutmeg with the cream.

Pumpkin & lentil soup

This soup is gently spiced but tasty and sustaining, especially when served with wholemeal breads, cheese and fruit. It's popular as a casual meal with teenagers, as well as adults.

Serves 6. Freezes well.

3–4 Tbsp oil
2 medium-sized onions
1 tsp cumin seeds
1 tsp fennel seeds
1 Tbsp ground coriander
1 kg pumpkin
¾ cup red lentils
5 cups vegetable stock or water
freshly ground black pepper
1½ tsp salt or to taste
4 tsp brown sugar
½ tsp chilli powder
unsweetened yoghurt
fresh chopped coriander to garnish

Heat the oil over a gentle heat in a large saucepan. Peel and slice the onions, and crush the cumin and fennel seeds with a mortar and pestle (or very finely chop the seeds with a sharp knife).
Sauté the onion in the oil with the seeds until the onion has softened, adding the ground coriander for the last few minutes.
Meanwhile, peel the pumpkin and cut into 3-cm chunks. Rinse the lentils in a sieve under cold running water and drain, discarding any grit you may find.
Stir the lentils into the onion and spice mixture with the prepared pumpkin and the water. Cover and simmer for about 15 minutes, until the pumpkin is tender. Stir once or twice during this cooking time, to ensure that the lentils are not catching on the bottom of the saucepan.
Stir in the freshly ground black pepper, salt, sugar and chilli powder.
Transfer the mixture into a food processor and blend. You may have to do this in two lots. Transfer the puréed soup back into the saucepan and reheat gently, stirring. When the soup is piping hot, adjust the seasonings and ladle it into heated serving bowls. Drizzle 2–3 tablespoons of yoghurt into each bowl and garnish with finely chopped coriander.

Roast capsicum soup

This soup is a gorgeous colour and has a smooth, rich texture. It can be enjoyed all year round as it is just as delicious served chilled, at room temperature or reheated. The only cautionary note is that it definitely benefits from being made the day before it is needed, as the flavours intensify overnight.

Serves 4–6. Suitable to freeze.

4 large red capsicums
2 Tbsp oil
1 medium-sized onion, peeled and finely chopped
1 red chilli, seeded and finely chopped
1 tsp dry-roasted cumin seeds, ground
2 cups vegetable stock
400-g tin peeled tomatoes, with juice
1½–2 tsp salt or to taste
lots of freshly ground black pepper
⅓ cup sour cream (or 'lite' cream)
fresh coriander, finely chopped (or Italian (flat-leaf) parsley, or chives)

Preheat the oven to 190°C.
Place the capsicums in a roasting pan and roast for about 25 minutes, turning once, until the skin has blackened and blistered away from the flesh.
Cool until you can handle them safely. Place them in a sieve over a bowl, to catch any juices (reserve for adding to the soup with the stock). Peel the capsicums, and discard the skins, seeds and core. Chop the flesh roughly and set aside with the reserved juices.
Heat the oil in a large, heavy-based saucepan over a medium heat. Sauté the onion, chilli and ground cumin seeds until the onion softens, then transfer to a food processor with the prepared roast capsicum and their juice, and the tomatoes with their juice.
Purée and transfer the mixture to the saucepan with the stock. Cover and simmer, stirring occasionally, for 15 minutes.
Stir in the salt and pepper and adjust if necessary.
The soup can be cooled and refrigerated, covered, at this stage — the flavour will improve if left overnight. It can then be served reheated, or at room temperature.
Ladle into individual bowls and serve garnished with a swirl of sour cream and finely chopped coriander, parsley or chives.
Serve with hot crusty ciabatta or baguette.

Green sauce

This super-easy basic sauce is guaranteed to lift the profile of almost anything, from eggs (hard-boiled to omelettes/frittatas), breads (wraps/pitas/breads for dunking), potatoes (boiled/baked or salad), or vegetables (as in crudités/fritters/roasted). Toss it into hot pasta, drizzle it over vine-ripened tomatoes on grilled ciabatta, or serve as a dip.

Ensure the herbs are dry before chopping, as a food processor can bruise or mash them if moist, and may cause a bitter taste.

1 generous cup Italian (flat-leaf) parsley, chopped
1 generous cup fresh basil, chopped
1 Tbsp finely chopped mint
2 Tbsp finely chopped chives (or spring onion)
2 large cloves garlic, peeled
½ tsp salt or to taste
freshly ground black pepper
1 Tbsp capers, drained well
1½ Tbsp lemon juice (about ½ lemon)
½ cup extra virgin olive oil

Place all the herbs and garlic in a food processor and process until finely chopped though not puréed. Add the seasoning, capers and lemon juice and blend until smooth. Pour the oil in last, through the feed tube.
Store, covered, in the refrigerator. This sauce will keep for 5 to 6 days.

Black raspberry vinaigrette

It's surprising how many salads suit a dressing of raspberry vinaigrette, and Black Raspberry Vinegar* is so simple to make from either frozen or fresh raspberries. Use it to enhance kumara salad, mixed roast vegetable salad, mesclun/feta salad, and many more.

¼ cup Black Raspberry Vinegar (page 179)*
¼ cup olive oil (scant)
salt to taste
freshly ground black pepper
½ tsp Dijon mustard
½ tsp sugar

Place all the ingredients in a jar with a screw-top lid and shake well to combine. Store in the refrigerator indefinitely.

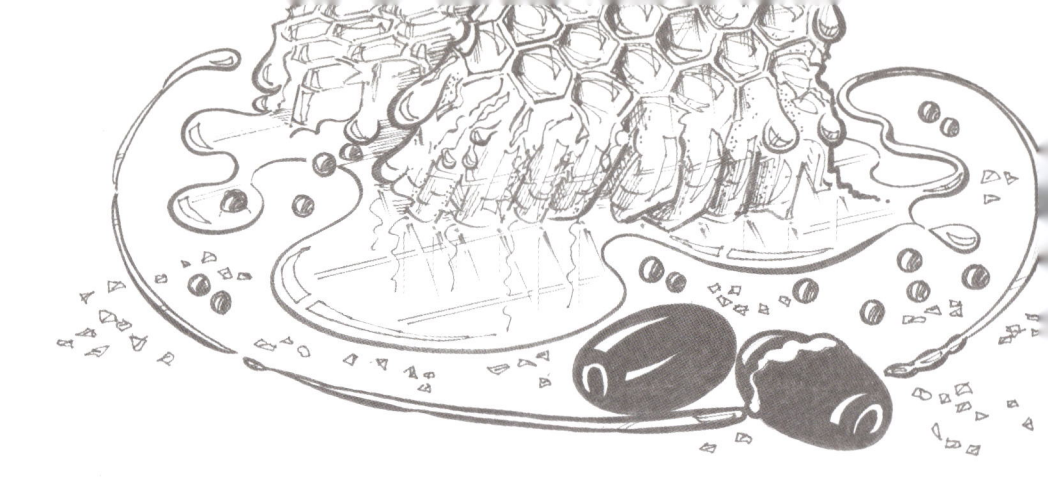

Honey cider vinaigrette

Simple but lovely on bitter greens (rocket, radicchio etc.), or watercress.

⅓ cup cider vinegar
⅓ cup olive oil
1 Tbsp warmed, clear honey
salt and freshly ground black pepper to taste

Combine all the ingredients in a screw-top jar or whisk together to combine well.

Aïoli

We still tend to be timid in our use of fresh herbs and spices, but it's only when introduced to authentic French food that you appreciate just how cautious we are with garlic. I've been making aïoli for 30 years now and include it in every book or column I write, but after visiting Provence I've upped the ante in terms of the amount of garlic I use.

This recipe is quite subjective; extra virgin olive oil is too strongly flavoured for my taste, and egg yolks instead of whole eggs make the mayo too thick and rich. The secret is to be patient when dribbling the oil slowly through the feed tube. If the aïoli is too thin, you've dribbled too fast. Any neutral oil is fine — personally I like equal quantities of olive pomace and rice bran oils.

Make plain mayonnaise simply by omitting the garlic. This recipe is easily doubled, and is an essential ingredient of dips and the best salad sandwiches.

---

1 egg
3 cloves garlic, peeled
2 Tbsp lemon juice
½ tsp salt or to taste
1 cup neutral oil such as sunflower or rice bran (or ½ cup olive pomace oil and ½ cup neutral oil)

Place all the ingredients except the oil in a food processor and process for 1 minute until well combined.
Leaving the motor running, dribble the oil through the feed tube very slowly. Taste and add a little more lemon juice if you wish.
Transfer to a jar with a lid and keep refrigerated for up to 8 days.

Caramelised balsamic vinegar

This caramelised balsamic may not be quite as good as the boutique variety, but it does make a fair substitute. Lightly drizzle watercress or any salad containing predominantly bitter greens (rocket, radicchio, etc.) with extra virgin olive oil, then toss with an equal quantity of caramelised balsamic.

3 Tbsp balsamic vinegar
2 Tbsp white sugar
2 Tbsp extra virgin olive oil

Heat the balsamic vinegar and sugar together, stirring to dissolve the sugar. Cool, then combine with the oil. Store in a bottle or jar at room temperature.

Summer mayo

Lovely with potatoes, or served simply as a mayonnaise, dip or spread, this is especially good with summer dishes; for picnics, barbecues and lunches. Substitute some of the herbs for others — basil is delicious instead of the tarragon, for example — but don't change the base of Italian (flat-leaf) parsley, some onion and garlic.

⅓ cup rocket
2 Tbsp roughly chopped fresh tarragon or ⅓ cup fresh basil
¼ cup finely chopped chives or 1 spring onion, chopped
2–3 cloves garlic
8 mint leaves, roughly chopped
1 cup packed Italian (flat-leaf) parsley, chopped
1 egg
1 Tbsp capers, rinsed and drained
2 tsp horseradish cream or sauce (optional)
2 Tbsp lemon juice
½ tsp salt or to taste
1 cup neutral oil such as pomace olive or rice bran

Pour enough boiling water over the rocket to cover, leave for 1 minute, drain, refresh under cold water, squeeze dry, then chop. This removes any possible bitterness and 'fixes' the colour. (See Glossary, page 183–184.)
Place the tarragon, chives or spring onion, garlic, mint and parsley in a food processor. It's important that all the herbs are dry or they won't chop finely. Chop briefly (don't purée) before adding the egg, rocket, capers, horseradish if using, lemon juice and salt. While the motor is running, drizzle the oil through the feed tube very, very slowly — if the mixture doesn't thicken, you've drizzled too fast.
Transfer to a jar with a lid and store in the refrigerator for up to 1 week.

Herb mayo

Herb mayonnaise is still the first thing our now adult children look for when they come home, just as they did as children when they were first persuaded to enjoy carrot and celery sticks by using them as 'dippers'.

½ cup finely chopped Italian (flat-leaf) parsley
2 cloves garlic, peeled
2 Tbsp finely chopped chives or spring onion tops
½ cup of finely chopped basil or a mix of herbs such as oregano, a little mint, pizza thyme, chervil*
1 egg
2 Tbsp lemon juice
½ tsp salt or to taste
1 cup neutral oil such as sunflower or rice bran, or ½ cup olive pomace oil and ½ cup neutral oil

*Ensure the herbs are dry before chopping, as a food processor can bruise or mash them if moist, producing a faintly bitter taste.

Place all the herbs and the garlic in a food processor, process until very finely chopped but not puréed, then add the egg, lemon juice and salt. Process to combine, then drizzle the oil in very slowly through the feed tube while the motor is running. If the mayo doesn't thicken, you've drizzled the oil in too fast.

Chermoula

Chermoula shines as a dressing for any roast vegetable salad, a dip for hot crusty ciabatta, or drizzled over a tomato/cucumber/capsicum/feta salad. It also makes a tasty dressing for potato, rice and lentil salads. Keeps refrigerated for up to 5 days.

1 tsp cumin seeds, toasted and ground
1 tsp turmeric
2 large garlic cloves, peeled
1 cup finely chopped fresh coriander, including stalks
½ cup chopped Italian (flat-leaf) parsley
½ cup finely chopped mint
1 tsp salt or to taste
1 tsp ground coriander
½ tsp chilli powder
1 tsp sweet paprika
juice and zest of 1 lemon
1 cup extra virgin or pure olive oil

Toast the cumin seeds in a dry frying pan over a medium heat until fragrant. Grind in a mortar and pestle or chop finely/crush with a heavy knife. Place all remaining ingredients except the olive oil in a food processor. Blend until puréed, then drizzle in the oil through the feed tube while the motor is running. Transfer to a bowl and cover or place in a jar with a lid and refrigerate until needed.

Satay sauce

This peanut sauce is quick to make and lovely as a sauce for Rice Paper Salad Rolls (see page 20), shallow-fried or baked tofu, or vegetarian kebabs.

■ **Recipe is easily doubled.**

¾ cup coconut cream plus 2 Tbsp extra
1 tsp red curry paste
1 Tbsp kecap manis*
salt to taste
2 Tbsp peanut butter
1 Tbsp tamarind concentrate**

Heat the coconut cream in a small heavy-based saucepan and bring to simmer point. Combine the curry paste with the extra 2 tablespoons coconut cream to make a slurry. Whisk in the red curry paste slurry, followed by the remaining ingredients. Ensure that the sauce is whisked smooth and that there are no lumps.
Simmer over a low heat stirring regularly for about 5 minutes, or until the sauce reaches the desired thickness.

* *Kecap manis is a sweet soy sauce.*
***Tamarind pulp is available in blocks from any Asian store and is preferable to the concentrate or pulp in jars. Break up and soak a 125-g block in 1 cup hot water for 10 minutes, then strain through a sieve into a bowl. Any extra can be frozen for adding to sauces, stews, lentils, etc., or buy a good quality tamarind concentrate (see Glossary page 185).*

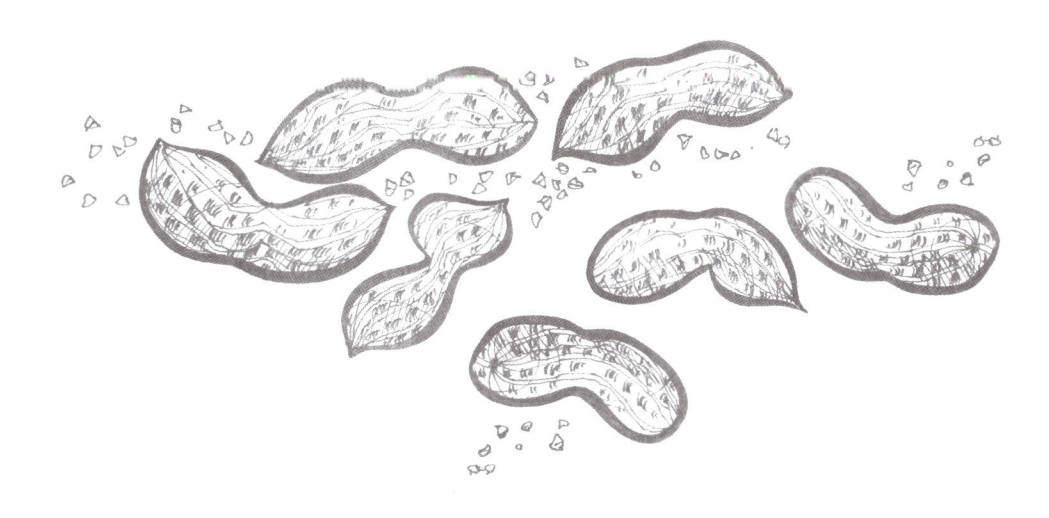

Tamarind mint sambal

Try this with any curry, and also enjoy with pastries such as samosas. It's a great combination of sour and sweet, lifted by the fresh herbs.

½ cup tamarind concentrate (see Glossary, page 185)
3 Tbsp brown sugar
1 tsp finely chopped or minced fresh ginger
1½ Tbsp finely chopped fresh coriander
1½ Tbsp finely chopped fresh mint

Stir to combine, cover and refrigerate until needed.

Tomato pasta sauce

This sauce is so simply made and so much better than the vast majority of store-bought pasta sauces. Do include the parsley stalks/branches if you have them as they enhance the flavour.

This recipe produces an all-purpose sauce, one that is especially good on pasta and polenta. Doubling the quantity and freezing the excess works well for planning ahead.

■ **Makes about 3–4 cups. Freezes well.**

2 Tbsp olive oil
1 small onion, peeled and finely chopped
4 cloves garlic
3 x 400-g tins peeled, chopped tomatoes with juice
   or 1.2 kg fresh peeled tomatoes, chopped
2 bay leaves
2 Tbsp fresh chopped fresh basil or 1 tsp dried basil
2 stalks parsley
1½–2 tsp sugar
1½–2 tsp salt or to taste
freshly ground black pepper

Heat the oil in a heavy-based saucepan over a low heat. Sauté the onion and garlic slowly until well softened.
Stir in the tomatoes, bay leaves, basil, parsley stalks, sugar, salt and pepper. Add the smaller amount of sugar and salt until you have tasted it — tomatoes vary in acidity. Raise the heat a little and simmer, uncovered, for 20 minutes, stirring occasionally. Discard the parsley stalks and bay leaves, then transfer to a food processor and purée until smooth. You should have about 3–4 cups of sauce.
Return the sauce to the pan and simmer for about 10 minutes longer over a gentle heat.

Paul's tropical dressing

Food writers are shameless when it comes to garnering ideas and hints from other cooks. Some really great home cooks, though, have an infuriating habit of creating the most wonderful concoctions, with that special 'spark' — but they can't tell you how they did it because they didn't measure!

This dressing was created by a very intuitive cook, for a large mixed green salad containing mesclun and romaine, radicchio, watercress, capsicum, rings of finely sliced red onion and fresh herbs, and yes, the mustard quantity is correct. There has been a small liberty or two taken, but this is pretty much how it went.

⅓ cup thinly sliced glacé pineapple (40 g)
juice of 2 large lemons (⅓ cup)
2 Tbsp Dijon mustard
1 tsp salt or to taste
generous grinds of black pepper
1 tsp tomato paste
1 cup olive oil

Place all ingredients in a food processor and process for a couple of minutes or until very well combined.
Transfer to a jar with a lid. Refrigerate, but bring to room temperature before using, if you remember.

Yoghurt sauce/dressing

Delicious with wraps, fritters, oven-baked eggplant slices, curries and anything Mexican.

---

2 cups plain Greek-style yoghurt
4 cloves garlic, peeled and very finely chopped (not crushed)
4–5 Tbsp lemon or lime juice
1 tsp salt or to taste
½ tsp freshly ground black pepper
¼–½ cup finely chopped fresh coriander or mint

Stir or whisk to combine thoroughly.

Roast capsicum & almond sauce

This roast capsicum/tomato/almond sauce is a version of the Spanish Romescu sauce, and is a great complement to eggplant fritters (slices of eggplant dipped in seasoned flour, lightly beaten egg and dried breadcrumbs then shallow fried), steamed green beans or asparagus. It's also good as a dip, with some chopped fresh coriander added if you like.

Mellow but complex flavours in this sauce are captivating, and accentuated by roasting the capsicums and the tomatoes. Make it when capsicums and tomatoes are inexpensive and readily available.

■ **Makes about 1–1½ cups. Freezes well.**

4 large red capsicums
4 large tomatoes, preferably acid-free
½ cup whole blanched almonds, roasted
3 cloves garlic, peeled
2 Tbsp balsamic vinegar
1 tsp lemon juice
¼ tsp chilli powder
½ tsp salt or to taste
⅓ cup olive oil

Heat the oven to 190°C.
Cut the capsicums in half, discarding the core and seeds. Cut the tomatoes in half.
Place both the capsicums and the tomatoes cut-side down on a baking tray or trays, in single layers, and roast for 30 minutes. Remove from the oven and discard the skins (and some of the tomato seeds, without making an issue of it!) when cool enough to handle.
While the tomatoes and capsicums are baking, toast the almonds on a separate tray for 7 minutes or until lightly golden. Remove and cool.
Transfer the toasted, cooled almonds to a food processor and grind finely but leave in the food processor bowl.
Transfer the tomatoes and capsicums to the food processor, on top of the almonds. Add the garlic cloves, balsamic vinegar, lemon juice, chilli powder, salt and olive oil and purée until smooth.
Transfer the sauce to a serving bowl or jug, cover and refrigerate until needed.
Bring to room temperature before serving.

mains

Briam 52
Asparagus flan with cashew nut pastry 54
Asparagus combo 56
Mushroom galette 57
Fast-lane lasagne 58
Stuffed red capsicums 60
Orzo, mushroom & thyme 62
Mediterranean pasta salad 63
Layered eggplant Napoli 64
Crisped polenta 65
Tofu, lemon & herb lasagne 66
Whole mushrooms en croûte 67
Mushroom tapenade pasta with scorched cherry tomatoes 68
Caramelised shallot tarte tatin 69
Pasta with spinach, cherry tomatoes & creamy blue sauce 70
Polenta primo 71
Smokin' beans 72
Mexican pumpkin pie 73
Mexican mole 74
Mushroom risotto 76
Falafel 77
Pizza 78
Summer picnic pie 80
Tuscan tart 81

Szechuan 'clay pot' casserole 82
Sesame noodles with seared tofu 83
Saag 84
Madras chickpeas. eggplant & spinach 85
Malai kofta 86
Cauliflower & almond curry 88
Chickpea, zucchini & herb fritters 89
Tunis roast vegetables with chickpeas 90
Kumara fritters with toasted cumin 91
Corn & coriander fritters 92
Bean & feta fritters 93

Briam

Briam is a personal favourite, a vegetarian dish served throughout the Mediterranean basin in various interpretations.

In essence, layers of different vegetables are slowly baked with olive oil and stock and herbs, very simply, until everything has reduced and the flavours have infused to create a dish that tastes stunningly good. None of the components is precooked, it is just as seductive at room temperature as it is hot or warmed, and it's an excellent dish to cook a day ahead to enhance the flavours. Adjust it according to what you have on hand — vary the herbs used, and either fresh or frozen broad beans are a nice addition, as are a few sliced mushrooms.

Briam is almost always served with bread, such as hot crusty ciabatta, and a Greek salad if desired.

Use pure or extra virgin olive oil for this dish. The dish size used is important; if a smaller dish is used the cooking time will be longer, as the Briam will be deeper. A metal roasting dish is recommended as this conducts heat more efficiently; if a ceramic dish is used, allow for a longer cooking time.

■ **Serves 6–8 depending on appetites. Freezes well.**

¼ cup extra virgin or pure olive oil (first measure)
¾ cup loosely packed Italian (flat-leaf) parsley
¾ cup fresh basil, dill or fennel* leaves, roughly chopped
500 g potatoes, unpeeled weight (about 3 medium to large)
1 large eggplant (400–450 g)
4 medium-sized zucchini (500 g)
2 medium-sized onions, peeled
8–10 cloves garlic, peeled and sliced into long slivers
4 red, yellow or orange capsicums, cored, seeded
   and roughly chopped or sliced lengthways
4 large tomatoes, sliced**
salt and freshly ground black pepper
2 tsp dried oregano or basil
3 bay leaves
1 cup water or vegetable stock
1½ cups tomato purée or tomato pasta sauce
¾–1 cup olive oil (second measure)

Preheat the oven to 170°C.
Pour ¼ cup olive oil into the bottom of a medium-sized
roasting pan, about 30 cm x 30 cm.
Prepare and measure the fresh herbs.
Don't peel the potatoes if thin-skinned or new season, but cut in half lengthways then slice across thinly, as you would for scalloped potatoes (about 2 mm thick). Cut the eggplant into quarters lengthways, then slice thinly as for the potatoes.
Cut the zucchini in half lengthways and slice across into thicker slices, about 1 cm.
Slice the onions thinly and prepare the garlic, capsicums and tomatoes.
Layer the vegetables into the roasting pan in the order given, sprinkling each layer with salt and pepper and some of the fresh and dried herbs. Tuck the fresh or dried bay leaves and garlic slivers among the layers as you go.
Combine the stock or water with the tomato purée/pasta sauce and pour evenly over the top. Follow this with the second measure of olive oil.
Cover with aluminium foil and bake for 2 hours, resisting any temptation to stir the mixture. Remove the aluminium foil after 1 hour, and as the layers slowly cook down, press lightly with a fish slice or similar every so often, to ensure that the top layers benefit from cooking in the delicious oil/stock and the flavours infuse.

*Fresh fennel loses much of its anise flavour when cooked.
**Fresh tomatoes are best, especially acid-free, but may be replaced with 1 cup of tinned chopped tomatoes with juice.

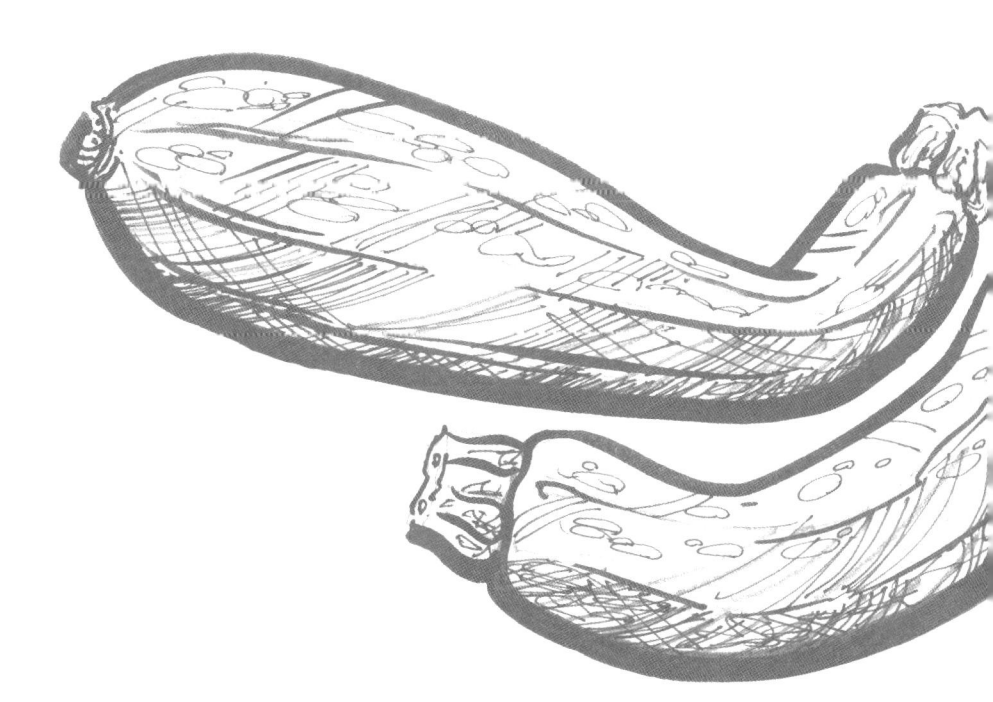

Asparagus flan with cashew nut pastry

Fresh asparagus should be eaten in every conceivable form while in season: risottos, pastas, salads, steamed and served with hollandaise, or baked in a pie, flan or quiche. The only caution is that too often asparagus cooked in pastry gets lost in translation and can be diminished in the process.

This flan is simplicity itself to make, but showcases the colour, texture and sweetness of the asparagus, as it rightly should.

■ **Serves 4–6. Not recommended for freezing.**

Cashew nut pastry, page 150

Filling
500 g medium–thick asparagus spears
2 small or 1 medium–large zucchini
1 cup grated Parmesan (or substitute tasty Cheddar)
¼ cup roughly chopped fresh basil (optional)
125 g (½ cup) sour cream or soft goat's cheese
2 tsp lemon juice
½ tsp salt or to taste
lots of freshly ground black pepper
2 garlic cloves, peeled and crushed
1½ Tbsp rinsed and well drained capers
1 Tbsp olive oil

Pastry
Preheat the oven to 200°C.
Make the pastry, as directed on page 150.
Lightly grease or spray a 32 cm x 22 cm springform flan tin. Turn the pastry out onto a well-floured bench and roll out to a rectangle about 4 mm thick (or a circle if you are using a round flan tin). Slide a long-bladed lifter under the pastry if necessary to ensure it doesn't stick.
Transfer the pastry into the prepared tin by wrapping one end around the rolling pin and positioning. Ease the pastry into the tin, taking care to 'fit' into the corners, and trim the top flush with the sides of the tin.
Prick the base and sides all over with a fork and place in the freezer for 15 minutes.
Transfer to the preheated oven and cook for 10 minutes, or until lightly golden. Allow to cool while preparing the filling.

Filling
Preheat the oven to 210°C.
Snap the bottoms off the asparagus spears. Drop the spears into lightly salted, boiling water and cook for 1–2 minutes once the water has returned to the boil. Plunge immediately into a sink of very cold water to stop further cooking, drain and wrap in paper towels to dry.
Trim the zucchini, then slice very thinly, on a slight diagonal.
Evenly distribute the cheese into the prepared pastry in the flan tin, followed by the zucchini slices and the basil, if using.
Combine the sour cream or goat's cheese and the lemon juice, salt, pepper and garlic. Drizzle this over the zucchini slices. Spread as evenly as possible, then sprinkle the capers over.
Toss the prepared asparagus in the olive oil and a little extra salt and pepper. Arrange the asparagus in a single layer on the top of the flan.
Bake at 200°C for 40–45 minutes, until the sour cream layer begins to bubble. Turn down to 180°C for the last 10 minutes if the crust is browning too fast, or cover loosely with aluminium foil.
Serve hot, warm or at room temperature, with shaved Parmesan if wished.

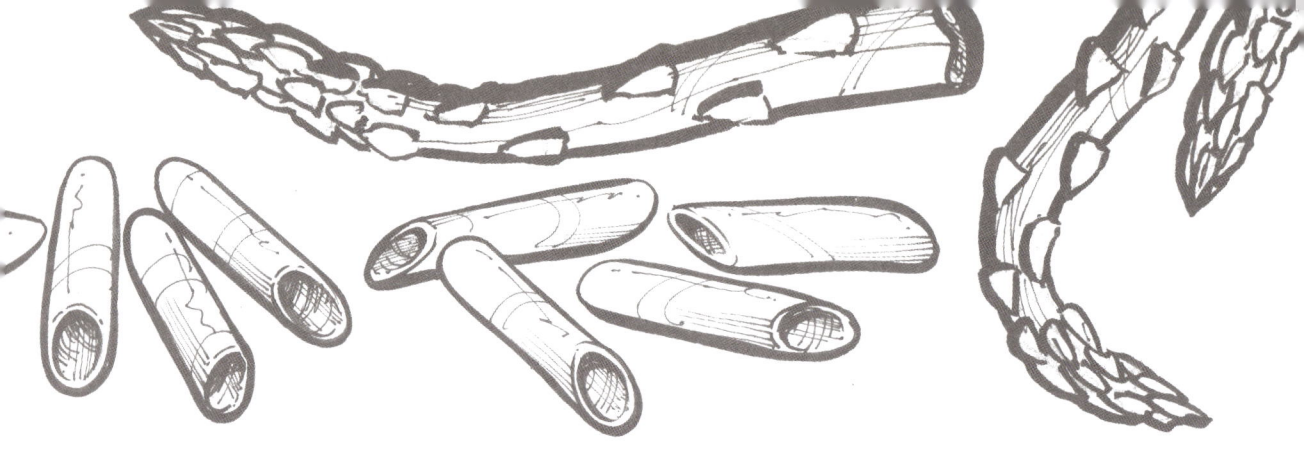

Asparagus combo

This dish celebrates spring, lighter meals and warmer weather. It's unusual in that it combines cooked pasta and potatoes together, but these partner well with roast asparagus and zucchini, lemon and fresh mint. Use waxy potatoes and dress while hot so they absorb as much flavour as possible. Serve with hot crusty bread such as ciabatta, and another salad such as fresh tomato, avocado, toasted almonds and feta. Roast baby beetroot also team very well with the combo.

■ **Serves 4. Not suitable to freeze.**

---

350 g small to medium-sized waxy potatoes (about 5–6 gourmet)
juice of 1½ large lemons
½ cup olive oil (approx.)
½ cup finely chopped fresh mint or coriander
salt to taste
freshly ground black pepper
100 g spiral or penne pasta
400 g slim asparagus spears or beans*
400 g zucchini (4 medium-sized)
2 hard-boiled eggs, peeled and quartered (optional)
½ cup black olives (optional)

*When the asparagus season finishes, try substituting beans instead — they're also great roasted.

Preheat the oven to 190°C.
Cook the potatoes until just tender. Drain, then slice into small bite-sized portions and immediately toss them in 2 tablespoons of the lemon juice, 2 tablespoons of the olive oil, 2 tablespoons of the finely chopped fresh mint leaves, about ½ teaspoon salt and freshly ground black pepper. Set aside to cool. Meanwhile, cook the pasta to al dente, drain and immediately refresh in cold water to stop the cooking process. Toss in a little olive oil and a squeeze of lemon juice to prevent them sticking
Snap ends from the asparagus and place in a single layer on a baking tray. Toss in 1–2 tablespoons oil, ½ teaspoon salt and freshly ground black pepper — the oil should very lightly coat the asparagus. Trim the zucchini and slice each thinly down its length. Take another baking tray and toss the zucchini slices in oil, salt and pepper, as for the asparagus. Place the two trays of vegetables in the preheated oven and roast, tossing once, for 7–12 minutes.
Transfer the pasta and potatoes to a large serving platter and pile the roasted asparagus and zucchini slices on top, with the hard-boiled eggs, if using.
Just before serving, toss everything with the remaining lemon juice, the remaining olive oil and finely chopped mint leaves, salt and pepper to taste and black olives if using. Check the balance of lemon, oil and seasoning and adjust to taste.

Mushroom galette

A galette can be thought of as a free-form tart, and may be either sweet, with a fruit filling such as apple, or savoury. Mushroom Galette makes a stylish lunch or light dinner dish, rich tasting but not too heavy. Some of the mushrooms may be replaced with chilli beans in sauce for a more substantial, albeit casual, result.

■ **Serves 6. Freezes well. Reheat in oven from frozen.**

Yoghurt pastry, page 151 (or two sheets pre-rolled puff pastry)*

Filling
3 Tbsp oil
30 g butter
2 red onions, peeled and sliced
4 cloves garlic, peeled and crushed
800 g mix of Portobello and button mushrooms, sliced thinly
8–10 sun-dried tomatoes in oil, drained well and sliced thinly
3 Tbsp roughly chopped fresh rosemary leaves (or 1½ Tbsp dried rosemary)
1–1½ tsp salt or to taste
lots of freshly ground black pepper
1 cup loosely packed Italian (flat-leaf) parsley
150 g mozzarella, grated or shaved
egg yolk for glaze

Preheat the oven to 190°C. Lightly grease or spray an oven tray.
Heat the oil and butter in a large shallow frying pan, add the onions and garlic, sauté over a low heat until soft. Stir in the mushrooms, turn up the heat to medium and toss or stir until they release their juice. Stir in the sun-dried tomatoes, rosemary, and the salt and pepper. Cook, stirring regularly, for 15–20 minutes over low–medium heat, until the liquid has evaporated.
Transfer the mushroom filling to a bowl to cool for 10 minutes. Stir in the parsley, two-thirds of the mozzarella and check seasonings.
Roll out the pastry to make one large circle approximately 38 cm in diameter. Transfer to a lightly greased baking tray (wrap the top over the rolling pin then lift to the tray). Spread the mushroom filling over the middle of the pastry, leaving a 10-cm margin around the sides. Sprinkle most of the mozzarella over the filling, reserving about ¼ cup. Fold the sides up over the filling, pleating as you go to make it fit, but leaving the centre of the pie uncovered. Brush the pastry top and sides with the reserved egg yolk and distribute the remaining mozzarella over the open top and pastry 'pleats'. Bake at 190°C for 30–40 minutes, or until golden brown and crisped on the bottom. If it browns too quickly, turn the heat down to 180°C after 20 minutes.
Transfer the galette to a serving platter or board and serve hot, warm or at room temperature, accompanied by a green salad.

*Yoghurt pastry is preferred, but if time is short, two sheets of pre-rolled puff pastry can be substituted if one of the sheets is cut to make one large 'square' with the other. Join seams with a smear of water and press firmly.

Fast-lane lasagne

Only the mushrooms are precooked in this delicious lasagne, making assembly merely a matter of layering the various ingredients into the dish — so easy and so tasty! Use oven-ready lasagne sheets, rather than fresh (if using fresh you may need slightly less liquid).

Serve simply with a green salad, or add grilled tomatoes and hot crusty bread for a heartier meal.

Frozen spinach** is specified here for expediency — or use 500 g fresh, lightly cooked spinach, refreshed, squeezed and chopped. Similarly, use a good store-bought tomato sauce or preferably make your own (page 48). Substitute cottage cheese for the ricotta if you wish.

■ **Serves 4–6. Freezes well.**

2 cups tomato pasta sauce
1 cup water
4 Tbsp olive oil
2 medium-sized onions, peeled and sliced finely
2 tsp crushed garlic
350 g Portobello mushrooms, thinly sliced
¾–1 tsp salt or to taste
freshly ground black pepper
250 g ricotta or cottage cheese
200 g creamy feta*
250 g zucchini
1 cup grated mozzarella
300 g frozen spinach, defrosted**
3 Tbsp basil pesto
salt and freshly ground black pepper, extra
6 sheets instant dried lasagne
½ cup each grated mozzarella and Parmesan

Preheat the oven to 180°C.
Lightly grease or spray a 20 cm x 30 cm baking dish.
Combine the tomato pasta sauce with the water.
Heat the oil in a large frying pan over a low–medium heat.
Sauté the onions and garlic until soft, then stir in the thinly sliced mushrooms, salt and pepper. Turn up the heat and cook until softened and most of the liquid has been absorbed.
Cream the ricotta or cottage cheese and feta in a food processor.

*A mild, creamy Greek feta such as Domyati is ideal for this dish, but any creamy feta will work.

Slice the zucchini on a diagonal into very thin slices. Grate the mozzarella.
Squeeze the spinach to remove all liquid, chop finely, and mix with the basil pesto, salt to taste and pepper.

Assembly
Spread 1 cup of the tomato pasta sauce on the bottom of the baking dish.
Cover with a layer of lasagne, followed by the mushrooms and another layer of lasagne.
Spread the creamed cheese mix evenly over this second layer of lasagne, followed by the zucchini.
Season lightly and top with the grated mozzarella. Distribute the spinach/pesto mix over the mozzarella.
Top with the final layer of lasagne and the remainder of the tomato pasta sauce.
Sprinkle with the extra mozzarella and Parmesan.
The lasagne can be set aside at this stage until ready to cook.
Cover and refrigerate if not cooking within an hour. Bring to room temperature before cooking.
Loosely cover with aluminium foil and bake at 180°C for 20–25 minutes, then uncover and bake for a further 30 minutes.
Rest for 10 minutes before serving, if time allows.

Stuffed red capsicums

Stuffed capsicums make a memorable main, teamed with couscous or a pasta dish, and they also partner well with potatoes, pulses and salads. The sweetness of red capsicums is a lovely contrast with both fillings. For something special, make half quantities of each stuffing mixture and enjoy both . . .

Fresh vegetables are best, but as the nutritional values are comparable, economies of time and cost justify the use of frozen vegetables such as spinach on occasion.

■ **Serves 4–8, depending on serving sizes. Not suitable for freezing.**

Spinach, nuts & feta stuffing
Spinach and nuts spiked with currants are a wonderful combination of crunch, soft, sweet and salt — take it a bit further with garlic, herbs and feta to create taste magic.

6 large or 8 medium-sized red capsicums
⅓ cup olive oil
½ cup currants
1 large red onion, peeled and finely chopped
4 cloves garlic, peeled and chopped small
2 medium-sized tomatoes, seeded and chopped small
¼ tsp chilli powder
½ cup flaked almonds (or pine nuts or chopped walnuts)
1200 g fresh spinach or 600 g frozen spinach, thawed
⅓ cup Italian (flat-leaf) parsley, chopped
⅓ cup fresh coriander (or basil), chopped
1 tsp salt or to taste
freshly ground black pepper
100 g feta, diced very small
2 Tbsp olive oil, extra

Preheat the oven to 190°C.
Choose capsicums with stem attached if available. Slice each capsicum in half lengthwise, including through the stem. Carefully remove the core and seeds of each half without splitting the 'case'. Place in a single layer on a baking tray, uncovered, and roast at 200°C for 12–15 minutes, until softened but not limp.
Heat the oil in a frying pan over a low heat, add the currants and warm them before sautéing slowly with the onion and garlic until the onion is soft. Stir in the tomatoes and chilli powder. Cook for a few minutes then mix in the nuts.
If using fresh spinach, blanch or microwave briefly and refresh under cold water. Squeeze then chop the thawed or fresh cooked spinach finely and stir into the onion mixture, loosening the spinach to break up any clumps.
Stir in the herbs, salt, pepper and feta.
Spoon the spinach mixture into the capsicum halves, place in a single layer in a baking dish and drizzle with extra olive oil. Cover firmly with foil and bake at 190°C for 25–30 minutes.

Spinach, ricotta & fresh herb stuffing
6 large or 8 medium-sized red capsicums
3 spring onions
4 cloves garlic
300 g frozen spinach, thawed (or 600 g fresh spinach)
500 g ricotta (or 300 g cottage cheese and 200 g cream cheese)
2 eggs, lightly beaten
½ cup finely chopped Italian (flat-leaf) parsley
½ cup finely chopped fresh basil
2 tsp salt or to taste
freshly ground black pepper
2 Tbsp olive oil, extra

Preheat the oven to 190°C.
Prepare and roast the capsicums as outlined in the previous recipe. Finely chop the spring onions and crush the garlic. Squeeze the defrosted spinach or prepare fresh spinach as outlined in the previous recipe. Chop the spinach finely.
If you are using a mix of cottage and cream cheese instead of the ricotta, beat or process together until creamy.
Combine all ingredients thoroughly then spoon the mixture into the capsicum halves, place in a single layer in a baking dish and drizzle with extra olive oil.
Cover firmly with foil and bake at 190°C for 25–30 minutes.

Orzo, mushroom & thyme

It may just be imagination, but orzo 'grains' seem to absorb flavour more readily than spiral or tube pasta. They also cook very quickly and are excellent for a salad base or for a hot dish such as this one, cooked similarly to a risotto but without the vigilance required.

Serve with other roast vegetables, and/or fritters, and a green salad.

■ Serves 4–6. Not suitable to freeze.

---

2 cups orzo
3 Tbsp oil (first measure)
1 large red onion, peeled and diced
5 large cloves garlic, peeled and finely chopped
3 Tbsp fresh thyme or rosemary (or 2 tsp dried thyme)
500 g Portobello mushrooms
oil (second measure)
salt
freshly ground black pepper
squeeze of lemon juice (optional)

Bring 6 cups salted water to the boil in a large saucepan. Add the orzo and cook on medium–high for about 8 minutes or until the orzo 'grains' are just cooked. Drain, refresh under cold water and drain again before setting aside.
Heat the oil in a large frying pan over a low heat, adding a little more oil only if you need to. Sauté the onion, garlic and thyme slowly, until well softened and the onion is lightly caramelised.
Preheat the oven to 180°C. Put a quantity of oil in a bowl, dip mushrooms both sides, wiping off any excess oil on the lip of the bowl. Place on a baking tray and season with salt and pepper, remembering that mushrooms can cope with quite generous seasoning. Bake for 8–12 minutes or until softened. Remove from the oven and slice each mushroom diagonally into 4–8 slices, depending on the size of the mushroom. Transfer the orzo to the frying pan with the onion mixture, and combine with about half of the mushroom slices. Turn the heat up a little and heat through, stirring constantly. Check the seasoning and finish with a squeeze of lemon if you wish. Either serve the orzo from the pan or transfer to a heated serving plate, topped with the reserved mushroom slices. Serve immediately.

Mediterranean pasta salad

The fresh, clean, piquant tastes of lemon, capers, olives, fresh basil and sun-ripened tomatoes complement the pasta in this salad perfectly, and it is especially good served with a platter of roast vegetables, Chermoula dressing (page 46) breads and a green salad.

■ **Serves 6. Not suitable for freezing.**

400 g large spiral pasta, cooked al dente
2/3 cup extra virgin olive oil
6 Tbsp lemon juice (1/3 cup)
2 tsp Dijon mustard
1 tsp salt or to taste
1 tsp freshly ground black pepper
1/3 cup drained and roughly chopped capers
3/4 cup finely chopped Italian (flat-leaf) parsley
1/2 cup olives, black or green
3/4 cup fresh basil, roughly chopped
1 cup sliced button mushrooms
1/2 cup roast salted nuts such as almonds or cashews
150 g diced feta (or lightly fried haloumi)
8 cherry tomatoes, halved

Refresh the pasta, drain well and transfer to a large serving platter.
Combine the oil, lemon juice, mustard and seasonings in a screw-top jar. Shake well; pour over the cooked and drained pasta and toss.
Add the capers, half the parsley, the olives and half the basil. Toss again. Cover with cling wrap and leave for up to an hour if possible, to enable the pasta to absorb the flavours — although the dish can be served at once if time is short.
Toss again and add the mushrooms, nuts, cheese and tomatoes and sprinkle over the remaining parsley and basil as a garnish.

Layered eggplant Napoli

In this delicious dish, eggplant slices are tossed in seasoned flour, dipped in lightly beaten egg and then coated with dry (preferably wholemeal) breadcrumbs, sealing them so they absorb very little oil. The eggplant is then layered with a mixture of cottage cheese (or ricotta), egg and feta to add interesting texture as well as nutritional balance.

■ **Serves 6. Freezes well.**

2 large eggplants, about 500 g each
½ cup flour
1 tsp salt or to taste
freshly ground black pepper
2 eggs, lightly beaten
¼ cup milk
1½ cups fine dry breadcrumbs (preferably wholemeal)
3 cups tomato pasta sauce (preferably
    home-made, see recipe page 48)
⅓ cup oil, more as needed
½ cup loosely packed Italian (flat-leaf) parsley
½ cup loosely packed fresh basil (or oregano)
¾ cup cottage cheese (or ricotta)
120 g feta, grated
1 large egg
½ cup fresh grated Parmesan or mozzarella

Preheat the oven to 180°C.
Trim the eggplant and slice into rounds about 1.25 cm thick. There is no need to salt the eggplant slices for this dish if they are fresh.
Toss the eggplant slices in the flour seasoned with salt and pepper. Combine the lightly beaten eggs with the milk and dip the eggplant slices in this, then coat each slice with the breadcrumbs.
Measure the pasta sauce and set aside.
Heat the oil to medium high in a large frying pan — an electric frying pan is ideal. Shallow-fry the eggplant slices on both sides until golden and cooked through. Drain on paper towels.
Place a layer of cooked eggplant slices on the bottom of a 30 cm x 20 cm lasagne or baking dish. You may have to cut some of the larger slices in half or quarters to achieve an even layer. Pour 1½ cups of the tomato pasta sauce evenly over the eggplant.
Roughly chop the parsley and basil and distribute half over the tomato sauce.
Whisk the cottage cheese or ricotta, feta and egg together or beat with a fork. Place large spoonfuls over the tomato sauce/herb layer then gently smooth over.
Now distribute the remaining herbs over the cheese/egg layer, followed by the remaining eggplant slices. Pour the last of the tomato sauce evenly over the top and sprinkle with the Parmesan or mozzarella.
Bake, uncovered, at 180°C for 40–45 minutes or until the top is bubbling and golden.

Crisped polenta

Crisped polenta teams well with vegetables such as slow-roasted or grilled tomatoes, sautéed or baked mushrooms, and watercress salad drizzled with extra virgin olive oil and caramelised balsamic vinegar (page 45). Or, spoon a simple tomato pasta sauce (page 48), over the cooked polenta and accompany it with a salad of rocket, olives and scorched cherry tomatoes. Or try it cut into 8-cm rounds and shallow fried for brunch; topped with fresh rocket leaves and a poached egg or two and garnished with shaved Parmesan, it makes a gorgeous, feel-good start to a lazy day.

The inclusion of saffron is not strictly necessary, although it does accentuate both the colour and flavour of the polenta.

Tasty Cheddar may be substituted for the Parmesan, although Parmesan is preferable.

■ **Serves 4–6. May be frozen.**

4 cups unsalted vegetable stock or water
1½ cups polenta, regular or instant*
pinch saffron (optional)
2 tsp salt or to taste
freshly ground black pepper
60 g butter, diced
⅓ cup finely grated Parmesan (or tasty Cheddar)
1 Tbsp fresh rosemary leaves, roughly chopped (or 1 tsp dried rosemary)
olive oil

Bring the stock or water to the boil over a medium heat. Use a large, heavy-based saucepan, as boiling polenta is hot and spatters. Crush or crumble the saffron and soak in 2 tablespoons hot water for 5 minutes.
Gradually add the polenta to the boiling stock or water, stirring constantly. Stir in the saffron and soaking water, salt and pepper. Cook, stirring frequently, over a low heat until the polenta is thick and pulls away from the sides of the saucepan. This should take 20–25 minutes. Stir in the diced butter, Parmesan and rosemary.
Transfer to a baking sheet and spread to 2–3 cm thick. Cool. Cover and refrigerate if necessary until ready to cook.
Stamp the polenta into rounds or slice into triangles. Shallow fry in a little oil until golden, 3–4 minutes each side over a moderate heat.
Serve immediately.

*If using instant polenta, cook for the recommended time.

Tofu, lemon & herb lasagne

This vegetarian lasagne is light and fresh, showcasing herbs and a touch of lemon that, in combination with the other key ingredients, make this dish a star. Try it partnered with sautéed mushrooms and hot ciabatta buns. Pre-made tomato pasta sauce (page 48) and frozen spinach speed up preparation time for this lasagne.

■ **Serves 6. Suitable to freeze.**

9 squares oven-ready lasagne (or enough for 3 layers)
3 Tbsp olive oil
1 large leek, white part thinly sliced (2 cups) (or 1 large onion, peeled and sliced)
3–4 cloves garlic, crushed
finely grated zest and juice of 1 large lemon
250 g firm fresh tofu, diced small (½ cm)
3 Tbsp fresh basil, chopped (or 2 tsp dried basil)
3 Tbsp fresh oregano (or 2 tsp dried oregano)
1 tsp salt or to taste
freshly ground black pepper
½ cup cottage cheese
1 cup grated tasty Cheddar
  (or ½ cup grated mozzarella and ½ cup grated Parmesan)
300 ml (1¼ cups) 'lite' cream or cream
600 g fresh spinach, steamed, refreshed under cold water and drained
  (or 300 g frozen spinach)
2 cups tomato pasta sauce
130 g feta, grated or crumbled
1 cup grated mozzarella

Preheat the oven to 180°C. Lightly grease a 23 cm x 30 cm lasagne or baking dish. Heat the oil in a frying pan and sauté the leek (or sliced onion) and garlic gently until tender.
Stir the lemon zest, juice and the tofu into the leek mixture, followed by the basil, oregano, salt and pepper. Cook just for a minute or two, then remove from the heat. Combine the cottage cheese, Cheddar and ½ cup of the cream. Stir into the leek mixture and set aside.
Chop the spinach.

Assembly
Evenly cover the bottom of the lasagne dish with 1 cup of the tomato pasta sauce. Cover with a layer of lasagne sheets and evenly spread over the leek filling. Place another layer of lasagne over the leeks, followed by the prepared spinach and then the feta.
Place another layer of lasagne sheets over the spinach/feta filling and spread this evenly with the remaining cup of tomato pasta sauce. Ribbon the remaining cream over, then top with the grated mozzarella.
Bake at 180°C for 45–50 minutes.

Whole mushrooms en croûte

This recipe makes a great entrée to a special meal or the anchor for a lunch or light main. It's ideal for preparing the day before, looks impressive and is not only a wonderful flavour combination but also a textural delight — a combination of herbs and fleshy mushroom encased in crisp puff pastry. Choose fleshy mushrooms, not thin flat ones, as they have a distinct 'cavity' that is easier to fill.

Rocket leaves and pizza thyme are used here, but use herbs of preference or availability. One thing to remember is that mushrooms not only cope with robust flavours, for true appreciation they need the extra boost — in other words, don't skimp on the garlic or the salt in this recipe!

■ **Serves 6. Not suitable to freeze.**

6 fleshy Portobello mushrooms, about 80 g each
sliced Camembert to fit inside mushroom cap — about 100 g
6 Tbsp finely chopped rocket and pizza thyme leaves (3 Tbsp of each),
   or herb combination of your choice
4 large cloves garlic, peeled
¾ cup roasted salted cashew nuts
¾ cup fresh, roughly grated Parmesan
1½ tsp salt or to taste
freshly ground black pepper
500 g flaky puff pastry, approximately, (or 780 g pre-rolled sheets if you
   don't mind wasting some)
1 beaten egg yolk

Preheat the oven to 200°C.
Trim stalks off so they sit flush in the underside of each mushroom cap. Line the mushroom 'cavity' with slices of Camembert, (not too thick), in a single layer.
Measure the herbs after chopping finely.
Place the prepared garlic and herbs, cashews, Parmesan, salt and pepper in a food processor and chop until finely ground, creating a dry pesto without oil.
Divide the pesto evenly between the mushrooms and lightly press over the Camembert.
Roll the puff pastry out thinly — if you are using pre-rolled sheets, roll them a little thinner. Cut 6 saucer-sized rounds of pastry to fit over the filling and enclose the entire mushroom. Brush the pastry join underneath with a little cold water to seal.
Decorate the tops with small pastry leaves or festive twists, then brush lightly with beaten egg yolk and place the mushrooms on a baking tray (seal side down), leaving a gap between each. If preparing ahead, cover with cling wrap and refrigerate overnight.
Bake at 200°C for 20 minutes or until the pastry is crisp and golden.

Mushroom tapenade pasta with scorched cherry tomatoes

This delicious pasta is surprisingly quick to make, and creates a lively pastiche of colour and flavours complemented by scorched cherry tomatoes.

Serve with chopped spinach sautéed in olive oil and hot, crusty ciabatta.

Instead of grilling the tomatoes to scorch them, a kitchen micro torch may be used (with care).

■ **Serves 4. Not suitable to freeze.**

400 g spaghetti

Sauce
⅓ cup olive oil
3 cloves garlic, peeled and chopped fine
1 tsp fresh seeded chilli, chopped fine (or ⅓ tsp chilli powder)
3 cups finely sliced button or field mushrooms (about 250 g)
lots of freshly ground black pepper
½–¾ tsp salt or to taste
¾ cup pitted and chopped good quality black olives*
1 punnet (15–18) cherry tomatoes
½ cup Italian (flat-leaf) parsley, roughly chopped
fresh Parmesan shavings, and extra to grate
fresh basil or rocket (optional) and/or 2–3 Tbsp basil pesto or rocket pesto (page 17)

*Use good quality Kalamata olives or equivalent for this dish — cheaper Spanish olives lack the flavour needed here.

Heat the olive oil in a large frying pan over a low heat and slowly sauté the garlic and chilli until fragrant.

Turn the heat to medium–high and stir in the mushrooms with lots of black pepper and salt to taste. Sauté for 5 minutes or until the mushrooms are cooked through.

Transfer half the cooked mushrooms to a food processor and pulse with the olives until quite smooth but not puréed. Return this mix to the pan with the remaining mushrooms and reheat, stirring gently, when the spaghetti is almost cooked.

Cook the spaghetti to al dente in lots of salted, boiling water.

While the spaghetti is cooking, heat the grill to its highest setting and grill the tomatoes until the skins split and blacken lightly.

Drain the pasta and transfer to the pan containing the mushroom/olive mixture. Toss to combine well, adding a little extra virgin olive oil if required.

Either transfer to a heated dish or serve the pasta from the pan, topped with the parsley, scorched tomatoes, fresh Parmesan shavings, fresh basil leaves and/or pesto.

Serve with extra finely grated Parmesan at the table.

Caramelised shallot tarte tatin

Simplicity but lots of interest in terms of taste, texture and visual appeal are keynotes here — and a watercress/mesclun salad, good bread and a slice of feta complement it perfectly; or serve with a salad of green leaves, crumbled blue cheese, and sliced fresh pear.

The shallots can be cooked ahead, then rewarmed before proceeding.

The cooked tarte tatin is equally as good eaten hot, warmed or at room temperature. Use shallots if they're available, because they look so good whole — otherwise a mixture of whole small pickling onions with red onions sliced into quarters or eighths can be substituted; or use all red onions, sliced lengthwise. Fennel loses much of its anise flavour when heated but adds interest and complexity to the taste.

■ **Serves 3–4 for lunch or a light meal with bread and salad. Add cheeses and fruit if something more substantial is needed. Not suitable for freezing.**

6 cloves garlic, peeled
500 g shallots, peeled
40 g butter
2 Tbsp oil
½ tsp salt or to taste
freshly ground black pepper
2 Tbsp brown sugar
1 Tbsp balsamic vinegar
1 cup dill leaves, roughly chopped (or fennel leaves with some top stalk)
1 square pre-rolled puff pastry, thawed
feta (optional)

Slice the garlic cloves into half lengthwise but leave the shallots whole, halving only those that are especially large. Set the shallots and garlic aside separately.
Melt the butter and oil in a 20-cm frying pan that will transfer to an oven. Cook the shallots over a medium–high heat, tossing and shaking the pan constantly, until they are well coloured and softening. Turn the heat down, add the garlic and continue cooking for another few minutes to soften and colour the garlic. Toss in the salt, pepper, sugar and balsamic and cook for just 2–3 minutes more, until the sauce is beginning to caramelise — it will continue this process in the oven.
Set aside to cool for 10–15 minutes while preheating the oven to 180°C. Stir the dill (or fennel) into the shallot mixture. Place the pastry over the top, trimming the corners and lightly tucking down the sides to secure. Make two or three small slits in the top of the pastry and place the pan in the preheated oven.
Bake for 25–30 minutes. Remove from the oven and immediately place a plate on top of the pastry and invert the pan so that the onion filling becomes the top of the tart. Serve hot or warm. Garnish with dill or fennel sprigs and accompany with feta if you fancy.

Pasta with spinach, cherry tomatoes & creamy blue sauce

It's reassuring to know that the love of cooking and good food has a legacy down through the generations, and kitchens can be very creative places. A mother/daughter effort produced this lovely combination of texture, taste, colour and style.

Buy the best quality creamy blue cheese you can afford — this dish is worth it; even those not too fussed about blue cheese love this combination.

Serve with salad and hot crusty ciabatta rolls to capture every drop of the sauce.

■ **Serves 4–6. Not suitable for freezing.**

½ cup walnuts, chopped
¼ cup olive oil
1 small onion, peeled and sliced
3–4 cloves garlic, peeled and chopped
1 medium-sized red chilli, seeded and diced (optional)
400 g pasta such as penne or spaghetti
300 g baby spinach leaves (or larger, fresh spinach leaves), roughly chopped
150 g creamy blue cheese, grated
3 Tbsp olive oil, extra
2 Tbsp pasta water
200 g cherry tomatoes, halved
salt and freshly ground black pepper to taste
½ cup shaved or finely grated Parmesan

Toast the walnuts in a shallow pan over low–medium heat, tossing regularly, until crisped and golden. Set aside. Set a large saucepan of salted water to boil for the pasta.

Heat the olive oil in a large shallow pan over a low heat and slowly sauté the onion, garlic and chilli until softened.

Start the pasta cooking in lots of well-salted boiling water, while you prepare the vegetables.

Add the spinach leaves to the onion/garlic mixture and turn up the heat to medium. Cook, stirring, until the spinach has wilted.

Turn the heat down immediately and stir in the blue cheese, the extra 3 tablespoons of olive oil, the pasta water (from the saucepan) and the tomatoes.

After the blue cheese has melted, season to taste with salt and pepper. You should now have a great tasting sauce in which to toss the pasta, and the tomatoes should retain their shape and structure.

Drain the cooked pasta and transfer to the pan containing the spinach/blue cheese sauce. Transfer to a heated serving dish, scatter the roasted walnuts over the top and serve immediately, accompanied by the Parmesan in a separate bowl on the side.

Polenta primo

This dish is traditional Italian — very simply constructed, but its attractive appearance, texture and great flavour ensure its popularity.

Use block mozzarella if possible, although tasty Cheddar or other cheeses will work. Nice with steamed broccoli or a watercress/mesclun salad with roasted walnuts, baked Portobello mushrooms and hot crusty breads.

Both the sauce and the polenta can be made ahead of time — in fact this sauce is well worth making in double or more quantities and freezing any excess for other uses. Instant polenta may be substituted for regular.

■ Serves 4–6. Freezes well.

4 cups water (1 litre)
2 tsp salt or to taste
1½ cups polenta or instant polenta*
300 g mozzarella sliced ½ cm thick

Tomato pasta sauce
See recipe page 48

Polenta
While the sauce is cooking, bring the water to boiling in a large saucepan (be careful — the polenta tends to spatter). Add 2 teaspoons salt and slowly stir in the polenta. Stir regularly, over a medium heat, for 20–25 minutes*, or until very thick and pulling away from the sides of the saucepan.
Transfer to a lightly sprayed or greased loaf pan and set aside to cool for at least 15 minutes, until firm. Turn out and slice across its width into pieces 1 cm thick.

Assembly
Preheat the oven to 190°C.
Lightly grease or spray a lasagne dish, about 30 cm x 20 cm.
Pour 1 cup of the tomato sauce into the bottom of the prepared dish, then place overlapping slices of polenta and mozzarella into the dish in a single layer. It doesn't matter if the cheese doesn't 'fit' the polenta exactly.
Pour over the remaining tomato sauce, weaving it so that the polenta/cheese layers are visible between thick ribbons of the sauce.
Bake uncovered at 190°C for 30–40 minutes or until the sauce and cheese are bubbling.

*If using instant polenta, cook for the recommended time.

Smokin' beans

Hot, smoky beans make a great family meal when everyone can create their own combo at the table. Provided plenty of serviettes are available, dribbles are allowed in the interests of a fun, flexible, inexpensive meal.

Place a large spoonful of beans along one side of a heated tortilla; spoon on some sour cream, grated cheese, carrot and shredded lettuce and perhaps some chilli sauce, plain yoghurt or aïoli (page 44). Fold up the bottom of the tortilla and roll.

If you have beans left over, add some chopped tomatoes and fresh coriander and spoon over baked potatoes. Serve with salads and a dollop of sour cream — delicious!

■ **Serves 4–6. Freezes well.**

---

5 cups cooked pinto beans*
2 Tbsp oil
2 medium-sized onions, peeled and finely chopped
6–8 cloves garlic, crushed
8 small dried chillies, crushed or minced with a sharp knife
1 Tbsp ground coriander
2 tsp ground cumin
2 tsp paprika
½ tsp sweet (dulce) Spanish smoked paprika
1 capsicum, seeded and diced
425-g tin peeled tomatoes, chopped, with juice
425-g tin tomato purée
1½ tsp salt or to taste
lots of freshly ground black pepper
fresh coriander, finely chopped

Heat the oil in a large saucepan and sauté the onions and garlic over a gentle heat until the onion begins to soften. Stir in the chillies, coriander, cumin, paprika, smoked paprika and capsicum. Continue to sauté gently for a few more minutes.
Add the tomatoes, tomato purée, and the salt and pepper. Simmer for 10 minutes with the lid on, stirring occasionally. Stir the cooked beans into the chilli mixture, cover and simmer for a further 15 minutes.
Garnish the dish just before serving with fresh coriander.

*Pinto beans have a milder flavour than red kidney beans and are preferred for this recipe. Two and a half cups dry beans should yield 5 cups cooked beans. Soak overnight then simmer for approximately 1½ hours or pressure cook, unsoaked, for 40 minutes.

Mexican pumpkin pie

It may not be exactly chic, but this pie looks awfully good when there are many mouths to feed and the priority is a dish that doesn't blow the budget but shows you care. It does use some shortcut ingredients, such as pre-rolled pastry and a can of Mexican chilli beans, but you can of course substitute home-made pastry and chilli beans if you wish.

Make it go further with baked potatoes or wedges, for example, and a tomato and avocado salsa or salad, or a combination of sautéed cabbage and mushrooms. Serve with chilli sauce on the side.

■ **Serves 6–8. Freezes well.**

3 sheets pre-rolled flaky puff pastry, defrosted
900 g seeded and peeled pumpkin
1 cup rocket, coriander, basil or Italian (flat-leaf) parsley (or a mixture)
1 tsp salt or to taste
freshly ground black pepper
2–3 cloves garlic, crushed
2 large eggs
250 g cottage cheese
400-g can of Mexican beans in spicy chilli sauce
1 generous cup tasty grated cheese
egg yolk for glaze

Preheat the oven to 200°C.
Cut the 3 pre-rolled sheets of pastry to form a square, sealing the edges together with a little water and pressing firmly. Transfer the pastry square to a lightly greased or sprayed oven tray and set aside.
Chop the pumpkin into bite-sized chunks and cook in salted water until tender. Drain and mash lightly.
Any mixture of the herbs may be used, but rocket must be wilted to avoid bitterness (see Glossary, pages 183–184). Pour boiling water over the rocket leaves, refresh under cold water and squeeze dry. Chop the herbs roughly and mix into the mashed pumpkin with the salt, pepper, garlic, eggs and cottage cheese with a fork. Spoon the pumpkin mix onto the prepared pastry square, spreading evenly but leaving enough pastry at the edges to draw up over the pumpkin towards the centre of the 'pie' (about 6 cm on all sides of the filling).
Spoon the chilli beans, with their sauce, over the top of the pumpkin mix, sprinkle over the grated cheese and draw up the pastry sides so they overlap the filling but don't enclose it, pleating it to create a large circle as you go. Trim off any excess pastry.
Brush the top of the pie with lightly beaten egg yolk and bake at 200°C for 30 minutes. Turn the heat down to 180°C if the pie is browning too fast and bake for a further 15–20 minutes.
Remove from the oven and allow it to rest for 5 minutes before slicing.

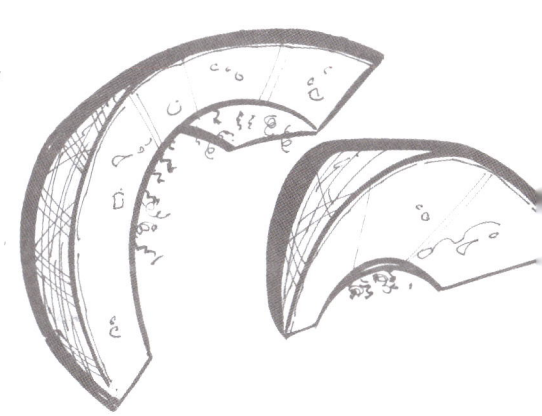

Mexican mole

Mexican cuisine is vibrant, showy and full of contrasts: think hot chilli salsa with cool guacamole, or avocado, tomato and fresh coriander spiked with lime. A meal is rarely about one dish in isolation, but more about an anchor main accompanied by side dishes.

Mole (pronounced mole-ay) is quintessentially Mexican; a traditional sauce where chilli is tempered by chocolate, and infused with notes of spice and smoke to create real character. It's different, delicious and, as with most Mexican food, inexpensive.

Mole is even better served the next day, when the flavours have found their rightful place in the scheme of things. Don't be tempted to take shortcuts with this mole — it's quick to assemble and well worth the cooking time.

■ **Serves 4–6. Suitable to freeze.**

---

1 x 400 g eggplant
¾ cup black turtle beans, soaked overnight
¼ cup oil (first measure)
salt
4 Tbsp oil (second measure)
1 large onion, peeled and sliced
5–6 red chillies, about 6 cm long, seeded and finely chopped
6 garlic cloves, peeled and finely chopped
2 large red capsicums, diced
1 tsp ground cinnamon
2 tsp ground coriander
1 tsp paprika
1 tsp sweet (dulce) Spanish smoked paprika
2 x 400-g tins peeled, chopped tomatoes
  or 1 kg fresh tomatoes, peeled and chopped
1½ cups water
30 g dark, 70% chocolate, finely chopped
salt and pepper to taste
fresh tomato salsa, sour cream, finely chopped coriander, lime or lemon

Preheat the oven to 190°C.

Slice the eggplant into 2-cm dice, toss with enough oil to lightly coat (about ¼ cup) and salt lightly. Transfer to an oven tray and roast for 25 minutes or until golden, turning once. Remove from the oven and set aside. Turn the oven down to 170°C.

Meanwhile, heat the 4 tablespoons oil over a medium heat in a large, heavy-based oven-to-table casserole dish with a lid. Sauté the onion and chillies, garlic and capsicums until well softened, adding a little more oil if necessary.

Stir in the cinnamon, coriander, paprika and smoked paprika and sauté for a few minutes more.

Add the tomatoes with their juice, and the water.

Stir in the soaked beans and the roasted eggplant. Heat to simmer point and stir in the chocolate. Cover the casserole dish and transfer to the oven. Bake at 170°C for 2 hours, stirring occasionally.

Taste, then add salt and pepper to your liking.

Serve with sour cream and/or fresh salsa as outlined below. Try it with nachos or baked potatoes, tortillas or any of the other suggestions.

Mole is especially good served simply with a dollop of sour cream, fresh chopped coriander and nachos. A fresh salsa is a good accompaniment: mix together seeded and chopped fresh tomatoes, peeled chopped garlic, finely diced red onion, seeded and minced fresh chilli (optional), a squeeze of lime or lemon juice, chopped fresh coriander, salt and pepper. Add diced avocado if you like, and partner it all with a spoonful or two of sour cream.

Mole is equally as good with tacos or tortillas, rice, baked potatoes or cornbread.

Mushroom risotto

Any mushrooms may be used here, although a combination of button, Portobello and oyster mushrooms looks interesting and adds textural interest. If this isn't possible, button mushrooms alone are excellent.

Either red or white wine may be used with excellent results; for taste, red is marginally better if you don't mind your risotto leaning towards a 'muddy' colour. Substitute ½ cup water with a tablespoon of lemon juice for the wine if you wish.

Serve with a hot crusty baguette and a salad.

The making of a good risotto used to be one of those culinary mysteries; so much so that most cooks can still remember their first attempt. Any wannabe risotto-makers can rest assured, however, that to be successful you need only arborio rice to achieve that wonderful traditional creamy texture, and a soupçon of confidence; the actual method is quite straightforward.

■ **Serves 4–6. Not recommended for freezing.**

---

3 Tbsp olive oil
1 onion, peeled and finely chopped
1 litre well-flavoured vegetable stock
3 cloves garlic, peeled and finely chopped
2 cups arborio rice
½ cup red or white wine (or ½ cup water and 1 Tbsp lemon juice)
salt to taste
lots of freshly ground black pepper
2 Tbsp margarine or butter
2 Tbsp oil, extra
1–2 Tbsp margarine or butter, extra
400–450 g mushrooms, chopped into chunks
Parmesan, very finely grated
chopped Italian (flat-leaf) parsley

Heat the oil in a heavy-based saucepan over a medium–low heat and sauté the onion until it begins to soften. At the same time, bring the stock to a simmer in a separate saucepan. Stir the garlic into the onions and sauté a few minutes more, then stir in the arborio rice. Cook, stirring, until all the grains are coated with oil. Stir in the wine and turn the heat up to medium. Stir in the salt and pepper.

When the wine has been absorbed, take a soup ladle of the simmering stock and add to the risotto, stirring. When this has almost been absorbed, add another, until all the stock has been added and absorbed. The process should take about 20 minutes, by which stage the rice grains should be cooked but still have distinct, individual character. They should not be so soft as to be mushy. Turn off the heat and vigorously stir in the first measure of butter. Add salt and freshly ground black pepper, to taste.

While the rice is cooking, heat the extra oil and butter in a pan and sauté the mushrooms briefly, with salt and pepper to taste, ready to add to the risotto as soon as the butter is added. The mushrooms are best lightly cooked, and should retain their shape. Don't overcook.

Grate the Parmesan on the smallest holes of a grater, used to zest lemons; chop the parsley and set these aside for garnish.

Mix the lightly cooked mushrooms into the risotto and serve garnished with parsley. Place the Parmesan in a dish on the table for each diner to help themselves.

Falafel

Traditionally, falafel are made from soaked but not cooked chickpeas (garbanzo beans) — however, it's hard to beat this version for reliability and taste.

■ **Makes 16–20 egg-sized falafel, enough for 4–6 people. Recipe is easily halved. Not suitable to freeze.**

2 x 400-g tins chickpeas, rinsed and drained (2½ cups cooked chickpeas)
4 cloves garlic, peeled and roughly chopped
1 tsp ground cumin
2 tsp ground coriander
1 tsp salt or to taste
½–1 tsp chilli powder
4 Tbsp lemon juice
4 Tbsp plain flour
4 Tbsp finely chopped Italian (flat-leaf) parsley
4 Tbsp finely chopped coriander
oil for shallow frying

Grind the chickpeas and garlic in a food processor until the mixture resembles breadcrumbs. Add the cumin, coriander, salt and chilli powder. Process to combine, then add the lemon juice and the flour.

Transfer to a bowl and stir in the parsley and fresh coriander.

Take an egg-sized portion of the mixture and squeeze lightly so that it sticks together. Form into a ball and flatten into a patty shape. Repeat with the remaining mixture.

Heat enough oil to just cover the bottom of a frying pan. Shallow fry the falafel until heated through and golden on both sides.

Drain on paper towels.

Stuff into wraps, pita bread or burger buns with a yoghurt and fresh mint sauce or chilli sauce, grated carrot and watercress.

Pizza

This pizza base recipe is hard to beat, and takes so little effort. It makes two 30-cm bases (or one large one), and rises in the time the two toppings are assembled. Double the topping quantities if you are making the same one for both pizzas.

■ **Serves 4, depending on appetites. Freezes well.**

Pizza base
1 cup plain flour
1 cup wholemeal flour
2 tsp instant yeast granules
1½ tsp sugar
½ tsp salt
1 cup warm water
½ cup (approximately) plain flour, extra

Lightly oil or spray two 30-cm pizza pans or oven trays.
Place the flours, yeast, sugar and salt in a medium-sized bowl and combine. Stir in the warm water (it should be just above blood temperature). Place the dough in a bread mixer with a dough hook or place on a lightly floured bench and knead, adding the extra flour while the dough is kneaded. This should only take 3–5 minutes by hand, until the dough is smooth and elastic (not sticky).
Place the dough into an oiled bowl, cover with a clean cloth and leave to rise in a warm place for an hour. Punch the dough down, turn out onto a lightly floured board and knead briefly. Preheat the oven to 210°C.
Divide the dough in two if making two pizzas, shape into smooth balls and roll each out thinly to fit the two pans, or simply roll out and transfer to oven trays.
Spread evenly with the base sauce of choice and one topping for each pizza, then bake at 210°C for 15–20 minutes.

Base sauces
2 large, red, roasted and peeled capsicums (from a jar is fine), lightly seasoned and puréed with a fresh, red, seeded chilli, finely chopped, or ½ tsp crushed chilli flakes
or
½ cup tomato concentrate or tomato pizza base sauce

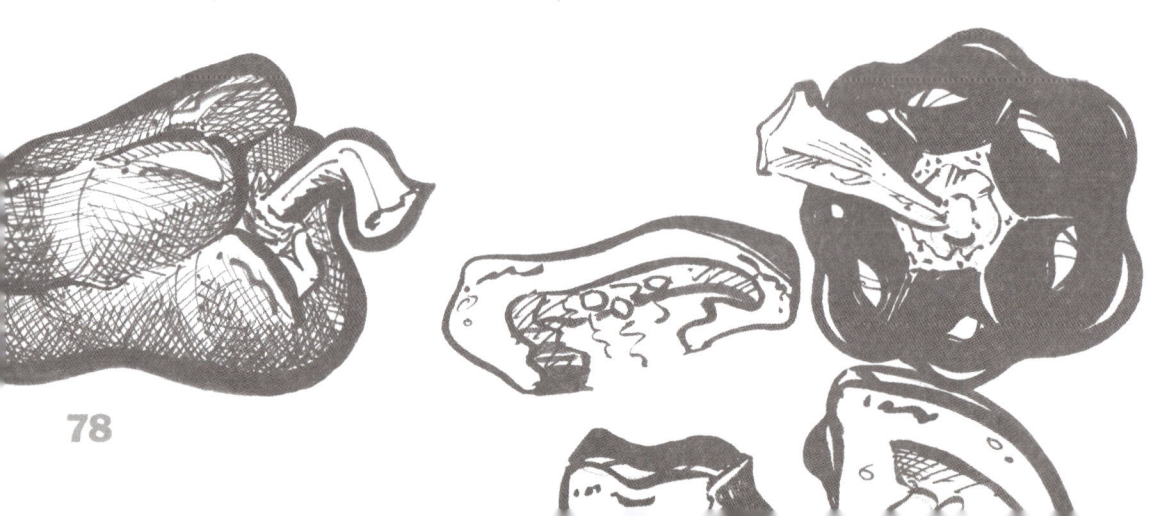

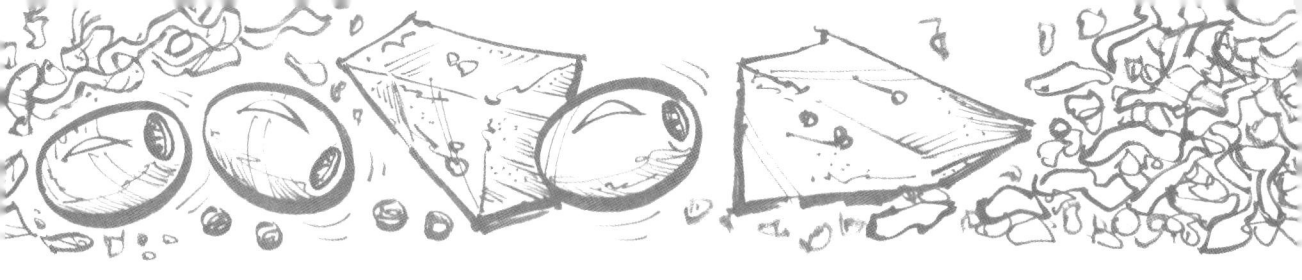

Spinach, feta, caper & cream topping

Spinach with feta sounds like a no-surprise topping, but when baked with a caper and sour cream garnish, a transformation occurs!

¼ cup roast capsicum or tomato base sauce
2 cloves garlic, peeled and finely sliced
250 g fresh spinach (or 150 g frozen spinach, thawed)
90 g feta, grated or crumbled
freshly ground black pepper
1 small red or yellow capsicum, cored and seeded
2 Tbsp capers, rinsed and drained
4 Tbsp sour cream

Evenly spread the sauce over the pizza base, and evenly sprinkle the prepared garlic over the top.
Wash and lightly steam fresh spinach, covered, for 2–3 minutes in a microwave. Refresh under cold water. Squeeze the fresh steamed or thawed spinach thoroughly, to remove any excess moisture, and chop finely. Place in a bowl and combine with the grated or crumbled feta and black pepper. Taste and add a little salt if needed. Distribute the spinach/feta mixture evenly over the top of the pizza.
Slice the capsicum into strips to top the spinach/feta. Sprinkle the capers over, then dot or drizzle the sour cream over the top, using a teaspoon.
Bake as directed above.

Zucchini, artichoke & blue cheese topping

A great topping garnished with fresh rocket after the pizza is cooked makes a delicious change.

¼ cup roast capsicum or tomato base sauce
1 zucchini, sliced thinly lengthways
2 tinned artichoke hearts, drained and quartered
90 g creamy blue cheese, sliced thinly
freshly ground black pepper
1 cup rocket leaves
2 Tbsp extra virgin olive oil

Evenly spread the sauce over the pizza base.
Arrange the zucchini slices in a spoke pattern, radiating out from the centre of the pizza, then place the quartered artichokes between the zucchini slices.
Distribute the blue cheese slices evenly over the pizza and grind over black pepper to taste.
Bake as directed above, and transfer to a board to cut and serve. Sprinkle over the rocket leaves and drizzle with the olive oil.

Summer picnic pie

This pie is good served hot or at room temperature, and is ideal for a casual meal, served with boiled new potatoes and a mixed green salad; or make ahead of time and take it on a picnic. The vegetables in this pie are grilled or roasted, as these methods need less oil than if the vegetables are fried. Although the debate still simmers on whether to salt eggplant or not, my take is that, while not strictly necessary, salting reduces the amount of oil absorbed during the cooking process.

■ **Serves 4 as a main, 6 as a light meal. May be frozen.**

Shortcrust pastry
Store-bought, pre-rolled savoury shortcrust or puff pastry may be used (350 g), or refer to recipe for light wholemeal shortcrust, page 150, and increase the quantity by a half to cater for the top of the pie.

Filling
1 large eggplant, about 500 g
500–550 g zucchini (4–5 medium-sized)
3–4 large red capsicums
125 g feta, grated or crumbled
½–¾ cup fresh basil, very roughly chopped
    (or 4 Tbsp basil pesto*)
salt and pepper to taste

*Rocket pesto (page 17) is just as good, or mint and almond pesto (page 12).

Preheat the oven to 190°C. Lightly grease or spray a 23-cm springform cake tin. Slice the eggplant into 5-mm slices, brush both sides with olive oil or dip into a bowl of olive oil and wipe off any excess on the lip of the bowl. Place in a single layer on a baking tray and bake until golden, about 25 minutes, or grill, turning once. Salt lightly and set aside.

Slice the zucchini into 5-mm slices and place on a baking tray in a single layer, toss lightly in olive oil and season with salt and freshly ground black pepper. Bake for about 20 minutes, or grill, turning once. Cool.

Cut the peppers in half lengthwise, remove the seeds and cores and place cut side down on a baking tray. Roast about 25 minutes, until the skin is blistered and lifting from the flesh.

Grate or crumble the feta and set aside. Measure out the fresh basil or basil pesto. Increase the oven temperature to 210°C.

Assembly
Roll out two-thirds of the dough thinly on a floured surface and line the bottom and sides of the tin. Roll out the remaining dough to form a top for the pie. Line the base of the pie with half the pepper slices, then half the zucchini slices, half the feta, half the basil or the pesto, then half the eggplant. Repeat the layers, place the top on the pie and pinch the sides together. Make three small slits in the top with a sharp knife and brush the top with some beaten egg.

Bake at 210°C for 20 minutes, then reduce heat to 200°C for another 20–30 minutes.

Tuscan tart

Tuscan tart can be served as an entrée, lunch, picnic or casual meal. The pastry base is coated with fine cornmeal, which enhances the colour and crispness of the base. The topping enhances the sweet onion filling and provides a contrast to the base and filling.

■ Serves 4–6. Not suitable for freezing.

Filling
¼ cup pure olive oil
750 g onions, peeled and finely chopped
3 cloves garlic, crushed
1 tsp freshly ground black pepper
2 Tbsp brown sugar
2 Tbsp balsamic vinegar
1 Tbsp fresh rosemary
1 medium-sized red capsicum
2 Tbsp extra virgin olive oil

Heat the oil in a heavy-based frying pan and cook the onions with the garlic and the pepper over a low heat for about 20 minutes, until the onions are very soft. Stir regularly. Stir in the brown sugar, vinegar and rosemary. Transfer to a dish to cool. Core and seed the capsicum and slice into long slices, about 1 cm wide. Transfer to a bowl, toss them in the extra virgin oil and set aside. Preheat the oven to 200°C.

Pastry
See Tuscan Pastry, page 151

Topping and assembly
Distribute the cooled onion filling into the pastry base. Arrange the capsicum strips over the top radiating out from the middle, like the spokes of a wheel. Drizzle any remaining oil over the top. Bake at 200°C for 40–45 minutes.

Topping
12 large black olives, stoned and halved
2 Tbsp extra virgin olive oil
2 Tbsp lemon juice
freshly ground black pepper
¼ cup finely chopped parsley, preferably Italian flat-leaved
80 g feta
1 cup rocket leaves

Place olives in a small bowl with the oil, lemon juice, pepper and parsley. Grate or crumble the feta and set aside. Chop or slice the rocket leaves and set aside. When the tart is cooked, stand for 5 minutes. Sprinkle the feta evenly over the tart then distribute the rocket over the feta. Spoon over the olives with their marinade.
Serve hot. If you are intending to serve the tart at room temperature, cool before adding the topping.

Szechuan 'clay pot' casserole

This casserole is a delectable combination of taste and texture with distinct Asian leanings. Modelled on Chinese clay pot cuisine, it is just as easily cooked in a casserole dish and well worth trying; a delicious, quite sophisticated dish, it is as simple to prepare as a stir-fry.

Szechuan peppercorns can be omitted but are a nice addition and available from Asian supply stores. They are neither peppery nor hot, but add a hint of citrus to augment the more traditional Asian flavours. Serve with plain steamed rice or hot crusty breads and a green, such as steamed bok choy.

■ **Serves 4. Not suitable for freezing.**

---

400 g eggplant, sliced into 5 cm long x 1 cm thick x 2 cm wide strips
1 tsp salt or to taste
4–5 Tbsp oil
1 onion, peeled and sliced
4 cloves garlic, peeled and finely chopped
2 tsp grated fresh ginger
1½ tsp toasted, lightly crushed Szechuan peppercorns
¾–1 tsp chilli powder
3 Tbsp kecap manis
2 Tbsp hoisin sauce
2 cups vegetable stock or water
2 Tbsp soy sauce
2½ Tbsp cornflour
150 g button mushrooms, halved
150 g green beans, fresh or frozen
200 g firm fresh tofu, sliced into strips about 5 cm long x 3 cm wide x 1 cm thick
salt and pepper to taste

Preheat the oven to 190°C. Prepare the eggplant, place the slices in a colander, sprinkle with salt and leave for 20 minutes, turning occasionally. Press with paper towels to remove excess liquid.

Heat 2 tablespoons of the oil in a wok or heavy-based frying pan and sauté the onion, garlic and ginger over a gentle heat until the onion is soft, taking care not to scorch. Stir in the remaining oil, eggplant, Szechuan peppercorns and chilli powder. Raise the heat a little and cook, tossing regularly, for 10–15 minutes, adding a little more oil if needed. Don't be tempted to shorten this step; the eggplant should be thoroughly cooked.

Mix in the kecap manis and the hoisin sauce. Reduce the heat to very low and cook, stirring, for a few minutes. Mix ½ cup of the stock or water, the soy sauce and the cornflour together and add to the wok with the balance of the stock or water. Turn the heat up a little and bring to simmer point.

Gently mix in the prepared mushrooms, beans and tofu. Transfer to a casserole with a lid and cook in the oven at 190°C for 35–40 minutes.

Sesame noodles with seared tofu

Toasted sesame seeds make an attractive garnish and add both texture and flavour. This recipe is for summer appetites and inclinations; light, delicious and versatile. Substitute green beans or mushrooms for the zucchini if you wish, or use more capsicum. Served in bowls accompanied by lightly sautéed spinach, this dish invites even the most jaded of appetites to partake. Serve it warm or at room temperature.

■ **Serves 4. Not suitable for freezing.**

---

500 g firm fresh tofu, sliced into 2-cm slices
¼ cup soy sauce (Kikkoman or tamari)
oil to shallow fry
2 tsp sesame oil
2 Tbsp light soy sauce
1 Tbsp lime juice (or lemon juice)
2 Tbsp oil
2 Tbsp sweet chilli sauce
3 Tbsp oil
1 onion, peeled and sliced thinly
3-cm piece of fresh ginger, peeled and minced
2 red capsicums, seeded and sliced
4 zucchini, sliced thinly on the diagonal (or 300 g green beans)
4 cakes 2-minute noodles (approx 320 g)
toasted sesame seeds, for garnish*
lightly sautéed spinach or steamed bok choy (optional)

*To toast sesame seeds, simply place in a dry frying pan over a low–medium heat and toss or stir continuously until fragrant and lightly golden.

Marinate the tofu in the soy sauce in a shallow, non-metallic dish for at least 1 hour, turning twice.
Combine the sesame oil, light soy sauce, lime juice, oil and sweet chilli sauce.
Heat the 3 tablespoons oil in a large frying pan and sauté the onion over a gentle heat. Stir in the ginger and continue cooking slowly until soft. Stir in the red capsicum and zucchini slices and sauté with the onion and ginger until just cooked.
Meanwhile, cook the 2-minute noodles in a large saucepan of salted water and drain. If you are not ready to add the noodles to the vegetables, refresh briefly under cold water to stop them cooking further and drain thoroughly.
Add the noodles to the pan containing the sautéed vegetables. Pour over the sesame dressing and mix very thoroughly with a pair of tongs.
Drain the sliced tofu, reserving the soy marinade. Heat some oil in a frying pan and shallow fry the tofu slices on both sides until golden brown, about 3 minutes each side. You may have to do this in batches, so keep the cooked slices warm.
While the tofu is cooking, reheat the noodle mixture in the pan, tossing, until warmed, then transfer to large individual serving bowls or a serving platter. Serve the noodles garnished with toasted sesame seeds and topped with the tofu. Drizzle the reserved soy marinade over and accompany with sautéed spinach or steamed bok choy, plus chilli or sauces of choice on the side if you wish.

Saag

Saag (spinach curry) is tasty and quick to prepare. Although it's delicious on its own, a complementary curry such as cauliflower and almond is always a welcome balance to the meal. Serve with rice and/or flat breads, raita and sambals. Traditionally paneer (a firm, low-fat Indian cheese) would be incorporated in this curry, but this is not always available; firm tofu or chickpeas are acceptable substitutes and provide protein content.

■ **Serves 4 (6 if serving more than one curry). Freezes well.**

700 g fresh spinach (or 350 g frozen)
2 Tbsp oil
1 medium-sized onion, peeled and sliced
2–3 large cloves garlic, crushed (2 tsp)
5-cm piece fresh ginger, peeled and minced (2 tsp)
½ tsp black mustard seeds
½ tsp cumin seeds
2 tsp ground cumin
½ tsp ground nutmeg
¾–1 tsp chilli powder
½ tsp freshly ground black pepper
1 tsp salt or to taste
¾ cup cream or 'lite' cream
1 cup water
¼ cup unsweetened plain yoghurt
150 g paneer (or firm tofu, diced small or ½–1 cup cooked chickpeas) (optional)

Wrench or cut off the roots of the fresh spinach, if still attached. Wash the leaves and shake off excess water. Place in a microwave-proof bowl, cover with cling wrap and microwave 3–4 minutes on high. Refresh in cold water, drain and squeeze to remove excess water. Chop roughly and set aside.

If you are using frozen spinach, defrost and squeeze to remove excess water.

Heat the oil in a medium-sized, heavy-based frying pan. Sauté the onion, garlic and ginger over a gentle heat until the onion softens. Stir in the mustard and cumin seeds and sauté for 2–3 minutes longer.

Stir in the ground cumin, nutmeg and chilli powder. Cook another couple of minutes before adding the pepper and salt followed by the cream, water and yoghurt.

Bring to simmer point and cook uncovered for 5–8 minutes, until lightly thickened. Transfer to a food processor with the prepared spinach and process until well combined and of a sauce consistency.

The saag can be set aside at this stage. Just before serving, add the diced paneer, tofu or the chickpeas, and gently reheat.

Madras chickpeas, eggplant & spinach

Madras chickpeas can either be a one-dish meal, served with flat breads or rice and a salad, or an accompaniment to other Indian or Middle Eastern dishes. It is also very good warmed and stuffed into pita breads.

The flavours and textures of this dish work well together — it's quick to make and is even better eaten the following day.

■ **Serves 4–6. Suitable to freeze.**

---

350 g eggplant*
2 cups cooked chickpeas
3 Tbsp oil (first measure)
4 cloves garlic, crushed
2 tsp minced fresh ginger
2 tsp ground cumin
1 Tbsp ground coriander
1 tsp chilli powder
1 tsp salt (generous)
2 x 400-g tins peeled, chopped tomatoes with juice
4 Tbsp oil (second measure)
300 g fresh spinach
1 tsp garam masala

Slice the eggplant into 1-cm thick slices, transfer to a colander and toss with a teaspoon of salt. Leave for 20 minutes then press firmly between paper towels to remove liquid and set aside.
Heat the first measure of oil in a large, heavy-based saucepan over a low heat and sauté the garlic and ginger for 1 minute. Add the cumin, coriander and chilli powder. Cook, stirring, until fragrant then stir in the cooked chickpeas and 1 teaspoon salt. Stir in the tomatoes and their juice. Simmer, uncovered, for 15 minutes, stirring regularly.
Heat the second measure of oil in a shallow frying pan over a medium heat and cook the eggplant slices on both sides until golden. Add more oil if necessary. Drain on paper towels, then slice into bite-sized pieces.
Wilt the spinach — wash, shake to remove excess water then microwave, covered, for 2–3 minutes on high. Refresh under cold water, drain and chop roughly.
Add the eggplant and the spinach to the chickpea mixture and return to a simmer. Stir in the garam masala and cook for a few minutes more. Taste and adjust seasonings if required.

*If eggplant is not available, zucchini may be substituted for a different but very good result.

Malai kofta

Tasty kofta (balls) cooked in a spunky Indian sauce are irresistible, either on their own with chapati and/or rice and sambals (chutneys), or with other curries as an Indian-inspired feast. The sauce is really the star of this dish; alive with chilli, creamy but not cloying, tangy but not sour. Spinach works best, but may be replaced with 300 g zucchini, grated and squeezed of excess liquid, or cooked, mashed pumpkin.

■ Serves 4–6. Freezes well.

Kofta
200 g frozen spinach, thawed and finely chopped
  (or 400 g fresh, wilted, squeezed dry and finely chopped)
3 cloves garlic, peeled and crushed
250 g sieved cottage cheese
¾ cup roast salted cashew nuts
1 seeded and finely chopped fresh chilli
  (or ½ tsp chilli powder) (optional)
1 tsp salt or to taste
¼ cup plain flour, sieved
1 egg yolk

Defrost the frozen spinach and squeeze to remove liquid, then chop finely, or wash fresh spinach, shake off excess water, chop roughly and microwave or steam until just wilted. Refresh, squeeze dry then chop finely.
Transfer the spinach to a medium-sized bowl with the garlic. Press the cottage cheese through a sieve and stir in.
Grind the cashew nuts finely in a food processor and add to the spinach mixture.
Stir in the chilli if using, the salt, flour and egg yolk.
Form into walnut-sized balls and set aside or refrigerate.

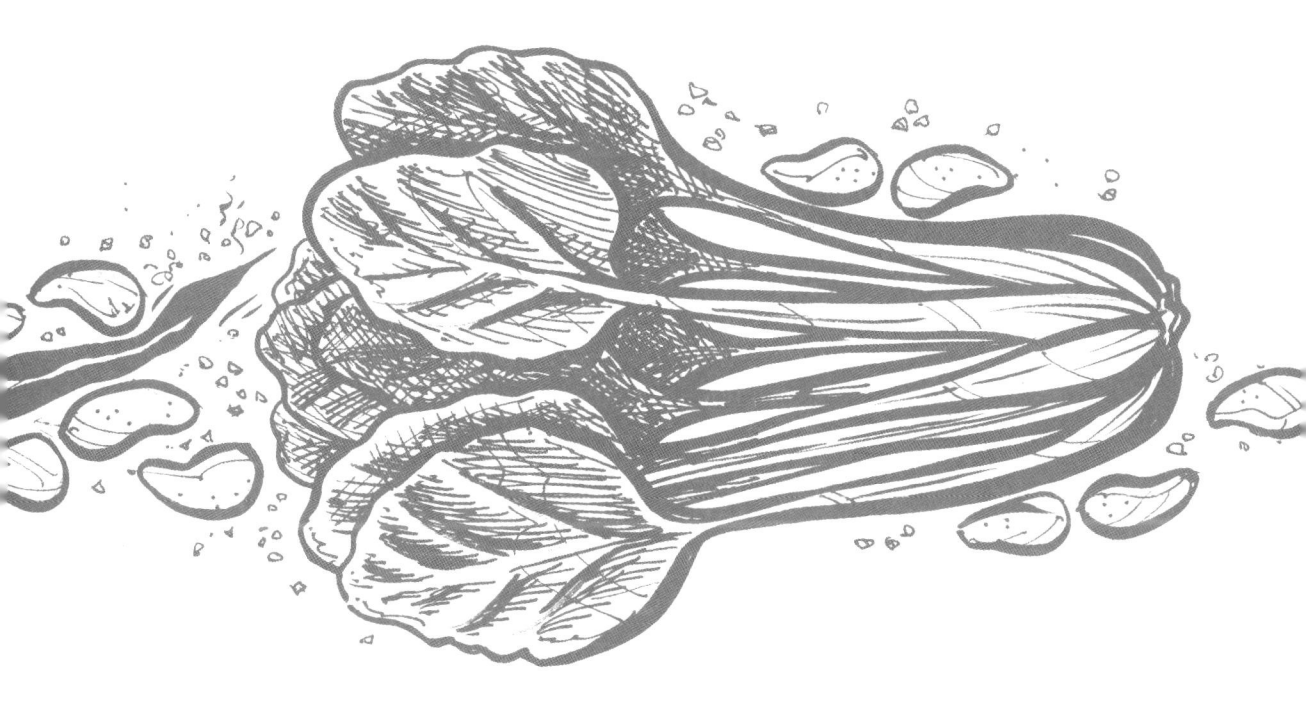

Sauce
¼ cup oil
1 large onion, peeled
1 red capsicum, seeded
6 cloves garlic, peeled and crushed
1 Tbsp peeled and finely chopped fresh ginger
1 Tbsp ground coriander
1 tsp chilli powder
4 tsp good-quality curry powder
2 tsp turmeric
1 tsp freshly ground black pepper
2 cups water
1 cup milk
½ cup plain unsweetened yoghurt
1 cup cream (or coconut cream)
1 tsp salt or to taste
2 Tbsp tomato paste
⅓ cup fresh mint, finely chopped
fresh coriander, finely chopped

Heat the oil in a large, heavy-based saucepan over a low–medium heat.
Slice the onion and capsicum into thin strips, then sauté with the garlic and ginger until softened.
Stir in the ground coriander, chilli powder, curry powder, turmeric and pepper and sauté for 2–3 minutes. Stir in the water, milk, yoghurt and cream. Don't panic if the sauce appears to split at this point — it comes back together as the sauce simmers and reduces. Stir in the salt, tomato paste and mint, then simmer, uncovered, for 20–25 minutes or until thickened.
Gently heat the kofta in the sauce. Garnish with the fresh coriander before serving.

Cauliflower & almond curry

Curries are a great way to entertain friends, not least because the flavours generally improve by making them the day before they are to be eaten.

This curry is simple and inexpensive, but contains a hint of luxury in its creamy texture and the inclusion of ground almonds. It's particularly good teamed with a vegetarian saag (spinach curry, page 84), but whether or not you team it with another curry, dress it up by adding flat breads as well as rice, chutneys, raita (grated cucumber and plain unsweetened yoghurt), and fresh chutneys. Instead of making flat breads, ready-made varieties are a major time-saver.

Small gourmet potatoes are ideal for this dish as they are thin-skinned and hold their shape.

■ **Serves 4, or 6 if serving more than one curry.**

4 Tbsp oil
1 small onion, peeled and sliced
1 tsp minced ginger
1 tsp crushed garlic
1 tsp each ground coriander, cumin seeds, and turmeric
¾–1 tsp chilli powder
2 tsp garam masala
200 g small waxy potatoes, unpeeled, cut into 2-cm dice
1½ cups water
¼ cup ground almonds
1½ cups coconut cream
1 tsp salt or to taste
freshly ground black pepper
350 g cauliflower, sliced into bite-sized pieces
fresh coriander, chopped, for garnish

Heat the oil in a heavy-based saucepan over a low heat. Sauté the onion slowly until it softens, stir in the ginger and garlic and sauté for another few minutes.
Stir in the coriander, cumin seeds, turmeric, chilli powder and garam masala. Sauté 2–3 minutes, then stir in the potatoes, water and ground almonds, followed by the coconut cream, salt and pepper.
Bring to simmer point and cook gently, covered, for 12–15 minutes, until the potatoes are just tender.
Stir in the prepared cauliflower, cover and simmer for another 10 minutes, or until the cauliflower is tender.
Remove from the heat and serve on rice, garnished with fresh coriander, as a stand-alone meal or with other curries.

Chickpea, zucchini & herb fritters

These fritters are quick to make, inexpensive but tasty, and the recipe extends well. Serve with boiled or mashed potatoes, thickly sliced sautéed mushrooms and a green salad; or try them in pita bread or wraps with salad vegetables, chilli sauce and plain yoghurt.

■ **Serves 4.**

400-g tin chickpeas (or 1 1/3 cups cooked chickpeas)
2 Tbsp oil (first measure)
½ medium-sized onion, preferably red
3 cloves garlic, peeled and finely chopped
1 medium-sized chilli, seeded and finely chopped (or ½ tsp chilli powder)
1/3 cup chopped coriander leaves and stalks
1/3 cup chopped fresh basil or oregano
2 zucchini, grated
1 egg
2/3 cup milk
½ cup flour
1 tsp baking powder
1 generous tsp salt or to taste
freshly ground black pepper
2 tsp sumac (or zest of ½ lemon)
1/3 cup grated tasty Cheddar
oil for shallow frying

Rinse and drain the chickpeas if using tinned. Grind the chickpeas in a food processor to the texture of breadcrumbs, then transfer to a medium to large bowl.
Heat the first measure of oil in a medium-sized frying pan and sauté the onion, garlic and chilli over a low heat until softened. Set aside.
Meanwhile, prepare the herbs and transfer to the bowl containing the chickpeas.
Grate the zucchini and discard any excess liquid by squeezing firmly. Add to the bowl along with the sautéed onion mixture. In a separate bowl, lightly beat the egg then combine it with the milk. Gently stir into the zucchini mixture in the bowl to combine.
Sift the flour, baking powder, salt, pepper and sumac and fold in, using a large metal or wooden spoon. Lastly fold in the grated cheese.
Heat oil over a medium heat in the same frying pan used to sauté the onion mixture. Cook large spoonfuls of the mix until golden brown on both sides and cooked through.

Tunis roast vegetables with chickpeas

Roasted ground cumin and lemon infuse this dish with North African/Mediterranean flavours. Although technically a roast salad, it can be served either straight from the oven or at room temperature.

Serve on a bed of couscous or with hot breads and salads such as tabouleh or Greek salad. Accompany with Chermoula (page 46) as an optional treat. Toast more cumin seeds than required, as any excess can be stored in an airtight jar until needed.

■ **Serves 4–6.**

---

1 Tbsp cumin seeds, toasted
2 medium to large Beauregard (orange) kumara (or pumpkin)
300 g eggplant
2 red capsicums
olive oil
salt and pepper
1 large or 2 medium-sized red onions, peeled and sliced
2–3 cloves garlic, peeled and finely chopped
4 Tbsp lemon juice
½ tsp chilli powder
1 cup cooked chickpeas or more if wished
500 g asparagus (or beans or broccoli)
¼ cup rinsed and drained capers (or ½ cup black olives) (optional)
Italian (flat-leaf) parsley for garnish (optional)

Preheat the oven to 200°C.
Toast the cumin seeds in a pan over a medium heat until fragrant. Cool, then crush with a mortar and pestle.
Peel the kumara. Slice in half lengthwise, then into 8 cm long x 1 cm thick strips. Slice the eggplant into similar-sized pieces. Seed the capsicum and slice lengthwise into 2 cm thick strips.
Toss the kumara, eggplant and capsicum in sufficient oil to coat, season with salt and pepper and roast in a large, shallow pan for 25–30 minutes or until the vegetables are cooked and lightly golden. Turn after 15 minutes.
Meanwhile heat oil in a frying pan and sauté the onion and garlic slowly over a low heat until well wilted and beginning to caramelise. Combine the lemon juice, chilli powder and toasted crushed cumin seeds.
Snap the asparagus (or beans or broccoli) and lightly cook in boiling salted water. Refresh briefly under cold water (it should still be crisp), and drain on paper towels. Combine the lemon juice mixture with the onions before tossing with the roast vegetables and the chickpeas.
Check for seasoning, and garnish with the capers or black olives and parsley if desired. Serve warm.

Kumara fritters with toasted cumin

These fritters are quick and easy, especially if served with a home-made chutney, plain yoghurt and fresh finely chopped coriander; otherwise, try them with the Coriander, Mint & Cashew Pesto, page 14.

Serve with steamed broccoli and oven-baked eggplant slices, or a green salad and Madras Chickpeas, Eggplant & Spinach, page 85.

---

2 tsp cumin seeds, toasted and crushed*
600 g peeled and grated Beauregard (orange) kumara
   (approximately 2 large kumara)
2 eggs, lightly beaten
2 Tbsp plain flour
1 tsp salt or to taste
freshly ground black pepper
oil for shallow frying
Coriander, Mint & Cashew Pesto (page 14) and/or sweet chutney

Toast the cumin seeds in a frying pan over a medium heat until fragrant, tossing constantly. Crush in a mortar and pestle or with the flat blade of a heavy knife.
Weigh the kumara after it has been peeled and grated.
Lightly beat the eggs in a medium to large bowl, then stir them into the grated kumara with the toasted cumin seeds and the flour, salt and pepper.
Heat the oil in a frying pan and shallow fry spoonfuls of the mixture on both sides, until golden.
Serve with the pesto and/or a chutney.

*Toast a larger quantity of cumin seeds than you need, and keep in an airtight jar.

Corn & coriander fritters

These corn and coriander fritters are great served with sweet chilli sauce (mix in some finely chopped Vietnamese mint leaves); or drizzled with a little pomegranate molasses and served with plain unsweetened yoghurt mixed with fresh, finely chopped coriander.

■ **Serves 4–6. Not recommended for freezing.**

3 eggs, lightly beaten
1½ cups creamed corn (400-g tin)
½ cup milk
1 finely chopped yellow or red capsicum
1 small onion, peeled and finely chopped
¾ cup plain flour
1 tsp baking powder
½ cup fine polenta (cornmeal)
1 cup grated tasty Cheddar
1 tsp salt or to taste
lots of freshly ground black pepper
½ tsp cayenne pepper
1 Tbsp sweet chilli sauce
¼ cup finely chopped coriander, including stalks
3 Tbsp finely chopped parsley
oil for shallow frying

Whisk the eggs in a medium-sized bowl and add the creamed corn, milk, capsicum and onion. Combine well.
Sift the flour and baking powder into the bowl. Mix in all the remaining ingredients except the oil. If fine polenta isn't available, blitz polenta in a food processor or use an extra measure of plain flour instead.
Heat 5 mm oil in a large, shallow frying pan or electric frying pan. Place spoonfuls of the mixture into the heated oil, using 2–3 tablespoons of mixture for each one.
Cook the fritters in batches over a medium heat for 3–4 minutes each side or until golden brown.
Drain the cooked fritters on paper towels and keep warm while the remaining mixture is cooked. Serve immediately.

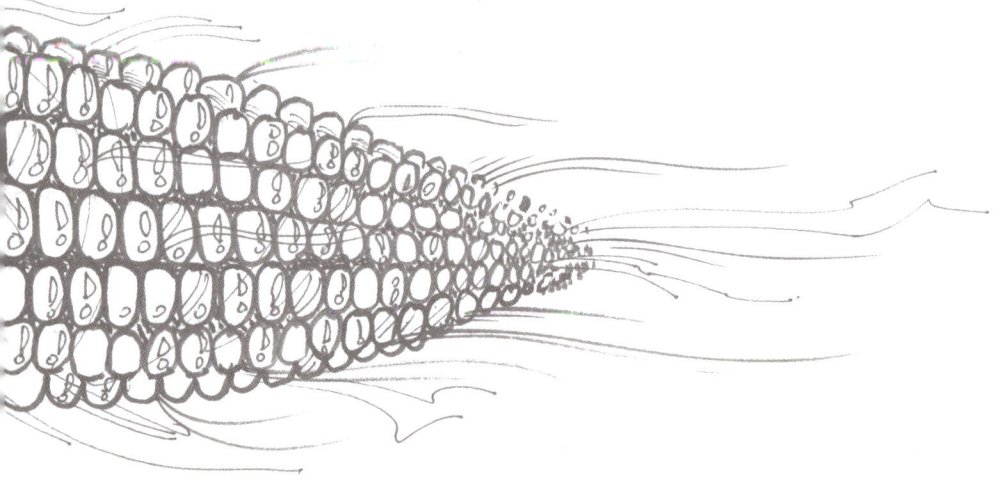

Bean & feta fritters

When a meat-loving son in his twenties was not only complimentary about these fritters but polished off most of the batch, this cook had to have a little lie down!

The inclusion of herbs and feta add zing to these tasty fritters. Serve them casually or give them a status lift by nestling atop a mesclun salad and serving with Puliyini (page 170) and scalloped potatoes.

Use a firm-textured feta, as small dice in these fritters is preferable to grated or crumbled. Pinto beans look very like kidney beans but are lighter in colour and not as strong in flavour. Almost any bean can be used for this recipe, though of course the flavour will vary slightly.

■ **Makes 6–8 medium-sized fritters. Serves 4. May be frozen. Recipe doubles well.**

---

3 cups cooked pinto (or other) beans, roughly mashed
1 onion, peeled and finely chopped
¼ cup finely chopped parsley
2 Tbsp fresh pizza thyme (or 1 tsp dried thyme)
1 tsp salt or to taste
1 tsp freshly ground black pepper
120 g feta, diced small
1 large egg
oil to shallow fry

Combine all ingredients except the oil in a medium-sized bowl.
Form into fritters or patties with your hands, according to the size you want and the number of people you are serving.
Heat about 3 tablespoons oil in a heavy-based frying pan (an electric frying pan is excellent for this). You will need to add more oil for the next batch.
Fry over a medium heat for 2–3 minutes on each side until golden and cooked through. Remove from the pan and drain on a kitchen towel. Keep warm until all fritters are cooked.

salads/sides

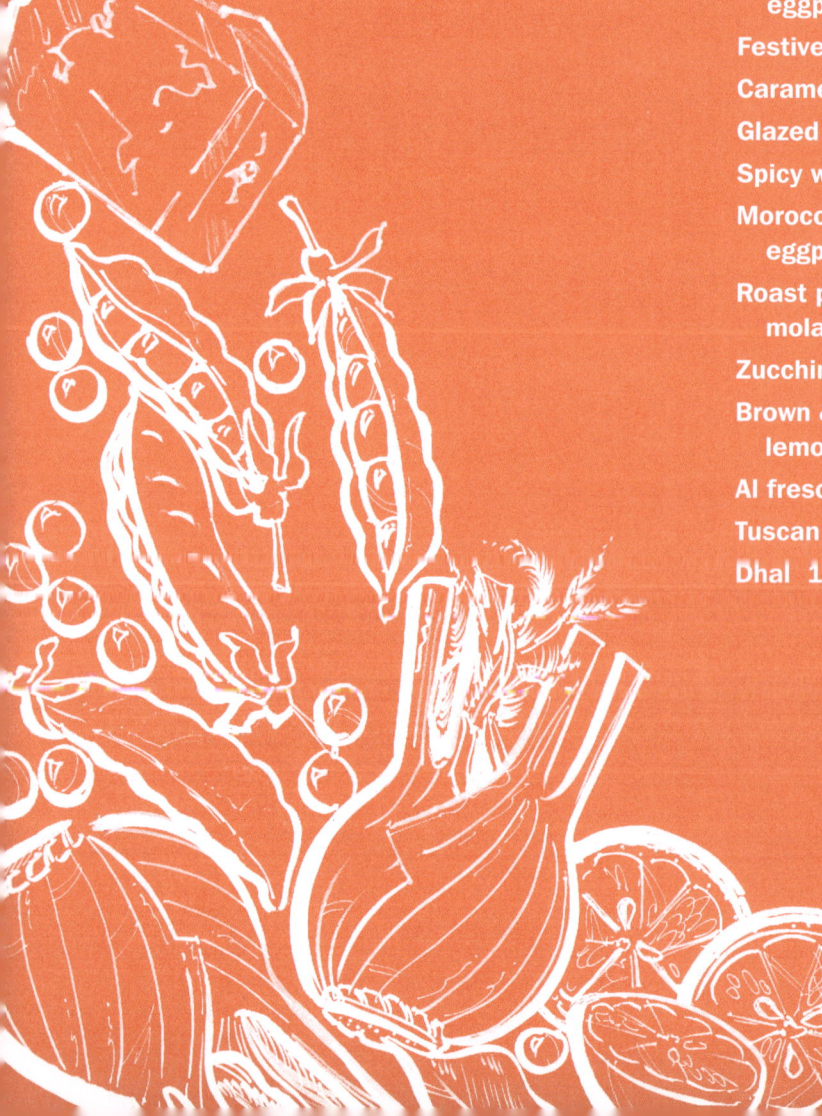

Lentil, caper & olive salad 95
Asparagus salad with lime, ginger, soy & sesame 95
Lentils 'n' thyme 96
Sahara carrot sauté 97
Burghul, couscous or quinoa tabouleh 98
Quinoa salad with broad beans, mandarins, mint & sesame 98
Mango, fennel & watercress salad 100
Eggplant salad with yoghurt mint dressing 100
Artichoke gratin 101
Brown rice & seaweed salad 102
Florence fennel & pea salad 103
Roast eggplant & pomegranate with tzatziki-style dressing 104
Roast kumara, nut & feta salad with raspberry vinaigrette 105
Curried okra 106
Rock melon or mango salad with Asian dressing 107
Piperade 108
Creamed parsnip & leek with toasted cumin seeds 109
Mediterranean fava bean salad with sumac, mint & eggplant 110
Festive Moroccan couscous 111
Caramelised tomatoes 112
Glazed beetroot salad 112
Spicy wedges 113
Moroccan spice & honey eggplant 114
Roast pumpkin with pomegranate molasses 115
Zucchini salad 115
Brown & wild rice with roast lemon 116
Al fresco potato salad 117
Tuscan broad beans 118
Dhal 119

Lentil, caper & olive salad

Puy lentils have a light, slightly peppery flavour and firm texture. Brown lentils may be substituted, though the flavour will be more 'earthy' and the texture softer.

Lentils work well with the contrast of capers, green olives, lemon and fresh herbs. Try this salad with foccacia, baked potatoes, an omelette or frittata.

■ **Serves 4. Not suitable to freeze.**

1 cup Puy lentils (or brown lentils)
2½–3 cups stock and/or water
1 bay leaf
½ cup green stuffed olives* chopped
2 Tbsp well-drained small capers
2 cloves garlic, crushed
½ cup chopped Italian (flat-leaf) parsley
¼ cup lemon juice (generous)
2 Tbsp extra virgin olive oil
¾ tsp–1 tsp salt or to taste
freshly ground black pepper

*Olives stuffed with pimiento inject some colour into the mix but any stuffed olives would work.

Rinse and drain the lentils then place in a heavy-based saucepan over a low heat with the stock or water and the bay leaf. Cover and simmer slowly for 25 minutes or until tender, stirring occasionally. Rinse under cold water, drain well and discard the bay leaf. Transfer to a serving bowl and combine with the remaining ingredients.

Asparagus salad with lime, ginger, soy & sesame

Lime, ginger and sesame with sweet soy sauce complement asparagus beautifully.

1 kg asparagus

Dressing
1 Tbsp finely chopped fresh ginger
¾ tsp sesame oil
1½ Tbsp kecap manis
¼ cup lime juice
½ tsp sugar
salt and freshly ground black pepper to taste

Snap off the tough ends of the asparagus and drop the asparagus into 10–12 cm boiling water stems first. Cook for about 2 minutes. Drain immediately and refresh in cold water. Drain well, and dry well with paper towels. Combine all the dressing ingredients together in a screw-top jar and shake well. Arrange the asparagus on a serving platter and drizzle the dressing over.

Lentils 'n' thyme

Lentils generously flavoured with herbs are surprisingly good, and a simple but tasty vegetarian meal is to serve this dish warmed over a mesclun/green salad containing diced feta and dressed with Black Raspberry Vinegar (page 179) and extra virgin olive oil. Add some boiled new potatoes or a baked potato for balance; it's a fantastic combination. Puy, French green or brown lentils can be used, although the cooking times for each are slightly different so some adjustment may be required. Use either French green lentils or Puy for preference, as they hold their shape better than brown and have a less 'earthy' taste.

■ **Serves 4–6. May be frozen**

1¼ cups Puy or French green lentils
3 Tbsp olive oil
2 large cloves garlic, crushed
1 handful of pizza thyme*
2 Tbsp balsamic vinegar
2 Tbsp extra virgin olive oil
1 Tbsp lemon juice
1 tsp salt or to taste
lots of freshly ground black pepper
½ cup chopped Italian (flat-leaf) parsley

Rinse and drain the lentils, then transfer to a saucepan with 5–6 cups water. Bring to boiling point then simmer, uncovered, for about 15 minutes, until just cooked. Transfer them to a sieve, rinse in cold water and drain.

While the lentils cook, prepare the remaining ingredients. In the case of the thyme, a 'handful' is the only adequate description, and equates to about 1 cup of stalks. Tie the thyme stalks together at their base with some string, unless you can cope with the tedium of stripping the leaves off their stalks.

Heat the olive oil in a frying pan over a low heat and add the garlic and the thyme bundle. Sauté the garlic and thyme together, tossing the thyme to soften the leaves — but take care not to scorch the garlic. Stir in the lentils, then the balsamic vinegar, extra virgin olive oil, lemon juice, salt and pepper. Stir well and cook for 3–5 minutes over a low heat, then stir in the parsley and remove from the heat. The thyme leaves wilt and most will have dropped off the stalks during cooking. With a wooden spoon or tongs, press as many remaining leaves from the thyme bundle as possible and stir in, before discarding the thyme stalks.

Taste for seasoning before serving. A little more extra virgin oil and a dash more lemon are good if you are not serving the lentils with a dressed salad. Serve hot, warmed or at room temperature.

> **Pizza thyme is lovely to have growing near the back door; throw it into sauces and dressings, onto pizzas, into breads, and don't be timid — it complements rather than takes over. If you don't have access to pizza thyme, substitute other mild herbs such as basil or oregano (common thyme, rosemary and sage are all much more strongly flavoured).*

Sahara carrot sauté

Carrots cooked until just tender, still with a little crispness, and lightly flavoured with cumin and ginger, are refreshing and delicious; a perfect balance for Moroccan and other North African dishes in particular.

■ **Serves 6. Not suitable to freeze.**

600 g slim carrots, peeled
2 Tbsp olive oil
30 g butter
2 tsp finely chopped fresh ginger
¾ tsp sugar
½ tsp toasted cumin seeds
½–¾ tsp salt or to taste
freshly ground black pepper
2 Tbsp roughly chopped Italian (flat-leaf) parsley

Slice the carrots in ½-cm thick slices on a diagonal. Melt the butter and oil together in a heavy-based pan or saucepan. Stir in the ginger, sugar, cumin seeds, salt and pepper, followed by the carrots. Sauté, stirring, for 5–7 minutes over a medium heat, or until just tender but still with a light crunch. Transfer to a heated serving dish, garnish with the parsley and serve immediately.

Burghul, couscous or quinoa tabouleh

Tabouleh (Tabouli) is a salad to return to, especially in summer. It's worth trying it with couscous or quinoa, however, for a different result than with the more familiar burghul. (One cup raw quinoa produces 3 cups of cooked; one cup raw burghul or couscous produced 2 cups of soaked grain.)

■ **Serves 4–6.**

1 cup burghul or couscous (or ²/₃ cup quinoa, black* or white)
2 cups finely chopped parsley
⅓ cup finely chopped mint
3 spring onions, finely chopped
¼ cup lemon juice
¼ cup olive oil
1 tsp salt or to taste
freshly ground black pepper
3 firm tomatoes, seeded and diced

*Black quinoa makes a very attractive tabouleh.

Cover the burghul with cold water and leave for 30 minutes. If using couscous, cover with boiling water and stand for 7 minutes. For quinoa, cook in 2 cups salted water, uncovered, for 15–20 minutes until the 'curl' is released and the grain is al dente, before refreshing under cold water.
Drain thoroughly in a sieve, lightly pressing to remove all liquid.
Transfer to a serving bowl and add the parsley, mint and spring onions.
Stir in the lemon juice, oil and seasonings. Discard the seeds and juice from the tomatoes, dice the flesh and stir into the tabouleh.

Quinoa salad with broad beans, mandarins, mint & sesame

Broad beans have found new favour over the last few years, and rightly so. Among obvious attributes such as flavour and versatility, they are nutritious and easy to grow — sweet young beans can be used for this salad without having to be peeled. That said, however, frozen or mature fresh broad beans (cooked and peeled) make a perfectly adequate substitute.

Quinoa has been an important food for centuries. It is not strictly a grain, as it is not a grass, but the Incas referred to it as the 'mother of all grains', a reference to its nutritional importance. Only potatoes were valued more highly, as quinoa has higher protein content than grains such as wheat and rice and is more balanced in terms of nutrients (and it's gluten-free).

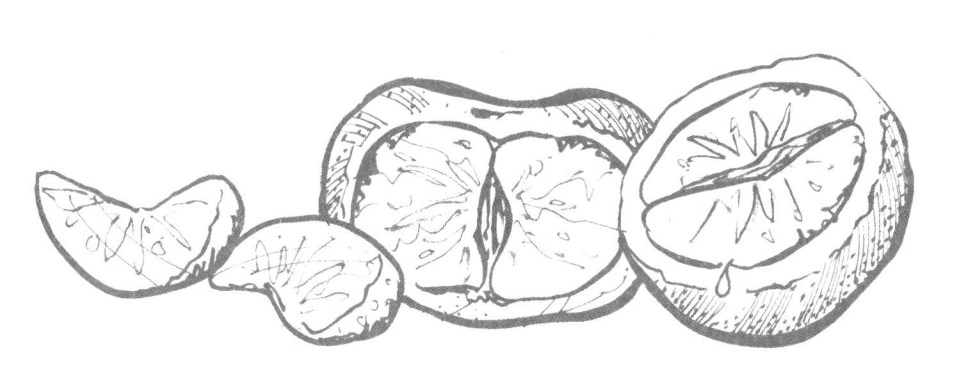

1 cup quinoa*
2 cups water
1 cup lightly cooked, shelled young broad beans
   (or 250 g frozen broad beans, lightly cooked and peeled)
3 mandarins, peeled
2 Tbsp sesame seeds
¼ cup almonds, blanched or unblanched (can use slivered almonds)
¼ cup finely chopped fresh mint (first measure)

Dressing
2 Tbsp fresh orange juice
2 tsp honey
½ tsp sesame oil
2 tsp cider vinegar (or lemon juice)
¼ cup finely chopped fresh mint (second measure)
salt to taste
freshly ground black pepper

Rinse and drain the quinoa. Place in a saucepan with 2 cups of salted water and simmer on a low heat 15–20 minutes, uncovered, until the quinoa is tender with a light crunch, as with al dente pasta. Pour into a sieve and hold under running cold water briefly to stop further cooking. Drain well, pressing with the back of a spoon if necessary.
Lightly cook the broad beans by simmering in water (3–4 minutes). Refresh under cold water and drain. Peel the beans only if they are mature and skins are thick.
Cut the mandarins in half through the equator, discarding any obvious seeds. Break into segments.
Toast the seeds and the almonds separately in a dry frying pan until golden, or place separately on an oven tray and toast about 10 minutes at 180°C. Slice the almonds lengthwise (or use slivered almonds).
Place all the salad ingredients in a serving bowl except for the almonds and ⅓ cup of the broad beans.
For the dressing, warm the orange juice and the honey together until the honey melts. Stir in all the remaining ingredients and combine. Pour the dressing over the salad just before serving, tossing to combine.
When ready to serve, sprinkle the reserved broad beans and the almonds over the top as a garnish.

*Couscous or orzo would make a good substitute for quinoa.

Mango, fennel & watercress salad

It's great when friends do their own thing with your ideas. This is one Gill is justifiably proud of.

■ **Serves 4. Not suitable to freeze.**

2 ripe mangoes, peeled (or tinned mangoes, drained)
1 fennel bulb, trimmed and cored
¼ medium-sized red onion, peeled and finely sliced
4 cups watercress

Slice the flesh from the mango on a diagonal. Discard the stone. Cut the prepared fennel in half lengthwise and slice finely. Wash and dry the watercress, discarding any thick stems before measuring.
Place the mango, fennel and onion in a bowl.
Transfer the watercress to a serving platter.

Dressing
juice of 2 limes
2 tsp white balsamic vinegar
½ tsp honey
2 tsp wholegrain mustard

Whisk together until well combined.

Assembly
Combine the mango, fennel and onion mix with the dressing and place on top of the watercress.

Eggplant salad with yoghurt mint dressing

This dish is lovely as the centrepiece of a vegetarian meal, served with other salads and a potato or grain dish such as tabouleh or couscous.

■ **Serves 4–6. Not suitable to freeze.**

500 g eggplant (1 large)
1 tsp salt (first measure)
¼ cup flour
1 tsp ground coriander
1 tsp turmeric
½ tsp salt (second measure)
freshly ground black pepper
oil for frying

Slice the unpeeled eggplant into 1–1.5 cm thick rounds and salt lightly on both sides with 1 teaspoon of salt. Place in a colander to drain for 30 minutes. Pat dry with paper towels.

Combine the flour, coriander, turmeric, ½ teaspoon of salt and the pepper in a small dish. Dredge the eggplant slices in the flour mixture and shake off any excess.

Heat enough oil to shallow fry the eggplant — you may have to add more oil during the cooking time. Fry the eggplant until golden brown and crisp on both sides. Drain on paper towels before transferring to a serving dish (either warm or at room temperature). Drizzle with Yoghurt Mint Dressing.

Yoghurt mint dressing

½ cup plain unsweetened yoghurt
1 large clove garlic, crushed
1 tsp caster sugar
2–3 Tbsp finely chopped mint (or coriander)

Combine all ingredients.

Artichoke gratin

Jerusalem artichokes deserve a much wider fan base than they currently enjoy, and one of the reasons for this is that they will thrive in the most neglected corner of the garden — just be aware that they grow tall and they spread. In addition, these gnarly tubers are both nutritious and versatile; they make a wonderful soup, are a delicious addition to roast vegetables (try them with roast baby beetroot, for example), can be grated into raw salads, sliced thinly, drizzled with olive oil, seasoned and roasted in a single layer or made into a dauphinoise.

Replace the 1¼ cups milk with 1 cup milk and 4 tablespoons cream if you wish.

■ **Serves 4–6. May be frozen.**

---

750 g Jerusalem artichokes*
1½ cups grated tasty cheese
salt to taste, and freshly ground black pepper
1¼ cups milk
finely chopped fresh parsley for garnish

Scrub but don't peel the artichokes, although any particularly knobbly bits can be pared off as they can be difficult to scrub clean.

Slice thinly and layer into a lightly greased or sprayed ovenproof dish, sprinkling each layer with some of the grated tasty cheese and salt and pepper. Top with the rest of the cheese after you have poured over the milk.

Cover tightly with a lid or with foil and bake for 1¼ hours at 190°C. Serve with parsley as garnish

*If you are working ahead, allow for the fact that once the artichokes are sliced they do discolour if left uncooked for an hour or more. The way to get around this is to par-cook in advance.

Salads & sides

Brown rice & seaweed salad

This salad has quite subtle flavours but is also refreshingly different. Serve it lightly warmed or at room temperature as a light meal or lunch with fritters or salads or as a contribution to a buffet. If preparing ahead, reserve at least half of the pumpkin seeds and the nori until just before serving. Pumpkin seeds may be dry roasted in a large frying pan, tossing constantly, if preferred.

Red radishes are preferable here for colour as well as flavour and texture, but if they are not available, substitute peeled, thinly sliced daikon (Japanese radish) or something with 'crunch' such as mung bean sprouts, julienned carrots or celery.

---

1 cup brown rice
2½ cups water
1 cup pumpkin seeds
1 Tbsp soy sauce
1–2 spring onions, sliced thinly
²/₃ cup finely sliced red radishes (about 4)
1 cup thawed frozen peas
3 Tbsp finely slivered, pickled sushi ginger
   or 1 Tbsp peeled and grated fresh ginger
3 Tbsp mirin* (or lemon juice)
1 tsp sesame oil
2 Tbsp oil
1 Tbsp soy sauce, second measure
¾–1 tsp freshly ground black pepper or to taste
salt to taste
⅓ cup very finely shredded or cut nori**

Place the rice and water into a straight-sided bowl and microwave uncovered, on high, for 30 minutes. The water should be absorbed at this point and the rice tender.

While the rice is cooking, heat the oven to 180°C. Spread the pumpkin seeds out onto a tray or dish and toast for approximately 12 minutes, tossing occasionally, until they are golden brown. Immediately transfer to a bowl and pour over the soy sauce, mix well then set aside to cool. The hot seeds will quickly absorb this dressing and — be warned — they make a scrumptious nibble.

Prepare the vegetables and ginger and combine the mirin or lemon juice, sesame oil, oil and soy sauce.

Stir all the ingredients into the rice, except half the toasted pumpkin seeds and the finely shredded nori. Transfer to a serving dish.

Just before serving, stir in most of the pumpkin seeds and half the nori. Taste and adjust the balance of lemon and seasoning if needed.

Scatter the remaining pumpkin seeds and nori over the top of the rice as a garnish.

* Mirin is a Japanese rice wine vinegar.
**Nori is dried seaweed sheets used for making sushi. Toast over a gas flame to freshen and curl if desired. Use scissors to shred the nori.

Florence fennel & pea salad

Fennel salad is delicious, and possibly even addictive. This particular version features thawed frozen peas, but fresh orange or mandarin slices are also good, as are toasted slivered almonds, sliced dates, feta instead of Parmesan, and a host of other combinations. The finely shaved fennel benefits from marinating.

Getting your hands on some Florence fennel presents the dilemma of how to use it — the decision to roast, sauté or salad is not one to be cavalier about because all are equally delicious. In the end, of course, the answer has to be that such a decision should be one of the moment.

---

2 medium-sized bulbs Florence fennel (approximately 2½ cups sliced)
4 Tbsp extra virgin olive oil
2 Tbsp white balsamic vinegar
½ tsp salt or to taste
lots of freshly ground black pepper
2 cups frozen peas, thawed
1 cup rocket leaves (preferably), or mesclun
¼ cup roughly chopped Italian (flat-leaf) parsley
juice of ½ a large lemon
shaved Parmesan to garnish

Trim the stems off the fennel bulbs and slice the stems finely to add to the salad later, if wished. Slice the bulbs in half lengthwise, cut out the core and discard.
Using a very sharp knife, slice the bulbs as thinly as possible lengthwise, and transfer to a medium-sized bowl.
Combine the olive oil, white balsamic vinegar*, salt and pepper in a screw-top jar or with a small whisk. Pour over the prepared fennel and marinate for 1 hour.
Combine with the frozen thawed (not cooked) peas, the rocket or mesclun and the parsley. Check the seasoning.
Transfer to a serving dish and squeeze over the lemon juice.
Garnish with the shaved Parmesan and serve immediately.

*White balsamic vinegar will not stain light-coloured foods.

Roast eggplant & pomegranate with tzatziki-style dressing

Any dish that can be prepared ahead is a bonus, but part of the attraction of this dish is the combination of taste and texture — velvety roast eggplant slices drizzled with creamy yoghurt containing the surprise zing of fresh minced garlic. The final touch is a garnish of bright crimson pomegranate seeds. These sweet/tart seeds are reminiscent of red currants, and visually and taste-wise are the perfect complement to the other ingredients. Serve with rice, lentil or pulse dishes and, for example, slow roasted tomatoes and a Mediterranean green salad with olives and Parmesan. It is not strictly necessary to salt fresh, firm, unblemished eggplant but for this dish it is recommended. Tzatziki is a Greek-style yoghurt sauce where the inclusion of fresh, minced garlic is important for authenticity and to give real zing to the dish.

■ **Serves 6. Not suitable for freezing.**

500–600 g eggplant (1 large)
½ cup oil (approximately)
1 cup plain Greek-style yoghurt
2–3 cloves garlic, peeled and minced
seeds of ½ pomegranate, for garnish

Preheat the oven to 190°C.
Slice the eggplant 2 cm thick, sprinkle lightly with salt and place in a colander to drain for 30 minutes. Use a paper towel to pat dry.
Eggplant absorbs oil readily. To counteract this, pour some neutral oil into a bowl wide enough to fit the widest slices. Dip each eggplant slice into the oil, wipe off any excess oil on the rim of the bowl and place in a single layer on a baking tray. Bake the eggplant slices for 25–30 minutes, turning once during cooking time. When golden brown on both sides, transfer to a kitchen towel to drain.
Combine the yoghurt and garlic.
Arrange overlapping slices of eggplant on a serving platter, drizzle the yoghurt and garlic mixture down the centre and scatter pomegranate seeds over.
Serve at room temperature.

Roast kumara, nut & feta salad with raspberry vinaigrette

The flavour and visual appeal of orange-fleshed kumara is particularly attractive with raspberry vinaigrette, toasted walnuts and feta.

■ **Serves 6. Not suitable to freeze.**

3 red onions, peeled and cut into quarters or eighths
oil for roasting
salt and pepper
700 g Beauregard (orange) kumara, peeled
60 g roasted walnut pieces
2 Tbsp olive oil
3 Tbsp Black Raspberry Vinegar*
½ tsp Dijon mustard
1 cup rocket leaves
1 tsp salt or to taste
freshly ground black pepper
100 g mild goat's feta, crumbled

Preheat the oven to 200°C.
Toss the prepared red onions in a little oil, salt and pepper on a large shallow oven tray. Roast at 200°C while you prepare the kumara. Cut the peeled kumara into 3-cm dice, toss lightly in oil to coat, sprinkle with a little salt and pepper, then transfer to the tray with the partially cooked red onions. Roast until just tender, about 20 minutes, but don't overcook — the kumara shouldn't be too soft. Cool.
Roast the walnut pieces in a very small amount of oil in a frying pan while the kumara is cooking (about 6 minutes), salt lightly and drain on a paper towel.
Combine the olive oil, raspberry vinegar and mustard and set aside.

Assembly

Place the kumara and onions (warm or at room temperature) in a serving bowl with the rocket leaves and dress with the oil/vinegar/mustard dressing. Add the salt and pepper and combine lightly but thoroughly.
Garnish with the roasted walnut pieces and the crumbled feta.

*Make your own from fresh or frozen berries, page 179.

Curried okra

Curried okra is quick to prepare and teams well with other curries and/or dhal, or as a sauce to serve with roast eggplant slices. It's also good on its own, served with chapatis or rice; for a main dish, add some diced paneer or firm, diced tofu, at the end of cooking time. When cut, okra exudes a slightly sticky liquid that thickens stews and sauces naturally, as in gumbo and other African/Caribbean dishes. As a vegetable it has a mild flavour and teams well with tomatoes, corn, onion, garlic, peppers and eggplant.

■ **Serves 4. Freezes well.**

3 Tbsp oil
1 medium to large onion, peeled and sliced
5 cloves garlic, crushed
2 tsp very finely chopped fresh ginger
2 green chillies, seeded and finely chopped
½ tsp chilli powder
1 tsp cracked fenugreek (optional)
4 tsp ground cumin
4 tsp ground coriander
800 g peeled chopped tomatoes or 2 x 400-g tins peeled chopped tomatoes with juice
3 Tbsp tamarind concentrate*
1–2 tsp brown sugar
1 cup unsalted vegetable stock or water
1½ tsp salt or to taste
freshly ground black pepper
400 g okra, washed thoroughly
fresh coriander for garnish

*Make your own, see Glossary, page 185, or buy some very good quality concentrate.

Heat the oil in a heavy-based saucepan over a low heat. Sauté the onion, garlic, ginger and chillies gently, until the onion is well softened. Stir in the chilli powder, fenugreek (if using), cumin and coriander and sauté for 2–3 minutes, adding a little more oil if necessary.

Stir in the tomatoes, tamarind, brown sugar, stock or water and the seasonings. Cover and simmer gently for 10 minutes, stirring once or twice.

Meanwhile, wash the okra thoroughly, trim the stalk end and slice each okra in half on the diagonal. Stir the okra into the sauce and simmer on low, uncovered, for about 30 minutes or until the okra is tender. Add a little more stock or water during cooking if the sauce seems too thick.

Taste and adjust the seasonings for your preference. Garnish with chopped fresh coriander to serve.

Rock melon or mango salad with Asian dressing

This salad is perfect to serve as the weather warms up, as a rather elegant entrée to a slice of quiche, for example, or as a welcome contribution to a buffet, barbecue or picnic. Despite the rather unusual ingredient pairings, it's refreshingly different, adding a festive note with tropical overtones and brought together by the Asian-inspired dressing. Include an avocado if you wish.

Florence fennel is included mainly for texture, although its light anise taste also adds a refreshing note to the flavour spectrum of the salad. Celery can be substituted for the fennel and will make a contribution to texture balance.

■ **Serves 6.**

---

1 rock melon or 2 mangoes, ripe but firm
2 cups loosely packed rocket leaves or watercress
1 avocado, peeled and sliced into 2 cm x 5 cm pieces (optional)
1 bulb Florence fennel (or 1 cup celery), sliced thinly on a diagonal
¼ cup roasted salted peanuts (or cashews), for garnish

Dressing
2 Tbsp lime juice, preferably (or lemon juice)
1 tsp light soy sauce
3 Tbsp olive oil (not extra virgin)
½–1 tsp honey (or sugar)
1 tsp fresh chilli, seeded and finely chopped (or ⅛ tsp chilli powder)
2 Tbsp flaked coconut (or coconut thread)
3 Tbsp chopped fresh mint (8–10 leaves)

Peel and seed the rock melon or the mangoes. Slice the flesh into pieces approximately 2 cm x 5 cm.
To make the dressing, blend all the ingredients with an electric blender stick or in a blender or food processor until smooth. This quantity should be just enough to lightly dress the ingredients but not overwhelm them.
Arrange the rocket, avocado, fennel and melon or mango on a serving plate or bowl, and drizzle the dressing over. Toss lightly and serve immediately, garnished with the peanuts or cashews and a few extra mint leaves if wished, finely chopped.

Piperade

This is one dish that is a must to make every summer; a sweet capsicum sauté that sounds deceptively simple but is a truly sumptuous dish where slow cooking releases the sweetness of the capsicums and enhances the richness of the flesh.

Serve it as a side dish to accompany almost anything. Leftovers are great on pizzas, in pies, soups or sandwiches. Stir any leftover piperade in with some cooked or tinned, drained borlotti beans for dinner, Italian-style.

■ **Serves 4–6. May be frozen.**

4 large capsicums, red and yellow
1 Tbsp butter
3 Tbsp olive oil
4 cloves garlic, peeled and sliced thinly
½ tsp sugar
pinch of salt or to taste
freshly ground black pepper

Seed the capsicums and slice into long thin strips, then cut in half. Discard the seeds. Heat the butter and oil over a low heat in a heavy-based pan with a lid.
Sauté the garlic briefly, until it is fragrant, then stir in the capsicums. Place the lid on the pan and cook slowly over a low heat, stirring or tossing regularly until the capsicums start to release their liquid. Continue to cook, covered, for another 5–10 minutes, then either remove the lid or ease it to the side so that some of the liquid can evaporate off.
Stir in the sugar, followed by the salt and pepper if you wish — you may decide you don't need seasoning in this dish at all. Continue cooking slowly for another 20–25 minutes, then remove from the heat. It may be served hot but is at its best served at room temperature or slightly warm (with hot crusty bread to mop up the juices).

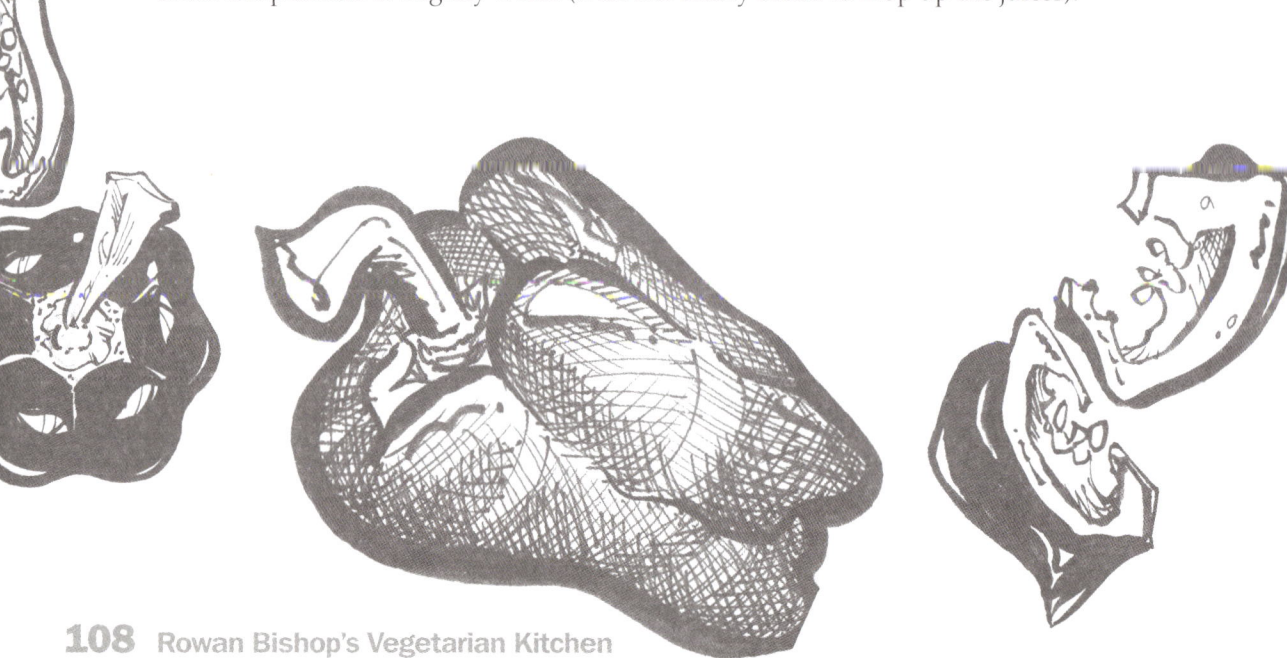

Creamed parsnip & leek with toasted cumin seeds

Parsnips and leeks are a great combination, and when the vegetables are 'pulsed' in a food processor to break up the leek and combine the flavours, the result is delicious. Toasted cumin seeds add interest as well as flavour.

Team with a casserole or pie for great 'comfort food'.

■ **Serves 6. Not suitable to freeze.**

4 large parsnips (800 g)
1 cup thinly sliced leek
3 Tbsp butter
¼ cup cream (or sour cream or milk)
1 tsp salt or to taste
¾ tsp freshly ground black pepper
1 tsp whole cumin seeds, toasted

Preheat the oven to 190°C.
Peel the parsnips and trim. Chop into quarters lengthwise, then into 2–3 cm chunks. Trim the leek(s) and slice into thin rounds, using mainly the white part. Bring salted water to the boil in a large saucepan and cook the parsnips and leek until tender. Drain, then transfer to a food processor and pulse the parsnips and leek with the butter and the cream or milk, salt and pepper.
Toast the cumin seeds in a dry pan over a medium heat, taking care not to burn them. Toss regularly.
Transfer the creamed mixture to an oven-to-table serving dish. Sprinkle the cumin seeds over the top as a garnish. Bake, uncovered, for 20–25 minutes if the mash is still hot, or 45–50 minutes if the mash has cooled before baking. The mixture will puff a little and turn lightly golden.
Serve immediately.

Mediterranean fava bean salad with sumac, mint & eggplant

Colourful, delicious and nutritious, a combination of good looks and great taste — what more could you want? Vibrant green beans add sparkle, while lemony sumac and mint add zing to the eggplant and lentils. The finished dish looks and tastes wonderful as part of a buffet, barbecue or themed dinner, and for lunch the next day stuff it into pitas or enjoy on its own.

■ Serve 6 or more. Not suitable to freeze.

---

1 cup Puy or French green lentils
500 g eggplant, about 1 large or 1½ medium
1 Tbsp sumac
½ tsp salt
⅓ cup oil
500 g fava (broad) beans, fresh or frozen*
  (or 250 g broad beans and 250 g fresh or frozen peas, thawed)
3 Tbsp liquid honey
grated zest of 1 lime (or small lemon)
¼ cup lime (or lemon) juice
½ tsp chilli powder or to taste
⅓ cup finely chopped mint
¾ tsp salt or to taste
freshly ground black pepper

Preheat the oven to 200°C.
Rinse and drain the lentils, then simmer, covered, in 3 cups of water for 20–25 minutes or until just tender. Refresh under cold water and drain very thoroughly before transferring to a serving bowl.
Chop the eggplant into 2-cm dice and toss in the combined sumac, salt and oil. Transfer to an oven tray lined with baking paper and spread out in a single layer. Roast at 200°C for 20–25 minutes or until lightly browned and crisped. Toss 2–3 times during cooking. Cool, then gently combine with the lentils.
Boil the fava beans in lightly salted water until just cooked (2–3 minutes). Refresh

under cold water and drain. Unless the beans are fresh and very young, slip off the grey skins and discard. There is no need to cook frozen thawed peas for this salad, but blanch fresh peas if you wish. Combine the prepared beans (or beans and peas) with the lentils and eggplant.

For the dressing, combine the honey, zest, lime or lemon juice, chilli powder, mint, salt and pepper.

Toss the dressing with the vegetables to combine.

Serve warm or at room temperature.

> *Fresh young beans can be used for this salad without having to be peeled after cooking, although frozen or mature fresh beans, cooked and peeled, are perfectly adequate.

Festive Moroccan couscous

Enriched with the colour and flavour of precious saffron, and studded with dried fruits and toasted nuts, this couscous is almost a feast in itself. It's a lovely addition to a Moroccan menu or served with vegetable casseroles or stews, or presented at a barbecue. Adapted from a recipe by Ghillie Basan.

■ **Serves 6. Not recommended to freeze.**

2 cups couscous
½ tsp saffron, crushed
2½ cups hot water
1 tsp salt or to taste
4 Tbsp olive oil
1 Tbsp butter
½ cup slivered almonds
½ cup dried cranberries
½ cup dried apricots, slivered
2 tsp cinnamon

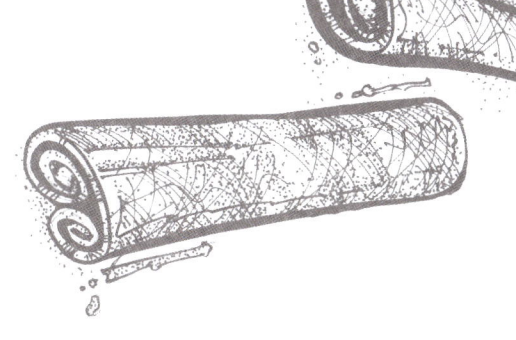

Place the couscous in a bowl. Crush the saffron with a mortar and pestle and soak in ½ cup of the hot water for 5 minutes. Combine the water and saffron with the remaining 2 cups hot water, the salt and 2 tablespoons of the olive oil.

Pour over the couscous and leave to stand for 5–10 minutes. Fluff up with a fork to combine thoroughly.

Heat the remaining 2 tablespoons olive oil in a small, heavy-based frying pan over a low–medium heat and sauté the slivered almonds until lightly brown. Lift from the oil and drain on paper towels. In the same pan and oil, stir in the mixed dried fruits and cook gently until the fruit plumps, about 5 minutes. Stir the almonds and plumped fruits into the couscous and combine.

When ready to serve, heat, covered, in a microwave or transfer to an ovenproof dish, cover and bake at 180°C for about 20 minutes or until heated through.

Turn out and shape into a mound on a warmed serving plate, and sprinkle the cinnamon down the sides in 'stripes'.

Caramelised tomatoes

Traditional slow-roasted tomatoes are great, and this slightly sweeter version is also delicious, especially with Mediterranean dishes or stuffed into pita breads or spread as a pizza topping. Use acid-free tomatoes for best results.* If caramelised balsamic vinegar is not available, make a substitute mixture by heating 1 tablespoon white sugar and 1½ tablespoons balsamic vinegar together until the sugar is dissolved.

■ **Serves 4. Not recommended for freezing.**

6–8 acid-free (Roma) tomatoes
2 Tbsp caramelised balsamic vinegar*
2 Tbsp extra virgin olive oil
salt to taste and freshly ground black pepper

Preheat the oven to 160°C.
Slice the tomatoes in half lengthwise and place in an ovenproof dish to fit. Make a small incision in each tomato half with a sharp knife, then combine the caramelised balsamic vinegar, oil and seasonings. Drizzle over the tomatoes.
Bake, uncovered, for 1½ hours.
Serve hot, or at room temperature.

Glazed beetroot salad

When prepared like this, beetroot retain their plump texture to produce a visual feast as well as a great-tasting salad. Serve with steamed new potatoes and a mesclun or rocket salad for a light lunch or as a side dish at a buffet or barbecue. If you wish, garnish with feta or soft goat's cheese and toasted walnuts for a different look and taste.

■ **Serves 4–6**

4 medium-sized beetroot, trimmed but not peeled
1 large red onion, peeled
2 Tbsp oil
1 tsp salt
freshly ground black pepper
2 Tbsp brown sugar
1½ Tbsp balsamic vinegar
extra balsamic vinegar and seasoning if desired

Place the beetroot in a single layer in a microwave-proof dish with ¼ cup water and microwave, covered, for 8–10 minutes, or until just tender. Check after 5 minutes. Don't overcook, as they have yet to be roasted. Alternatively, place the beetroot in a roasting pan with sufficient water to just cover the bottom of the pan. Cover tightly with aluminium foil and bake at 190°C for 50 minutes–1 hour, or until just tender when pierced with a sharp knife or skewer.

Protect your hands from staining by wearing gloves.
Peel the beetroot and slice into wedges 1–2 cm thick. Cut the onion into 8 segments, each with a piece of root attached.
Toss the prepared beetroot and onion in the combined oil, salt, pepper, sugar and balsamic vinegar. Roast, uncovered, at 180°C for 25–30 minutes, or until the onion is soft and caramelised. Toss once or twice during the cooking time.
Cool. Taste and add extra balsamic and seasonings to sharpen the flavours if you wish. Transfer to a serving platter. This is especially delicious served on, or tossed with, watercress or rocket.

Spicy wedges

These lightly spiced wedges are a little different and quite irresistible. Serve them with tarts, pies, fritters, or to accompany an Indian meal.

Waxy or floury potatoes are suitable for this recipe.

■ **Serves 6. Not suitable to freeze.**

---

1 kg medium to large potatoes
4 Tbsp oil
2 tsp black mustard seeds
2 tsp cumin seeds
1 tsp turmeric
½ tsp chilli powder
1 tsp salt or to taste
freshly ground black pepper
2 Tbsp lemon juice
4 Tbsp finely chopped fresh coriander

Scrub the potatoes and slice lengthwise into wedges. Simmer the wedges in lightly salted water for about 15 minutes or until just tender. Transfer immediately to a colander to drain.
While the wedges are cooking, heat the oil to medium–hot in an electric frying pan, for preference, or a large, heavy-based frying pan. Stir in the mustard and cumin seeds and cook until the seeds begin to 'pop'. Turn the heat down, stir in the turmeric, chilli powder, salt and pepper and continue to cook for 1 minute.
As soon as the potatoes are cooked and drained, heat the oil and spice mixture in the frying pan, transfer the potatoes to the pan and toss gently with a fish slice until well coated with the spices.
Drizzle the lemon juice over the wedges, garnish with the finely chopped coriander and serve immediately.

Salads & sides

Moroccan spice & honey eggplant

Versatile, full of flavour and perfectly concluded by pomegranate molasses (see opposite), this dish can be served hot, warm or at room temperature to enhance almost any menu. It is, however, particularly good with Moroccan or North African dishes.

■ **Serves 4–6 as an accompaniment. May be frozen.**

700 g eggplant
oil
½ tsp salt or to taste
1 Tbsp olive oil
2 cloves garlic, crushed
1 tsp peeled and finely chopped fresh ginger
⅓–½ tsp chilli powder
1 tsp sweet paprika
2½ Tbsp clear honey
⅓ cup water
¼ cup orange juice
1 Tbsp pomegranate molasses
fresh coriander or Italian (flat-leaf) parsley to garnish

Preheat the oven to 190°C.
Slice the eggplant into 2-cm rounds and dip each slice into a bowl of neutral oil, wiping off any excess oil on the lip of the bowl.
Place in a single layer on an oven tray, sprinkle with the ½ teaspoon of salt and roast at 190°C for 20–25 minutes, turning once, until golden brown on both sides.
Meanwhile, heat the olive oil in a wide frying pan with a solid base. Gently sauté the garlic and ginger until fragrant, then stir in the remaining ingredients (except the coriander or parsley) and reduce by about a quarter. Transfer the eggplant pieces from the oven into the pan, preferably in a single layer.
Cook over a low heat, uncovered, for about 10 minutes. There should still be a little liquid left in the pan, but the eggplant will have absorbed most of this; what remains will have the consistency of a light syrup.
Serve garnished with a little chopped coriander or parsley.

Roast pumpkin with pomegranate molasses

Nothing could be simpler and quantities don't matter at all. Pomegranate molasses or syrup is essentially reduced pomegranate juice with sugar and lemon. It has a unique, tangy sweetness that enhances and complements the flavour of roast pumpkin, among many other dishes. Use it once and you'll find ways to use it again — on pies, steamed green beans and fried eggplant slices, for example.

Preheat the oven to 190°C.
Peel and cut pumpkin into the desired number of slices. Place in a single layer on a baking tray and coat or toss lightly in oil, then sprinkle with salt and freshly ground black pepper.
Bake for 25–35 minutes or until golden and tender, turning once.
Transfer to a serving dish and drizzle with pomegranate molasses.

Zucchini salad

Zucchini salad is fresh and simple, with a tropical touch provided by the inclusion of coconut threads and a sweet, gingered dressing.

Overgrown zucchini or even small marrows may be used for this dish by removing the centre core of seeds and spongy tissue.

■ **Serves 4–6. Not suitable to freeze.**

*450 g zucchini (trimmed weight), chopped into small dice,
   half the size of your small fingernail*
2 small apples or 1 large, preferably red-skinned
¾ cup coconut threads
¼ cup sultanas
1 Tbsp sour cream (optional)

Dressing
1 Tbsp lemon juice
2 Tbsp white wine vinegar
1 tsp fresh minced ginger
1 Tbsp sugar
¼ cup olive oil
½ tsp salt or to taste
freshly ground black pepper

Place all the dressing ingredients in a small screw-top jar and shake well.
Prepare the zucchini, then core the apples and chop into dice the same size as the zucchini. Place the zucchini and apple in a serving bowl then mix in the coconut threads, sultanas and the sour cream, if using. Pour over the dressing and mix thoroughly to combine. Cover with cling wrap and refrigerate until required. Bring to room temperature before serving.

Salads & sides

Brown & wild rice with roast lemon

This dish is wonderfully versatile — it can be served hot, warm or at room temperature and has a deliciously rich, nutty flavour thanks to the wild rice, for which there is no close substitute.

The roasted lemon slices (and other fruits such as oranges, peaches, etc.) can be pre-prepared — finely chopped and frozen for later use, or packed in small jars and covered in light olive oil for use in orzo, quinoa or couscous-based salads; pasta salads with fried haloumi and marinated artichoke hearts; or Greek salads with diced feta and olives. Roasting intensifies the flavour of fruits and removes any bitterness.

■ **Serves 6. May be frozen.**

½ cup currants or raisins, plumped in juice of 1 orange
2 lemons, roasted and finely chopped
olive oil
brown sugar
1 large onion, preferably red, peeled and finely chopped
4 carrots, peeled and chopped into small dice
1 cup pumpkin seeds (or cashews), toasted
30 g butter
2 Tbsp olive oil
1 cup wild rice
1 cup brown rice
3 cups vegetable stock
¼ cup finely chopped olives — reserve some for garnish
½ cup plucked Italian (flat-leaf) parsley
salt and freshly ground black pepper

Preheat the oven to 180°C.
Place the currants or raisins in a small bowl with the orange juice, cover with cling wrap and set aside.
Slice the lemons into 1-cm rounds, skin included. Place in a single layer on a roasting tray, then drizzle with olive oil and a dusting of brown sugar. Roast 20–25 minutes or until the fruit is well coloured and shrivelled (not scorched). Chop finely and set aside.
Prepare the onion and carrots. Heat the butter and oil in a casserole dish over a low–medium heat and sauté the onion and carrots, about 10 minutes.

Wash and drain the rices separately, then stir the brown rice into the sautéed vegetable mixture. Sauté for a few minutes longer, then stir in the stock.

Turn up the heat and bring almost to the boil. Place a close-fitting lid on the dish or cover tightly with aluminium foil. Transfer to the oven and cook for 10 minutes at 180°C. Stir in the wild rice at this point and cook for a further 30 minutes.

Transfer the cooked rice to a bowl and add the roasted lemon, currants or raisins with any remaining orange juice, chives, parsley and the toasted pumpkin seeds or cashews. Toss to combine. Season to taste.

Transfer to a large platter and garnish with the reserved, finely chopped chives. For individual servings, pack the salad into a small cup, turn it out into the middle of a large white plate, dust the plate with fresh, finely chopped herbs and drizzle some fruity green olive oil around the salad.

Al fresco potato salad

Potato salads are a great standby, and something most of us enjoy, especially in summer. This recipe is a great al fresco or buffet dish.

It is important to bring to room temperature before serving, and to use only waxy potatoes, so they don't break up. Also, be sure to make a batch of aïoli before you start — very few store-bought labels will 'cut it' for this recipe to be enjoyed at its best.

■ **Serves 6–8. Not suitable to freeze.**

---

1 kg waxy potatoes, peeled
1 cup aïoli* (page 44)
4 Tbsp whole seed mustard
2 Tbsp fresh lime juice (or lemon juice)
½ red capsicum, seeded and diced
½ cup finely chopped fresh coriander (or mint)
2 fresh red chillies, seeded and finely chopped
1 small red onion, peeled and sliced thin
1 tsp salt or to taste
lots of freshly ground black pepper

Dice the peeled potatoes into bite-sized pieces, about 2 cm. Drop the diced potatoes into boiling, lightly salted water to cook for 8–10 minutes, until they are just tender. Don't overcook, as they need to hold their shape. Drain immediately in a colander.

While the potatoes are cooking, mix the remaining ingredients together in a small bowl. As soon as the potatoes are well drained, transfer to a bowl and while they are still hot, mix the dressing through the potatoes gently, to ensure they are well coated. Cool. If the salad is to be refrigerated before serving, remember to bring it back to room temperature first. Mix gently once more and transfer to a serving bowl.

Garnish with extra coriander if desired.

Tuscan broad beans

One of the most delectable salads imaginable is singularly Italian, and simply too good to be served with any distractions. Serve it as an entrée or appetiser, with hot crusty ciabatta to mop up!

The cheese is optional, depending on appetites. The focus here is on the beans and the dressing (lime juice is recommended above lemon, if possible). Fresh broad beans (or fava beans as they are also known) are available for such a limited time that frozen are a very convenient alternative, even if they do need peeling.

Broad beans are full of protein so follow with a light main such as Briam (page 52) or Tofu, Lemon & Herb Lasagne (page 66).

■ **Serves 4. Not suitable to freeze.**

---

500 g shelled broad beans, fresh or frozen
lime juice (or lemon)
extra virgin avocado 'Zest' oil (or extra virgin olive oil)
pinch of chilli flakes
a few grinds of rock salt
freshly ground black pepper
3 Tbsp Italian (flat-leaf) parsley, chopped
feta (or soft goat's cheese, or shaved Parmesan) (optional)

Bring a medium-sized saucepan of salted water to the boil over high heat, tip in the beans and bring back to the boil. Simmer for 2 minutes, uncovered.
Refresh under cold running water and drain. If using mature fresh or frozen beans, peel off the outer skins and discard.
Pile onto a serving plate and dress with the lime juice followed by the oil, chilli flakes, salt, pepper and the roughly chopped parsley. The ratio of lime juice, oil and seasonings is a matter of personal choice in this dish, but a guide would be to toss the prepared beans with 3 tablespoons lime juice and 4 tablespoons avocado 'Zest' oil (or extra virgin olive oil). Garnish with the cheese, if using. Provide lime wedges and extra oil at the table, as well as rock salt and pepper.
Serve immediately, or bring to room temperature or slightly warm if preparing ahead. Accompany with hot, crusty ciabatta.

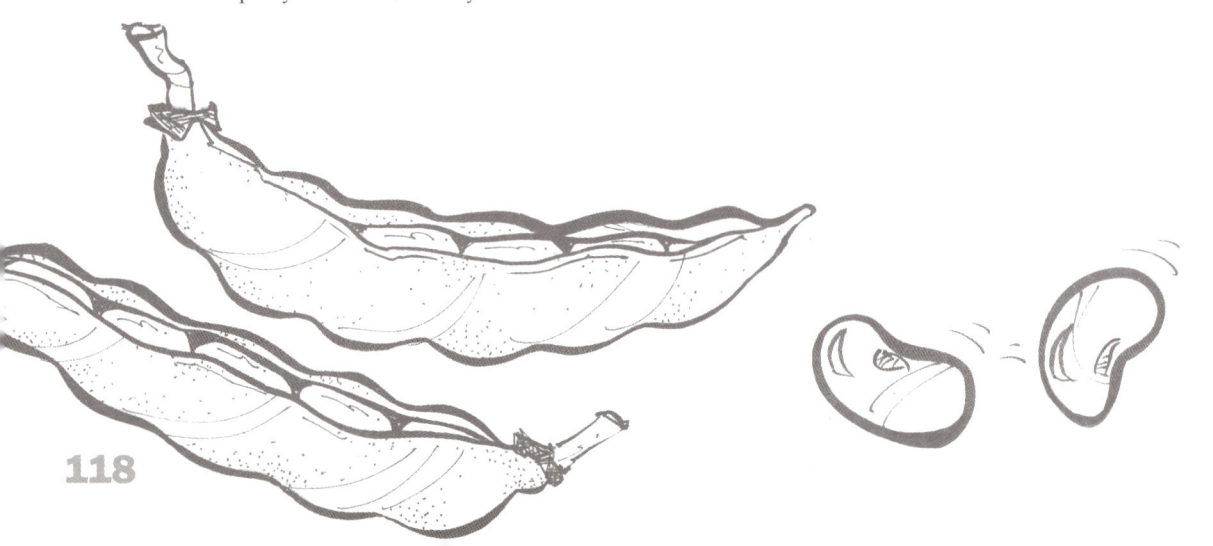

Dhal

Dhal is one of the true comfort foods of all time, right up with mash, and custard made with egg yolks. It's best known as a mild accompaniment to curries — very nutritious but generally taking a back seat to the stars on the plate. This is not, however, how true dhal lovers see the case — we bring it to centre stage so its true worth can be appreciated. Dhals are simply made from most pulses or lentils, but this version is particularly good — try it served with steamed brown rice, chopped fresh coriander and a few grinds of rock salt for that feel-good feeling (honestly — it's even good for breakfast!)

Alternatively, serve with any curry, accompanied by rice or naan, raita and sambals. This quantity makes 4 modest serves, or 6 if served with curries and rice/naan.

■ **Freezes well.**

---

1 cup yellow split peas*
2½ cups water
½ tsp turmeric
½ tsp fresh finely chopped ginger
1 tsp salt or to taste
2 Tbsp oil
½ tsp black mustard seeds
1 Tbsp butter
½ tsp cumin seeds
1 medium-sized onion, peeled and diced small
2 cloves garlic, peeled and finely chopped
1 green chilli (6–7 cm) seeded and very finely chopped

Soak the split peas overnight in enough water to cover well, unless you are using a pressure cooker. In hot weather, place in refrigerator to soak.

Rinse and drain the soaked peas, then place in a saucepan with the 2½ cups water, turmeric, ginger and salt. Bring to simmer point, turn heat to low and simmer, uncovered, for about 40 minutes, stirring regularly. At this point the peas should be soupy but not completely mushed.

While the peas are cooking, heat the oil in a medium-sized frying pan and cook the mustard seeds until the first seeds 'pop'.

Lower the heat and stir in the butter, followed by the cumin seeds. These need only a few seconds to brown (don't scorch), then quickly stir in the prepared onion and garlic. Cook on a very low heat, stirring regularly, until golden and soft. This should take about 20 minutes. Stir in the green chilli and sauté for 1 minute. Transfer the pea mixture into the pan with the onion/garlic and cook, stirring, for about 5–7 minutes or until the dhal reaches the consistency you prefer.

*The split peas must be soaked overnight, unless using a pressure cooker. Pressure cook for 12 minutes, unsoaked.

sweets

Citrus crème brûlée 121
Pear & lemon flan 122
Roast cherries with rum 122
Feijoa (or apple) coconut cake 123
Diva chocolate cheesecake with chocolate sauce 124
Rhubarb & feijoa pie 126
Ice cream 127
Tirami trifle 128
Chocolate feijoa cake 129
Kingston cake with grilled mandarins 130
Grilled mandarins 131
Fig & nut meringue torte 131
Raspberry sorbet 132
Macerated tamarillos 132
Venus cake 133
Orange blossom pannacotta with sweet clementines 134

Sweet clementines 135
Bev's feijoas in pink wine syrup 135
Gula melaka 136
Tart Madeleine 137
Sachertorte 138
Apple & cranberry custard pie 139
Rhubarb & strawberry pie 140
Kiwi cassata 141
Berry cups 142
Blackberry pie 143

Citrus crème brûlée

Crème Brûlée is a classic dessert that never strays far from favour, for the very good reason that few of us can resist the combination of a crisp toffee coating over cool, creamy custard.

In this version, orange and lime juices are reduced to intensify their flavours without diluting the texture of the custard, and lime gives the orange just the right amount of torque. Substitute fresh lemon juice for the lime if necessary, and soya milk may be substituted instead of the cream if a non-dairy option is preferred.

Quick, straightforward and impressive, this brûlée can be assembled the day before; all that's needed in terms of equipment are half-cup (125 ml) ramekins. Although a micro-torch is fun, it's really not essential as long as you have access to a hot grill.

■ **Serves 4 (or double the quantities to serve 8). Not suitable to freeze.**

½ cup fresh or pure orange juice
juice of 2 limes (about 4 Tbsp)
2 cups (500 ml) cream
⅓ cup caster sugar
5 egg yolks
2 tsp caster sugar per ramekin

Preheat the oven to 170°C.
Combine the orange and lime juices in a small saucepan and reduce over a medium–high heat until only ¼ cup remains.
While the juices reduce, heat the cream and sugar in a second saucepan to just below simmer point to dissolve the sugar. Don't let the mixture actually simmer, though. Meanwhile, pour about 5 cm hot water into a roasting pan or ovenproof dish and place in the oven.
Reserve the whites from five eggs (they can be frozen), and place the yolks in a medium-sized bowl. When the juices are reduced and the cream/sugar mixture is hot, whisk the juices and the cream mixture alternately into the yolks, whisking continuously.
Strain the mixture if you wish, although this isn't strictly necessary. Divide between four half-cup ramekins and transfer to the dish of hot water in the oven. The water level should come halfway up the sides of the ramekins.
Bake at 170°C for 35–40 minutes, until the custards have firmed but still have some 'wobble'. Take the pan from the oven but leave the ramekins in the hot water for 10 minutes before removing.
Cool, then cover with cling wrap and refrigerate until needed.
Just before serving, evenly sprinkle two teaspoons caster sugar over the top of each brûlée. Either place the ramekins under a very hot grill, or use a micro-torch to scorch the sugar until it melts and begins to bubble. This can take 1–3 minutes, depending on how close the sugar is to the flame. The sugar will harden very quickly as it cools.
Serve as is, without any distraction, or with fresh berries and/or a smidgen of crème fraîche or whipped cream.

Pear & lemon flan

Simple but stylish, pear and lemon is a dream team.

■ Serves 6–8. Not recommended for freezing.

Pastry*

Filling and assembly
2 large pears or 3 small
4 eggs
2 cups caster sugar
zest of 2½ lemons
5 Tbsp lemon juice
4 Tbsp custard powder

*Refer to page 152 for the recipe for semolina pastry or use pre-rolled shortcrust to line a lightly greased or sprayed, 25-cm loose-bottomed flan tin.

Preheat the oven to 190°C. Make the pastry and line the flan tin. Freeze for 15 minutes while preparing the filling.

Peel and core the pears, then slice lengthwise into thin slices. Arrange the pear slices so they overlap and cover the bottom of the flan.

Whisk the eggs lightly then beat in the sugar, zest, juice and custard powder.

Pour the filling evenly over the pears and bake for 45–50 minutes or until golden and lightly set. If the pie starts to brown too quickly after 20 minutes, lower the oven temperature to 180°C.

Serve at room temperature with mascarpone, plain yoghurt or lightly whipped cream.

Roast cherries with rum

So often the best 'afters' are very simple affairs that showcase our wonderful fresh produce, especially when the weather is hot and the outdoors beckons. This recipe works just as well with blackberries, boysenberries, halved plums, blackcurrants and others, but leaving cherries whole makes sense as stoning is fiddly. While extracting the stones at the table may be a little inelegant, it works perfectly well if a bowl for the stones is provided — as long as formality is not too much of an issue. Reduce the cooking time for the softer berries.

■ Serves 4. Suitable to freeze.

500 g black cherries, stemmed
½ cup white sugar
¼ cup rum, brandy, port or red wine
pomegranate seeds (optional)

Preheat the oven to 170°C.
Place the cherries or other fruit in a medium-sized roasting dish and toss them in the sugar. Roast at 170°C for 40 minutes, uncovered, or until the cherries are well heated through and the juices are released.
Stir in the rum (preferably), brandy, port or wine and toss. Roast for another 15 minutes until the cherries are cooked and starting to collapse. If you are using softer fruits, reduce the roasting time; for example, berries require only about half the total cooking time.
Remove from the oven and transfer to a serving dish to cool. Stir in some pomegranate seeds if available, for a great burst of flavour.
Serve spooned over plain vanilla ice cream.

Feijoa (or apple) coconut cake

This cake is moist but light, irresistible at any time and delicious as a casual dessert accompanied by lightly whipped cream or plain yoghurt.

■ **Serves 6–8. Suitable to freeze.**

175 g softened butter
1 cup sugar
3 eggs (preferably size 7)
1½ cups flour
2 tsp baking powder
½ cup milk
5–6 largish feijoas, peeled (or 2 large tart apples, peeled and cored)
1¼ cups desiccated coconut
¼ cup flaked almonds
2 Tbsp sugar

Preheat the oven to 180°C.
Lightly grease a 23-cm springform cake tin (check the size of your tin for best results).
Cream the butter and sugar together. Add the eggs one at a time and beat in.
Sift the flour with the baking powder and fold in alternately with the milk.
Cut the peeled feijoas into 1½-cm dice or slice the peeled apples into 5-mm slices, then into 2-cm dice. Fold into the batter with the coconut.
Pour into the prepared tin, sprinkle the almonds and sugar evenly over the top of the cake and bake 45–50 minutes, or until a skewer inserted into the middle of the cake comes out clean.

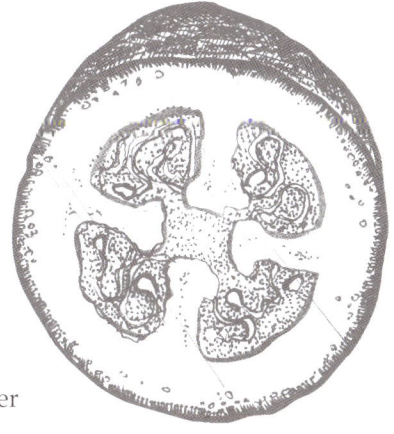

Diva chocolate cheesecake with chocolate sauce

Baked cheesecakes are the real deal, as opposed to their unbaked counterparts. In any case, this one is irresistible; velvet smooth and contains a hint of mocha beneath the rich chocolate flavour, but not overly sweet.

A luxurious conclusion to any meal, it's surprisingly quick to make as the base is not precooked and the filling is all mixed in a food processor. The sauce is an optional extra, but does add that extra touch of luxury — use a store-bought sauce if you wish.

■ **Serves 12. Freezes well.**

Base
2 cups Malt 'o' Milk biscuit crumbs (or any sweet plain biscuit)
2 Tbsp cocoa powder, sieved
60 g butter, diced
30 g dark chocolate, chopped

You will need most of a 250-g packet of biscuits. Place the biscuits in a food processor and blitz to fine crumbs. Transfer 2 cups of crumbs to a small bowl and mix in the cocoa.

Melt the butter and chocolate together on low power in a microwave or over a low heat in a saucepan on the stove, then thoroughly mix into the crumb mixture and press firmly into a deep-sided 25-cm springform cake tin. Set aside.

Filling
750 g cream cheese, diced
1 cup cottage cheese
¾ cup sugar
4 large (size 7) eggs
2 Tbsp cocoa powder, sieved
2 tsp granulated instant coffee (or 1½ tsp instant coffee powder)
1 Tbsp Crème de Cacao liqueur (optional)
200 g good quality dark chocolate, melted
2 Tbsp cocoa powder

Preheat the oven to 170°C. Pour hot water into a roasting pan to half full and set on the bottom rack of the oven.

Place the roughly diced cream cheese in a large bowl and soften on low power in a microwave, until just softened. Transfer to a food processor with the cottage cheese and the sugar. Process until well mixed, then add the eggs one by one.

Add the cocoa, instant coffee and the liqueur if using.

Melt the chocolate on very low power in a microwave or in a bowl over simmering water, and add to the filling mixture. Combine thoroughly in the food processor.

Pour the filling mixture on top of the prepared base, smooth over the top and bake for 1 hour at 170°C, or until the filling has risen and is firm to the touch but a skewer inserted into the middle exits with a little filling adhering to it — the filling should still have a little wobble in the middle. Don't worry if some cracks appear in the top as it cooks (a few cracks are unavoidable), but turn the oven down if the cake appears to be cooking too fast.

Cool in the tin before transferring to a serving dish. Cover and refrigerate until needed. Sieve cocoa powder over to 'dust' the top and serve with chocolate sauce.

Chocolate sauce

So simple and fast! (Next time you have leftover pouring cream, freeze it to make this sauce.)

1 cup chopped dark chocolate
¾ cup cream

Place both ingredients in a small saucepan over a low heat and heat to simmer point, stirring all the time.

Cool before serving. Cover and refrigerate for up to 1 week.

Rhubarb & feijoa pie

Tart fruit flavours have always been popular, but never more so than in today's café culture. Gooseberries, redcurrants and blackcurrants and rhubarb are incorporated into food chic like never before. Rightly so, too. These flavours are assertive in themselves, but sometimes just the right note can be struck by combining them with others.

Rhubarb combined with feijoa, for example, is superb in this pie. The distinctive rhubarb is present, but the flavour is enhanced when combined with feijoas; definitely a case of the whole being more than the sum of its parts.

Pre-rolled pastry sheets are stipulated here, purely in the interest of convenience; but refer to the recipe on page 152 if you prefer to make your own. No precooking of either fruit or pastry is required.

■ **Serves 6–8. Suitable to freeze.**

---

2 sheets pre-rolled sweet shortcrust pastry (or see recipe page 152)
300 g feijoa flesh
300 g trimmed rhubarb stalks
½ cup caster sugar
2 Tbsp cornflour
1 Tbsp beaten egg (or milk)
2 Tbsp granulated sugar

Preheat the oven to 220°C.
Lightly spray or grease a 25-cm pie or quiche tin.
Use one of the thawed pastry sheets to line the prepared tin — you will probably need to trim a 5-cm wide strip of pastry off the second sheet and use to extend this so it covers the bottom and sides of the tin (wet one edge and press together). Reserve the remaining pastry for the top of the pie.

Spoon out the flesh from the feijoas, then weigh it. Chop the flesh roughly and transfer to a bowl. Using a sharp knife, slice the rhubarb stalks thinly. Again, weigh after preparation.

Place the rhubarb in the bowl with the feijoa flesh and combine with the caster sugar and the cornflour.

Transfer the filling evenly into the prepared base, then cut the remaining pastry sheet into 7 strips. Use the strips to design a lattice top over the filling, then brush the strips with the lightly beaten egg or milk, using a pastry brush, and sprinkle with the granulated sugar.

Place the pie in the preheated oven and bake at 220°C for 10 minutes, then turn the heat down to 200°C.

Cover the pie with a sheet of aluminium foil at this point to stop it browning too fast. Bake for a further 40–45 minutes, uncovering the pie for the last 10 minutes of cooking to ensure the top is an even golden brown.

Serve at room temperature or slightly warm, accompanied by vanilla ice cream, plain yoghurt or lightly whipped cream.

Ice cream

Dead easy to make, no mixing or beating and absolutely luxurious — you really can't go wrong with this one. This ice cream has been a family favourite for decades, with everyone having their own preferred flavour. The only note of caution here is that it softens really quickly when taken from the freezer, so if you are planning to roll it into scoops for serving, it is advisable to do this ahead of time and return it to the freezer so you can present the scooped ice cream in perfect condition.

If a non-alcoholic batch is required, try the basic vanilla option or simply omit the liqueur from the other options. Or, fold in sweetened puréed berries or other fruit instead of the liqueur.

Base ice cream
600 ml cream
397-g tin sweetened condensed milk

Beat the cream until it thickens to soft peak stage, then pour in the sweetened condensed milk while continuing to beat, adjusting the pouring speed so that the cream is thickened but not stiff — it should be of a creamy consistency but not buttery. Fold in the flavouring ingredients or liquor/liqueur of choice (see below) and transfer the mixture to a 2-litre plastic container with a lid.

Freeze for 12 hours.

Vanilla: *1 tsp pure vanilla extract*
Coffee: *¼ cup white rum (or Crème de Cacao liqueur), 3–4 tsp instant coffee*
Licorice: *¼ cup white or black Sambuca liqueur, 150 g soft licorice, chopped or sliced thinly*
Whisky & Chocolate: *¼ cup whiskey, 70 g good quality (70%) dark chocolate, melted*
Limoncello: *¼ cup limoncello (see page 177)*

Tirami trifle

This dead-easy dessert started out as a trifle, endured the rejection of lemon curd and fruit as possible inclusions and ended up as a layered sponge hybrid — somewhere between a tiramisu and a trifle. The logic to this evolution is that the result is familiar but lighter than either tiramisu or trifle, and provides a platform for berries or other fresh, roasted or poached fruits to shine.

It's not suitable to freeze but is best prepared a day or two in advance, covered and refrigerated. Delicious and fast, fast, fast. Ideal for a light celebration dessert.

■ **Serves 6. Not suitable to freeze.**

---

300 g plain (or chocolate) sponge
½ cup unsweetened apple juice
4 Tbsp Cointreau (first measure)
150 g 'lite' cream cheese
⅓ cup caster sugar
2 tsp orange zest
¼ cup Cointreau (second measure)
300 ml cream
4 Tbsp cocoa, optional

Weigh the sponge and slice into 1-cm thick slices. Combine the apple juice and first measure of Cointreau in small bowl and set aside.
Beat the cream cheese with the sugar until smooth and creamy, then mix in the orange zest and the second measure of Cointreau.
Whip the cream to soft peaks and fold into the cream cheese mixture to combine.
Line the bottom of a serving bowl with some of the sponge slices, allowing the lengths to come about 2 cm up the sides. Cut the sponge to fit if necessary.
Moisten the sponge layer quite liberally with almost half of the juice/liqueur mix then spread with almost half of the cream mixture. Sift some of the cocoa over this layer, if using. Repeat the layers, finishing with the cream and topping with the cocoa.
Cover and refrigerate until ready to serve with fresh raspberries or other fresh, poached or roasted fruit.

Chocolate feijoa cake

Cakes that can be served as a casual dessert as well as something sweet to enjoy with a coffee, such as this one, are really useful. This simple recipe produces a cake that is moist and rich, without any cloying sweetness, and the recipe allows the unique aromatic tartness of the feijoas to work as a complement to the chocolate. Serve with lightly whipped cream or crème fraîche if serving as a dessert.

■ **Serves 6–8. Freezes well.**

1½ cups peeled, diced feijoas (approximately 8 egg-sized feijoas)
2 Tbsp brown sugar
½ tsp cinnamon (first measure)
185 g butter, softened
¾ cup caster sugar
2 eggs
1½ cups self-raising flour
½ tsp baking soda
½ cup cocoa powder
½ tsp cinnamon (second measure)
½ tsp ground nutmeg
½ cup sour cream

Preheat the oven to 180°C.
Lightly oil or spray a 23-cm springform baking tin. Line the bottom of the tin with baking paper. Peel the ripe feijoas using a sharp knife. Slice each feijoa in half lengthwise, then cut into 1-cm dice. Measure 1½ cups of the diced fruit and place in a bowl with the brown sugar and the first ½ teaspoon cinnamon.
Cream the softened butter and sugar in a small bowl with an electric beater. Beat in the eggs one after the other, then transfer the mixture to a large bowl. Stir in the prepared feijoas, sifted flour, baking soda, cocoa, second measure of cinnamon and the nutmeg alternately with the sour cream in two batches.
Transfer the batter into the prepared pan and smooth the top evenly.
Bake at 180°C for 50 minutes, or until a skewer inserted into the middle of the cake exits cleanly. Remove from the oven and stand for 5 minutes, then turn out onto a wire rack and remove the baking paper. Cool completely.
Cover the top and sides with the chocolate glaze.

Chocolate glaze
130 g dark chocolate
40 g butter

Place in a small microwave-proof bowl and heat on medium power for about 1 minute. Whip with a knife until smooth and shiny.

Kingston cake with grilled mandarins

Kingston cake is a Greek-style semolina cake that has orange syrup poured over while it is hot. It is quite a dense, textured affair; sumptuous but understated, and particularly good when teamed with mascarpone, crème fraîche or plain Greek-style yoghurt — add grilled or roasted fruit such as peaches or nectarines, or fresh fruit, such as blueberries or raspberries to really lift the ante. Grilled mandarins are a lovely complement, too, when fresh summer fruits are not available.

Always thinking of the next deadline, food writers sometimes forget to revisit past favourites. I first published this cake in a column in 1984 but forgot how good it is until it emerged recently — just as good as ever.

■ **Serves 6–8. May be frozen.**

165 g butter, softened (or margarine)
¾ cup caster sugar
3 eggs
1½ cups semolina
1½ tsp baking powder
185 g ground almonds
grated zest of 1½ oranges
3 Tbsp orange juice

Preheat the oven to 180°C. Lightly grease or spray a 23-cm cake tin, preferably springform. Line the base with baking paper.
Cream the softened butter and sugar together, then beat in the eggs one at a time. Mix the semolina, baking powder and ground almonds together and fold lightly into the creamed mixture, alternating with the orange zest and juice.
Transfer to the prepared tin and bake 35–45 minutes or until a skewer inserted into the middle of the cake exits cleanly. While the cake is cooking, make the syrup.
Transfer the cooked cake from the oven and place on a plate to catch any escaping syrup if you are using a springform pan with a removable base.
Prick the top of the cake a few times with a skewer then slowly pour the hot syrup evenly over the surface.
Cool in the tin. Turn out, remove the baking paper and place the cooled cake on a serving plate. Cover and refrigerate.
Bring to room temperature before serving with the grilled mandarins.

Syrup
*1½ cups fresh orange juice**
½ cup sugar

Place the orange juice and the sugar in a small saucepan, bring to a simmer over a medium heat and simmer for 5–6 minutes, uncovered.

*Bottled orange juice is fine, as long as it contains no added sugar or preservatives.

Grilled mandarins

Allow one per person. Use seedless mandarins if possible, and if they are thin-skinned, it's not necessary to peel them.

Peel, then slice, each mandarin in half through the equator and discard any obvious seeds. Slice a cross through the middle of each half, and sprinkle with about 1 teaspoon grated palm sugar.

Line the grill pan with aluminium foil, then place the mandarins on the pan and put under a hot grill until bubbling and starting to caramelise, 8–10 minutes.

Transfer to a serving dish and drizzle with a little Cointreau if desired.

Fig & nut meringue torte

This torte is divine; a favourite that can be whipped up in minutes and that showcases a crisp meringue crust enclosing a chewy fig/nut filling.

Top with sliced fresh fruit if you wish, or serve with whipped cream or ice cream and perhaps a drizzle of rum pot liqueur (page 178), macerated tamarillos or a berry purée such as a coulis. A fresh fruit topping can be dusted with icing sugar, drizzled with honey and/or liqueur or melted chocolate, or simply left au naturel — passionfruit, fresh figs, nectarines, peaches, raspberries, strawberries or whatever you fancy.

■ **Serves 6. Not recommended for freezing.**

4 large egg whites
¼ tsp salt or to taste
1 tsp malt vinegar
1 cup caster sugar
½ cup Brazil nuts (or blanched whole almonds)
½ cup thinly sliced dried figs
fresh fruit such as peaches or raspberries (optional)
200 ml cream, whipped (optional)

Preheat the oven to 150°C. Line a baking tray with baking paper or a Teflon sheet.

Beat the egg whites, salt and vinegar until stiff peaks form. Slowly add the sugar, ¼ cup at a time, beating thoroughly between additions. Continue beating until the mixture is very thick and stiff.

Place the Brazil nuts and the figs in a food processor and chop together until finely ground. Gently fold into the meringue mixture. Pile the meringue onto the prepared tray, into approximately a 25-cm circle, using a palette or flat-bladed knife. The sides should be about 4 cm high. The torte will spread, though, as it cooks.

Bake at 150°C for about 1 hour, until the meringue feels lightly crisp and is a light golden colour. Turn off the heat and allow the torte to 'dry off' in the oven for a further 1½ hours. Cool, then store in an airtight tin until ready to serve (up to 4 days).

Top with fresh fruit and cream or ice cream as detailed above if wished, or simply serve with whipped cream.

Raspberry sorbet

Raspberry sorbet is light but full-bodied and is a gorgeous, rich red colour. Sorbets are especially appealing when they follow a rich or spicy meal, and can be made using other fruits such as apricot, orange and kiwifruit. Use an ice-cream scoop to serve straight from the freezer, as it melts quickly.

½ cup water
¾ cup caster sugar
400 g fresh or frozen raspberries
juice of 1 medium-sized lemon
1 egg white

Combine the water and sugar in a small saucepan and stir, over a low heat without
boiling, until the sugar is dissolved. Now bring to the boil and simmer, uncovered, without stirring, for 5 minutes.
Place the raspberries in a food processor, add the lemon juice and the hot syrup, then process until smooth. Push the raspberry purée through a sieve, then place in a covered container and freeze until firm.
Remove from the freezer. Beat the egg white stiffly, then beat into the raspberry mixture with a fork or whisk, and return to the freezer immediately, until ready to serve.

Macerated tamarillos

Stunningly simple! Macerated tamarillos provide the perfect balance for a dessert such as fig and nut meringue torte, page 131. Pour boiling water over 8–10 tamarillos and leave for 2–3 minutes, until the thin skins readily peel off.
Slice thinly and arrange in overlapping slices, in layers, in a serving bowl. Sprinkle each layer with caster sugar, according to taste. A guide is about ½–¾ teaspoon sugar per tamarillo, depending on size Cover with cling wrap and refrigerate for 24 hours before serving.

Venus cake

Oranges, almonds and carrots may sound an unusual combination, but this moist, golden cake is irresistible.

Serve it on the day it is made, or cover with cling wrap and refrigerate, then bring to room temperature to serve the next day. Serve with crème fraîche, whipped cream or unsweetened yoghurt, and roasted, grilled or fresh summer fruits. A drizzle of Cointreau is an optional extra, and the cake keeps well, refrigerated, for up to 4 days.

■ **Makes 12–14 generous slices. Suitable to freeze.**

250 g softened butter
1½ cups sugar
6 large egg yolks
300 g carrots, peeled (about 2 cups once processed)
1 cup flour
1 tsp baking powder
4 Tbsp orange zest (no pith)
200 g blanched almonds, finely ground
½ cup fresh orange juice
6 large egg whites

Preheat the oven to 180°C. Lightly grease a 25-cm springform cake tin and line with baking paper. Cream the butter and sugar. Add the egg yolks one by one, beating well after each addition, and reserve the whites in another bowl. Peel and trim the carrots (about 2½ medium to large), weigh and then chop finely in a food processor but don't mush. Set aside.
Sieve the flour and baking powder and gently combine with the cake mixture, followed by the carrots, zest, ground almonds and orange juice.
Beat the egg whites to soft peaks and gently fold into the batter. Transfer to the prepared tin, pushing into the sides and smoothing the top.
Bake at 180°C for about an hour or until a skewer inserted into the middle of the cake comes out clean. Rest for 5 minutes before turning out on a cake rack to cool. Remove the baking paper and, when cooled, transfer to a serving plate.
Serve with the citrus sauce if wished — this is an optional extra.

Citrus sauce

1½ cups fresh orange juice
juice of 2 lemons (or limes)
½ cup sugar
2 tsp cornflour

Place the juices and the sugar in a small saucepan over a medium heat, reserving 2 tablespoons juice. Taste and add a little more sugar if desired. Moisten the cornflour in the reserved juice, stirring until smooth. When the mixture comes to a simmer, stir in the cornflour mix slowly, stirring briskly to avoid lumps. Bring back to simmer point, stirring, for 1 minute. Cool to serve with the Venus Cake at room temperature.

Orange blossom pannacotta with sweet clementines

Pannacotta is such an easy dessert, and always popular. The inclusion of orange blossom water here is lovely and gives a delicate hint of orange to balance the poached clementines, which have been poached in a syrup containing the lightest touch of anise. Omit the orange blossom water and either add another flavour for a change or serve the pannacotta plain but with a fruit coulis or syrup.

Individual pannacottas always look good, but another option that is perfectly acceptable, if less formal, is to serve from one elegant bowl.

■ **Serves 6. Not suitable to freeze.**

---

2 cups cream
2 tsp gelatine
½ cup sugar
1½ cups natural Greek-style yoghurt*
1 tsp orange blossom water**

Measure ¼ cup of the cream into a small bowl and sprinkle the gelatine over, without stirring.

In a medium-sized saucepan, dissolve the sugar in the remaining cream, heating to simmer point. Stir constantly and remove from the heat immediately. Whisk in the softened gelatin until completely dissolved.

Transfer to a large bowl and cool for 10 minutes, then stir in the yoghurt and orange blossom water to combine thoroughly.

Transfer to a serving bowl or to 6–7 individual ramekins. Cover and chill until set, at least 8 hours but preferably overnight.

If spooning from a bowl to serve, allow guests to help themselves; if serving individual portions, carefully run a knife around the edges of the individual ramekins or dip the ramekins to just below the rims in warm water, briefly, to loosen the pannacotta. Invert a plate over the mould and turn over. Lift off the mould.

Serve with a spoonful of sweet clementines (see opposite).

*Needs to be a whole-milk yoghurt, not 'lite'.
**Available from Mediterranean/Middle Eastern stockists.
   See Glossary page 182.

Sweet clementines

Clementines are a variety of seedless mandarin, but any mandarin can be substituted. Oranges may also be used, but mandarins tend to be easier to peel.

One and a half star anise is all that is needed to impart that distinctively Eastern taste — different but delicious, and a lovely match for the pannacotta.

1 kg clementines (or mandarins), peeled
½ cup water
½ cup sugar
1½ star anise

Slice the peeled clementines or mandarins into 1-cm thick rounds.
Bring the water, sugar and star anise to a simmer in a large, shallow frying pan. Dissolve the sugar, stirring, then place the fruit slices in the syrup and cook over a high heat for 10–15 minutes, until most of the syrup has evaporated.
Transfer to a serving dish to cool, then cover and refrigerate until required. Bring to room temperature before serving.

Bev's feijoas in pink wine syrup

It's refreshing to enjoy a dessert that is very simply and unpretentiously prepared. Feijoas poached in a light wine syrup are lovely, the fruit enhanced by a light pink syrup so that the dish is understated but elegant (the alcohol content is evaporated in the cooking).

■ **Serves 4–6. Suitable for freezing (but better with cereal and yoghurt next morning).**

6–8 large feijoas
¾ cup water
⅓ cup red wine
½ cup sugar
150 ml cream, whipped (or crème fraîche or plain unsweetened yoghurt)

Peel the feijoas and cut in half lengthwise.
Combine the water, wine and sugar in a saucepan.
Heat, stirring, to dissolve the sugar. Add the feijoas and simmer until just tender, 5–7 minutes.
Using a slotted spoon, transfer the feijoas to a serving bowl and pour over the syrup.
Serve at room temperature with the whipped cream, crème fraîche or yoghurt.

Gula melaka

Gula Melaka is the simplest of desserts to make, and is a light and refreshing finish to any meal, especially curries. Its appeal lies in the juxtapositions of temperature, texture and flavour — chilled jelly-like sago and chilled palm sugar syrup topped with a spoonful of velvety coconut cream at room temperature.

■ **Serves 6. Not suitable to freeze.**

100 g sago
400 ml water
1 Tbsp white sugar
pinch salt
250 g dark palm sugar*
200 ml water
1 cup thick coconut cream

Rinse the sago in cold water, drain, then soak in enough cold water to cover. Bring the 400 ml measure of water to the boil in a saucepan. Add the sugar and salt, then slowly add the drained sago to the boiling water, whisking continuously.

Reduce the heat and simmer, stirring regularly, until the sago is translucent and the mixture has thickened, about 10–12 minutes.

Take 6 individual jelly moulds and wet them (don't dry with a cloth). The moulds should hold about ¼ cup, or up to 75 ml of the sago. Or, aim to half fill ½-cup moulds. Divide the cooked sago mixture between the moulds and cover. Cool, then refrigerate for at least 2 hours.

Grate the palm sugar into a saucepan, stir in the 200 ml water and simmer, stirring, until the sugar has completely dissolved. Cool, then chill.

Unmould each sago into a small dish, pour over a generous amount of the palm sugar syrup and place the remaining syrup and the coconut cream separately on the table for guests to help themselves.

*Palm sugar is from a palm and is not the same as jaggery, which is derived from sugar cane.

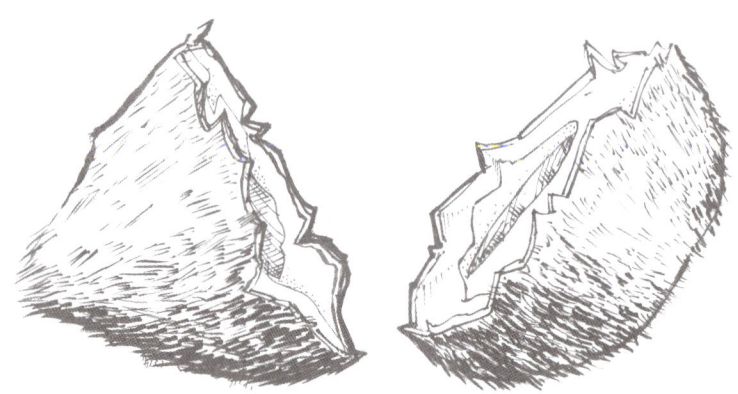

Tart Madeleine

This tart is the perfect finish to an informal meal; a lusciously light, citrus-flavoured tart that has long been a favourite. It can be made a day or two ahead and refrigerated.

■ **Serves 4–6. Suitable to freeze.**

Almond pastry (sweet shortcrust)
½ cup flaked or slivered almonds
1 cup plain flour
3 Tbsp caster sugar
90 g chilled butter, diced
3–4 Tbsp cold water

Process the almonds with the flour and sugar until finely ground, then add the butter and process until the mix resembles breadcrumbs. Pour the water in while the motor is running and process until it starts to 'ball'. Turn the dough onto a bench and form it into a ball. Place it in cling wrap and refrigerate for 30 minutes before rolling out.

Filling
3 Tbsp orange marmalade, preferably home-made
125 g butter, diced and softened but not melted
1 cup caster sugar
3 large eggs
zest and juice of 2 lemons
2 medium-sized tart apples, unpeeled and grated
3 Tbsp pine nuts (or flaked almonds)

Preheat the oven to 200°C.
Lightly grease or spray a 25-cm springform cake or flan tin.
Roll the pastry out thinly in a circle large enough to line the bottom of the tin and come 3 cm up the sides. Spread the marmalade evenly over the bottom of the pastry.
Cream together the butter and sugar, then beat in the eggs one at a time.
Stir in the lemon zest and juice, followed by the grated apples. Discard the cores.
Spread the filling evenly over the marmalade. Sprinkle the pine nuts or flaked almonds over the filling and bake at 200°C for 45–50 minutes (cooking time will vary a little depending on the size and juiciness of the apples).
Check after 20 minutes and turn the heat down to 180°C if the crust appears to be browning too fast. Cool in the tin.
Serve at room temperature or warmed, accompanied by plain, unsweetened yoghurt, or a little whipped cream.

Sachertorte

A special occasion dessert, Sachertorte is elevated from the ordinary by the zing of passionfruit beneath the chocolate glaze. It is moist and rich but not sickly sweet. Ideal for a crowd, it slices into 16, or more if served with another dessert.

Refrigerate, covered, for up to one week. Freezes well, although the glaze will dull just a little. This recipe for Sachertorte was originally published in *The Virtual Café* cookbook and was a signature dessert of Rowan Bishop Catering. It is included here by request.

---

225 g dark chocolate, chopped
8 eggs, separated
225 g butter, softened
1 cup sugar
2 tsp vanilla essence
225 g walnuts (or almonds)
⅓ cup flour
4 Tbsp sifted cocoa
½ cup sweetened passionfruit pulp, sieved

Preheat the oven to 180°C. Lightly grease or spray a 25-cm springform cake tin.
Melt the chocolate, either in a bowl over boiling water or in a microwave on low power for about 3 minutes. Stir after 2 minutes.
Separate the egg yolks from the whites and set aside in two bowls.
Cream the softened butter with the sugar and vanilla. Beat in the yolks one at a time, then beat in the melted chocolate.
Grind the nuts finely in a food processor before combining with the flour and the sifted cocoa. Stir into the creamed chocolate mixture.
Beat the egg whites to a soft peak. Fold one third of the beaten whites into the chocolate batter to combine, followed by the remainder.
Transfer to the prepared tin and bake at 180°C for 1 hour, or until a skewer inserted into the centre of the cake indicates it is just cooked, still moist but not sticky. Try to catch it at this stage. Cool in the tin, on a wire rack, for 20 minutes. Invert and turn the cake out onto the rack. Cool completely before brushing the sides and top with the sieved passionfruit pulp, using a pastry brush.
After 30 minutes the chocolate glaze may be applied with a flat-bladed knife or spatula.

Chocolate glaze
150 g dark chocolate, chopped
90 g butter

Melt the chocolate and butter in a microwave on low, stirring, for about 2 minutes.
Spread the glaze over the top and sides of the Sachertorte and allow to set.
Transfer to a serving plate and garnish with a sprig of green leaves such as angelica, or holly at Christmas time.
Serve with fresh berries or simply with whipped cream or crème fraîche.

Apple & cranberry custard pie

Tart fresh apples spiked with dried cranberries make a great team with custard and a crisp pastry base. Any tart apples, such as Granny Smiths, are ideal for this truly delicious dessert.

Serve warm with a spoonful of mascarpone, whipped cream or plain yoghurt on the side. If you're a fan of custard, this is a must-try.

■ **Serves 6–8. Not suitable to freeze.**

---

pre-rolled puff or short pastry (1 square plus one 3-cm wide strip)
½ cup chopped walnuts
1½ Tbsp brown sugar
1 tsp cinnamon
½ tsp nutmeg
2 tart apples, about 500 g
1½ Tbsp lemon juice
½ cup dried cranberries
250 g 'lite' sour cream
1 cup sugar
3 eggs (size 7)
3 Tbsp custard powder, sifted
1 Tbsp flour
1½ tsp baking powder
1 Tbsp melted butter

Preheat the oven to 190°C.
Roll out the square of thawed pastry a little thinner.
Grease or spray a 23-cm springform cake tin and line the bottom and two thirds up the sides with the pastry. Use the extra strip to 'patch' the sides. Even the sides with a knife so they are the same height all round, then place in the refrigerator while you prepare the pie filling.
Combine the walnuts, brown sugar, cinnamon and nutmeg and set aside. Peel, core and slice the apples thinly. Mix in a bowl with the lemon juice and the dried cranberries.
In another bowl, beat or whisk the sour cream and sugar together vigorously. Beat or whisk in the eggs, then the sifted custard powder, flour and baking powder.
Pour half the custard batter into the prepared pastry base, then gently arrange half the apple/cranberry filling on top. Sprinkle over half the walnut/spice mixture.
Repeat with the remaining batter followed by the rest of the apple/cranberries and then the remainder of the walnut/spice mix.
Drizzle the tablespoon of melted butter evenly over the top.
Bake at 190°C for 50 minutes–1 hour, or until the centre has firmed. Turn the heat down to 180°C if it browns too fast.
Leave to cool for 10 minutes before transferring from the tin and serving.

Sweets

Rhubarb & strawberry pie

This pie is a star! Strawberries and rhubarb make great partners; that's really all there is to be said. Guaranteed to win compliments, it's especially quick to prepare if you use pre-rolled pastry in the interests of convenience. No precooking of either fruit or pastry is required.

Most of us don't want to do anything more with the first strawberry crops than eat them fresh, perhaps with a little icing sugar and cream. It's only when they're at their cheapest and most plentiful that we cast around for sorbets, fools, coulis and pies.

■ **Serves 6–8. Suitable to freeze.**

2 sheets sweet shortcrust pastry*
300 g hulled strawberries
300 g prepared rhubarb stalks
½ cup caster sugar
2 Tbsp cornflour
¼ tsp nutmeg
½ tsp lemon zest
1 Tbsp milk
2 Tbsp sugar

Preheat the oven to 220°C.
Lightly spray or grease a 25-cm pie or quiche tin.
Use one of the thawed pastry sheets to line the prepared tin. You will probably need to trim a 5-cm strip of pastry off the second sheet and add it to the sheet so that it covers the bottom and sides of the tin (wet one edge and press together).
Hull the strawberries and slice large berries into quarters, and medium-sized into halves. Using a sharp knife, slice the rhubarb thinly, discarding any stringy pieces as you go. Weigh the berries and the rhubarb after preparation, as there is often some wastage that should be accounted for.
Place the prepared berries and rhubarb in a bowl and combine with the caster sugar, cornflour, nutmeg and zest.
Spread the filling evenly over the prepared base, then cut the remaining pastry sheet into 7 strips. Use the strips to design a lattice top over the filling, then brush the strips with the milk, using a pastry brush, and sprinkle with the sugar.
Place the pie in the preheated oven and bake at 220°C for 10 minutes, then turn the heat down to 200°C.
Cover the pie with a sheet of aluminium foil at this point to stop it browning too fast. Bake for a further 40–45 minutes, uncovering the pie for the last 10 minutes of cooking to ensure the top is an even golden brown.
Serve at room temperature or slightly warm, accompanied by vanilla ice cream or lightly whipped cream.

*For shortcrust recipe, see page 152.

Kiwi cassata

Traditional cassata can be a layered sponge and ricotta affair, more like a tiramisu, or a frozen layered ice cream, usually moulded into a round 'bombe' shape.

Both are perfect for summer eating, especially when teamed with a big bowl of fresh berry fruit. Ice-cream cassata can be made and frozen days or even weeks ahead for occasions such as Christmas.

■ **Serves 8–10. Keep frozen.**

¼ cup glacé cherries, chopped small
¼ cup dried cranberries, chopped
¼ cup Cointreau (or Grand Marnier, or orange juice)
½ cup flaked almonds, toasted
1 litre chocolate ice cream
80 g grated dark chocolate
300 ml cream
2 Tbsp caster sugar
80 g dark chocolate, chopped small

Marinate the prepared glacé cherries and cranberries in the Cointreau for 3 hours or overnight. Toast the flaked almonds in a dry pan, tossing constantly, until lightly golden — take care not to scorch.
Soften the chocolate ice cream then combine thoroughly with the grated chocolate. With a spatula, mould into a metal or plastic bowl about 20 cm in diameter, leaving a 'cavity' in the middle for the filling. The ice cream should come about 10 cm up the sides of a bowl of this diameter. Cover with foil and place in a freezer for at least 1 hour.
Whip the cream with the caster sugar until medium–firm peaks form. Fold in the marinated cherries, cranberries and toasted, cooled flaked almonds. Spoon into the centre cavity of the chocolate ice cream 'bowl' and cover with aluminium foil. Freeze for at least 4 hours or, preferably, overnight.
Unmould by sitting the bowl in hot water for a few seconds, then invert the cassata onto a double layer of cling wrap and enclose to freeze until ready to serve. Unmould onto a serving pedestal or platter. If freezing ahead, wrap in aluminium foil as well as cling wrap.
Slice and serve with a chocolate sauce or glaze and a big bowl of fresh berries, or garnish with curls of softened chocolate peeled with a potato peeler.

Chocolate glaze
This glaze is similar to the coating used for chocolate-coated ice creams, so is not a soft 'sauce' but forms a lightly crisp coating when cooled on top of the cassata.

100 g dark chocolate
40 g butter

Cover and melt together in a microwave on low power, or in a bowl over boiling water. Stir twice while melting. This should take 1–2 minutes in a microwave.

Berry cups

Individual jelly moulds look stylish and taste wonderful, especially when served with fresh berries and a good quality ice cream.

500 g frozen raspberries, thawed
½ cup sugar
6 tsp gelatine or agar agar
2½ cups blackcurrant or cranberry juice

Place the thawed raspberries and their juice in a large saucepan with the sugar. Soak the gelatine in ½ a cup of the blackcurrant or cranberry juice. Simmer the raspberry/sugar mixture for 1–2 minutes, remove from the heat and strain through a sieve on top of a bowl. Discard the seeds and return the sieved juice to the saucepan with the remaining 2 cups of blackcurrant or cranberry juice. Heat to simmer point, gradually stir or whisk in the soaked gelatine mixture until it is thoroughly dissolved, then pour into 6 x ½-cup moulds.
Cover and chill for 3–4 hours until set.
Unmould the jellies onto serving plates and garnish with fresh raspberries or berries of choice and crème fraîche or home-made ice cream.

Blackberry pie

As a kid, one of the things I looked forward to was late summer forays along isolated roadsides or climbing the hills at the back of our farm to pick plump, juicy blackberries warm from the sun. It didn't matter a jot that bare arms and legs emerged scratched, torn and stained — those pies, as I remember them, were worth almost any sacrifice.

Pre-rolled (frozen) pastry has been used here, purely in the interests of convenience. No precooking of either fruit or pastry is required. Even though this pie is made with frozen berries, it tastes almost as good as I remember. It's a little less sweet, as tastes have changed along with custom in that respect, but what you see is what you get — lots of berries in pastry — yum!

■ **Serves 6. Suitable to freeze.**

2 sheets sweet shortcrust pastry (or see recipe page 152)
1 kg frozen blackberries
½ cup caster sugar
2 Tbsp cornflour
1 Tbsp milk
1 Tbsp sugar

Defrost the blackberries in a colander or sieve over a bowl to catch the juice. Reserve the juice for the blackberry sauce.
Preheat the oven to 220°C. Lightly spray or grease a 25-cm pie or quiche tin.
Use one of the thawed pastry sheets to line the prepared tin — you will probably need to trim a 5-cm strip of pastry off the second sheet and use to extend this so it covers the bottom and sides of the tin (wet one edge and press together).
Place the defrosted berries in a bowl and toss or lightly combine them with the caster sugar and cornflour.
Spread the filling evenly onto the prepared base, then cut the remaining pastry sheet into 7–8 strips, about 1½ cm wide. Place the strips in a diagonal pattern across the top of the filling, then brush the strips with the milk, using a pastry brush, and sprinkle with the ordinary granulated sugar.
Bake at 220°C for 10 minutes, then turn the heat down to 200°C. Cover the pie with a sheet of aluminium foil at this point to stop it browning too fast. Bake for a further 40–45 minutes, uncovering the pie for the last 10 minutes of cooking to ensure the top is an even golden brown.
Serve at room temperature or slightly warm, accompanied by vanilla ice cream or lightly whipped cream.

Sauce
Measure the reserved juice — you should have a little over 1 cup. Take 2 tablespoons of the reserved juice and mix with 2 teaspoons cornflour in a small bowl. Place the remainder of the juice in a saucepan with ⅓ cup sugar and bring to simmer point, stirring. Whisk the combined cornflour/juice mixture in quickly, ensuring that no lumps form.
This sauce is a delicious accompaniment to the pie and can be served hot or at room temperature.

baking

Herb foccacia 145
Café gingerbread 146
Wild rice & pumpkin seed bread 147
Rhubarb & raspberry muffins 148
Portuguese custard tarts (pasteis de nata) 149
Cashew nut pastry 150
Light wholemeal shortcrust pastry 150
Yoghurt pastry 151
Tuscan pastry 151
Sweet shortcrust pastry with semolina 152
Brownie biscuits 152
Spiced gingernuts 153
Chewy chocolate chunk cookies 154
Cardrona chew 155
Persimmon spice cake 156
Christmas heaven cake 157

Herb foccacia

This lovely foccacia-style bread is as easy to make as a batch of scones, and absolutely a favourite with everyone. Team it simply with a dollop of aïoli (page 44); even just dipping it into extra virgin olive or avocado oil is a treat.

It's best eaten fresh, although it is great toasted next day, or reheated, uncovered, in an oven. The quantities given may be doubled and baked in one large shallow roasting pan or two 30-cm round 'pizza' pans.

For a quick herb fix, roughly chop 3 tablespoons fresh rosemary and add to the raw mix rather than making the herb-infused oil. Mix in some roughly chopped olives if you like.

---

1 large handful fresh pizza thyme (or herbs of choice)*
¼ cup olive oil
2 cups plain flour
2 tsp yeast granules
1 tsp sugar
1 tsp salt or to taste
1 cup warm water
rock salt
2 Tbsp olive oil, extra

*Vary the herbs but make allowance for more robust flavours such as common thyme, sage, and rosemary, reducing the quantity of these herbs accordingly.

A handful of pizza thyme is roughly equivalent to 1 cup of stalks and leaves. Tie the stalks with string to form a bundle. Larger leaved herbs such as sage could be stripped from their stalks before cooking in the oil.

Heat the olive oil in a small frying pan over a medium heat and 'sauté' the herb bundle, tossing constantly with tongs. The leaves will sizzle and pop as they heat, and darken; this will take only a few minutes. Set aside to cool. At this stage the leaves will have crisped, so it is now a very simple matter to strip them from the stalks back into the oil. Discard the stalks.

Place the flour, yeast, sugar and salt into a plastic or ceramic bowl and combine with the warm water (just a little above blood temperature) and the herb-flavoured oil. Cover with a clean tea towel and set in a warm, draught-free place to rise for about an hour. No kneading is required for this bread, just mix the dough with a clean hand for a minute or two, turning and folding. Oil a 30-cm round pizza pan or a similar-sized shallow pan with a lip.

Transfer the dough onto the pan and spread out to the edges of the pan with lightly floured hands. This dough can be a little resistant at this stage; if it is, let it rest for a few minutes before pushing to the edges of the pan.

Allow the bread to rise again for another hour or until doubled in size.

Preheat the oven to 210°C.

Poke the top of the bread gently with a finger, to create the hollows typical of foccacia-style bread. Grind rock salt evenly over the top of the bread and drizzle with the extra olive oil.

Bake for 15 minutes or until well coloured. Remove from the oven. Slide a fish slice under the bread and transfer to a rack to cool. Cut into wedges, or, if the quantities are doubled and cooked in a single large pan, cut into diamonds or squares.

Café gingerbread

This oldie has been given a new twist with the option of pomegranate molasses, the addition of crystallised ginger, and upping the ground ginger content; suddenly the flavour is café.

Gingerbread is very quickly prepared, and this quantity is ideal for a family as it makes 2 loaves. Pomegranate molasses is optional; it adds complexity and nudges the flavour towards tangy, but is not identifiable as a separate ingredient. The crystallised ginger, however, adds a whole new dimension.

■ **Freezes well.**

---

²/₃ cup crystallised ginger
250 g butter, diced
1 cup white sugar
1 cup dark cane (or brown sugar)
½ cup golden syrup*
   (or ⅓ cup golden syrup plus 3 Tbsp pomegranate molasses)
2 tsp baking soda
2 cups milk
2 Tbsp ground ginger
2 tsp cinnamon
2 Tbsp cocoa
4 cups flour

Preheat the oven to 180°C. Spray or lightly grease two loaf tins and line the bottom of each tin with baking paper.
Thinly slice the crystallised ginger, roughly chop the slices, then place in a saucepan with the butter, sugars and golden syrup (or golden syrup plus molasses). Melt over a low heat, or microwave in a bowl.
Stir the baking soda into the milk and set aside.

> **Take the lid off the syrup tin and place the tin in the oven as it is heating, to warm the syrup so that it pours easily.*

Sift the ginger, cinnamon, cocoa and flour together into a separate bowl. Stir the milk/baking soda mixture into the warm golden syrup mix (it will foam). Whisk in the sifted ingredients to combine thoroughly and ensure there are no flour lumps.

Pour the mixture equally into the prepared loaf tins, pushing the mix into the corners with a spatula. Smooth the top of each loaf.

Bake at 180°C for 50–60 minutes, testing with a skewer into the middle of each loaf. If it exits clean, the gingerbread is cooked.

Turn out on a cake rack and remove the lining paper.

Slice and spread thinly with butter when cool, or serve with custard, fruit and ice cream or yoghurt as a dessert.

Wild rice & pumpkin seed bread

The fragrance of fresh bread baking is the most welcoming smell imaginable, and it is so easy to make! Use 2¼ cups plain flour and omit the wholemeal flour if you want, and use all pumpkin seeds or all wild rice instead of a mix of the two. Wild rice looks attractive and has a pleasant nutty flavour, just a little crunchy in this bread when first baked but it soon softens. Replace the wild rice with kibbled wheat or rye if preferred.

■ **Makes one loaf or is easily doubled to make two. Freezes well.**

1 cup bran flakes
2 cups plain flour
¼ cup wholemeal flour
¼ cup wild rice
⅓ cup pumpkin seeds
1 Tbsp yeast granules
1 tsp salt or to taste
1 tsp sugar
1½ Tbsp olive oil
1¼ cups warm water

Grease or spray a loaf tin.

Combine all the ingredients and turn out on a lightly floured bench to knead for 2–3 minutes, to get the gluten working. The mix at this stage is a little sticky, but don't add extra flour unless you have to — the rising is better in a moist mix. Set aside in a warm, draught-free place to rise for about 1 hour or until doubled in size.

Sprinkle a little plain flour onto a bench and knead the dough for about 5 minutes, or until the dough is smooth and elastic, springing back when prodded. Work in up to ¼ cup flour as required.

Transfer the dough into the prepared loaf tin. Rise for about 1 hour, until doubled in size, then bake at 190°C in a preheated oven for 40–45 minutes, until the crust is golden and the bread sounds hollow when tapped.

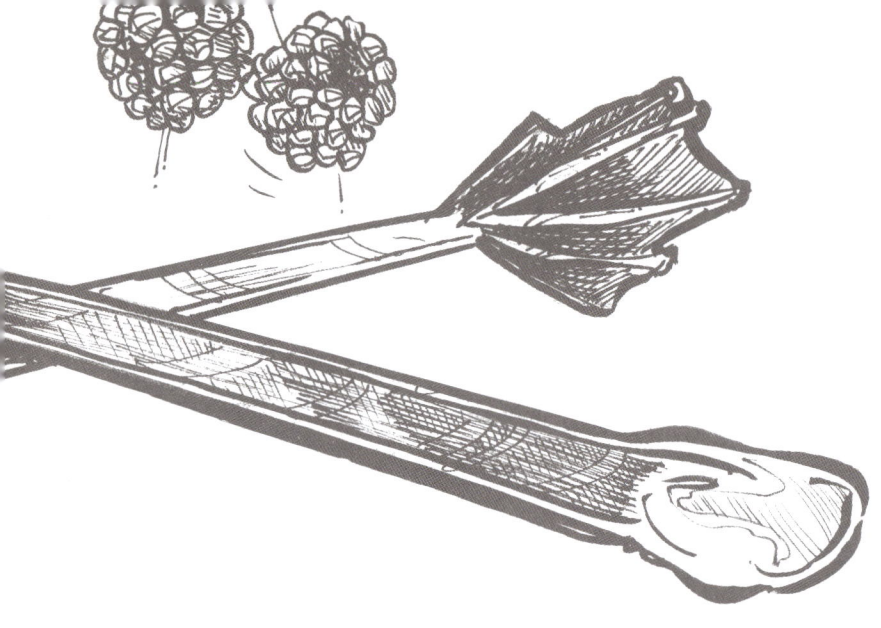

Rhubarb & raspberry muffins

The colour and texture of fine cornmeal works particularly well in these muffins, and rhubarb and raspberries are just the best combination, especially for those of us who love tart fruit flavours.

These muffins are straightforward and no-fuss — the rhubarb is added raw, and either fresh or frozen raspberries can be used. Don't, however, imagine that there'll be any left over to freeze, as they are very popular.

---

1 cup rhubarb, trimmed and diced small
½ cup sugar
1 cup fine cornmeal
1 cup flour
3 tsp baking powder
1 egg, lightly beaten
½ cup plain unsweetened yoghurt
½ cup milk
90 g butter, melted
⅔ cup raspberries, fresh or frozen

Preheat the oven to 200°C.
Lightly grease or spray a standard muffin tray.
Trim the rhubarb stalks and cut into small dice. Transfer to a bowl, toss in the sugar and set aside.
Sift the fine cornmeal, flour and baking powder into a medium to large bowl and combine. In a separate bowl, whisk the egg lightly with a fork, then whisk in the yoghurt and the milk. Melt the butter.
Make a well in the centre of the dry ingredients and pour in the egg, yoghurt, milk and melted butter with the rhubarb and sugar mix, and lastly the fresh or frozen raspberries. Combine the batter very lightly with a fork, until just mixed.
Divide the batter evenly between 12 muffin 'cups', and bake at 200°C for 20 minutes or until the muffins spring back when their tops are nudged. Leave to sit for a minute or two when removed from the oven, then transfer to a cake rack to cool.

Portuguese custard tarts (pasteis de nata)

It must be the combination of velvet smooth custard in crisp pastry that makes these delightful little tarts so addictive, along with the fact that they are not at all sickly but just sweet enough to be a treat.

I first tasted them in Sydney years ago, but really got enthusiastic about these tarts when visiting Macau, where they are sold in pie warmers on the streets everywhere you go.

They're straightforward to make, too, although recreating the brown caramelised 'spots' on the tops can be a struggle as most domestic ovens don't reach the heat required (this is, however, not an issue in terms of taste). A micro-torch is a last resort.

■ **Makes 12.**

---

puff pastry (2 sheets or 300 g), thawed
250 ml milk
250 ml cream
½ cup sugar
thinly pared rind of 1 orange
4 large egg yolks
1 egg
1 tsp rosewater (optional)
icing sugar and cinnamon to dust (optional)

To make the custard, place the milk, cream, sugar and orange rind in a saucepan over a medium heat and bring almost to the boil, stirring regularly. Watch carefully as it nears simmer point because there is a risk of splitting if it actually boils.
Meanwhile, whisk the yolks and the whole egg together in a bowl. Strain the hot milk through a sieve into the egg mixture, while whisking constantly. Discard the orange rind.
Return the mixture to the saucepan and heat, stirring, until the mixture thickens and comes just to simmer point.
Pour into a bowl and stir in the rosewater, if using. Cover the custard to prevent a skin forming and allow time for it to cool completely. It can be made the night before.
Preheat the oven to 250°C minimum. Lightly spray or grease standard-sized muffin tins. Lightly roll the thawed pastry sheets as thin as possible, then cut 12 x 10-cm circles using the open end of a jar, a cup or whatever is suitable. Line the muffin 'cups' with the pastry circles. You will probably have some pastry left over.
Pour the custard into the pastry cases, to 1 cm below the pastry rim. Place the muffin tray on the middle shelf of the preheated oven and bake for 10–12 minutes, until the pastry edges are puffed and well browned. Remove the tray from the oven, cool for a few minutes then transfer the muffins to a rack. Resist trying one when hot as they are at their best warm (and you might burn your tongue!).
Sprinkle with a mixture of icing sugar and cinnamon to serve, if you wish.

Cashew nut pastry

This pastry is a standard in my kitchen. The nuts add extra nutrients as well as flavour, and team well with fillings that showcase pumpkin, asparagus (page 54), cheeses, zucchini and spinach, just to mention a few.

½ cup roasted salted cashew nuts
½ cup wholemeal flour
1 cup plain flour
125 g cold butter, diced
½ cup cold water

Finely grind the nuts in a food processor,
then process again with the flours to combine.
Add the butter and process until the mixture looks like breadcrumbs.
Pour in the very cold water and process again to combine.
Turn out onto a floured bench and roll out to line a greased springform tin of choice — for example, a 32 cm x 22 cm rectangle or a 25-cm quiche tin. Prick the base several times with a fork, then freeze for 10–15 minutes before filling and baking.

Light wholemeal shortcrust pastry

Quiches, pies, flans — this is a very good all-purpose pastry for savoury dishes.

½ cup wholemeal flour
1 cup plain flour
¼ cup tasty grated cheese
80 g cold butter, diced
125 ml very cold water

Place all ingredients except the butter and the water into a food processor bowl. Dice the butter and place on top of the other ingredients.
Process until the mixture looks like breadcrumbs, then pour in the cold water through the feed tube, using the pulse control. You may not need to use the full amount of water; 3–4 quick pulses should be all you need before the mixture starts to 'ball'.
Press the moistened crumbs into a ball with your fingers and place in a plastic bag or cling wrap. Refrigerate for at least 20 minutes before rolling out.

Yoghurt pastry

Yoghurt pastry is lovely to work with. It is light, delicious and colours well without flaking. This pastry is ideal for pies and particularly good for dishes such as Mushroom Galette, page 57.

2 cups flour
1 tsp baking powder
1 tsp salt or to taste
80 g cold butter, diced
yolks of two eggs
¾ cup natural Greek-style yoghurt

Place the flour, baking powder, salt and butter in a food processor and process until the mix resembles breadcrumbs. Mix the yolks together with a fork but reserve about 2 tablespoons for glazing the pastry before baking. Add the remainder of the yolk and the yoghurt to the dry ingredients and process briefly until it starts to 'ball'.
Turn the dough out, form into a ball and wrap in cling wrap.
Refrigerate for about 30 minutes while you prepare the filling.

Tuscan pastry

This pastry is perfect for making Tuscan Tart (page 81) but also makes a tasty base with an interesting texture for all manner of toppings.

1½ cups flour
100 g chilled butter, diced
3–4 Tbsp cold water
¼ cup fine cornmeal for rolling
1 Tbsp pure olive oil

Grease or spray a 28-cm pizza pan.
Place the flour and the diced butter in the food processor bowl and process briefly, until the mixture resembles breadcrumbs.
Pour 3 tablespoons of the water through the feed tube while the motor is running. Remove the lid and press some of the dough between your fingers. If it sticks together, don't add the remaining 1 tablespoon water.
Turn the mixture out onto a bench or board and press into a ball.
Wrap in cling wrap and refrigerate for 30 minutes.
Sprinkle the bench and rolling pin lightly with cornmeal. Roll out the pastry thinly, about 5 mm thick. Turn the pastry over once or twice as you roll, sprinkling lightly with the cornmeal each time.
Place the pastry in the prepared tin, crimping the edges between your fingers. Brush the edges with the olive oil.

Sweet shortcrust pastry with semolina

Semolina shortcrust is an ideal crust for any sweet pie or flan. If you want a plain sweet shortcrust pastry, simply increase the quantity of self-raising flour to 1¾ cups.

¼ cup semolina
1½ cups self-raising flour
¼ cup caster sugar
90 g cold butter, diced
¼–⅓ cup cold water

Place the semolina, flour and sugar into the bowl of a food processor. Add the butter and process until the mixture looks like breadcrumbs. Add the cold water quickly through the feed tube while the motor is still running and process very briefly — just until the mixture is combined. You may not need to add all the water.
Tip the pastry out onto a lightly floured board and press into a ball.
Wrap in cling wrap and refrigerate for 20–30 minutes before rolling out.

Brownie biscuits

Brownie biscuits are an old favourite that no commercially produced wannabe has come anywhere close to reproducing, according to my admittedly biased stance on the matter. In any case, with a bit of help from modern technology, it takes no time at all to prepare these light, chocolatey, crisp biscuits with a hint of chew in the middle — so good!

■ **Recipe doubles well. Not suitable for freezing.**

125 g margarine or butter, softened but not melted
1 scant cup sugar
1 egg
1 cup flour
½ tsp baking powder
4 Tbsp cocoa
1½ cups unblanched raw peanuts (skin on)

Preheat the oven to 180°C. Lightly spray or grease an oven tray.
Cream the butter and sugar in a food processor until pale and most of the sugar has been dissolved. This will take a few minutes.
Add the egg and process briefly. Add in the sifted flour, baking powder and cocoa, then process just to combine.
Transfer the mixture to a bowl and fold in the peanuts until well combined.
Place the mixture in tablespoon lots onto the prepared tray, leaving a gap between each for spreading. Bake at 180°C for approximately 15 minutes.
Cool on a cake rack before storing in an airtight tin.

Spiced gingernuts

Along with her shortbread and caramel slice, my Gran's gingernuts were legendary. This is her basic recipe with just a light spin on the spices — still definitively ginger, although a hint of cardamom and allspice nudge the flavour towards the Dutch speculaas (spice) biscuit without compromising the original intent.

■ **Not suitable for freezing.**

125 g butter
1 cup sugar
1 large egg (size 7)
2 Tbsp golden syrup
1¾ cup flour
1 tsp baking soda
3 tsp ground ginger
1 tsp ground cardamom
½ tsp ground allspice

Preheat the oven to 180°C.
Dice and soften the butter without allowing it to melt (a good tip is to soften it in the oven as it's preheating).
Cream the butter and sugar together, beat in the egg, then the golden syrup (dip the spoon in hot water before measuring).
Sift in the dry ingredients and combine thoroughly with a large spoon.
Roll into walnut-sized balls and place on a lightly greased oven tray, allowing a space between each piece of dough. Flatten slightly with the ball of your hand.
Bake at 180°C for 20 minutes.
Transfer to a cake rack to cool then store in an airtight tin.

Chewy chocolate chunk cookies

These biscuits are the best! The most popular biscuit with friends and family and the most requested.

■ **Not suitable for freezing.**

1 cup white sugar
½ cup brown sugar
1 tsp baking soda
1 cup rolled oats
1½ cups plain flour
1 cup dried apricots, diced small
  (or dried cranberries)
1 cup coconut
1½ cups dark chocolate buttons
200 g butter, melted
1 tsp vanilla
2 Tbsp golden syrup
1 egg

Preheat the oven to 180°C.
Place the sugars, baking soda, rolled oats, flour, dried apricots or cranberries, coconut and chocolate in a medium-sized bowl.
Melt the butter then stir in the vanilla and the golden syrup. Whisk the egg into the melted butter with a fork or whisk, then pour into the dry ingredients and mix thoroughly with a large spoon.
Take walnut-sized pieces of the dough and squeeze lightly in your hand to roll into balls. Place on ungreased baking trays, flattening each piece with the flat of your hand and leaving a space between them.
Bake for 15–20 minutes at 180°C, or until a rich golden brown.
Transfer the biscuits to racks to cool. Store in airtight jars or tins.

Cardrona chew

This slice is nutritious, full of fibre and not overly sweet. It's great picnic fare, a tasty nibble for all ages, and is infinitely versatile — you can use whichever dried fruits you prefer, and even substitute chopped dark chocolate for some of the quantity if you wish.

Cousin Ken, who grew up in the Cardrona valley and is an accomplished chef, is the man behind the recipe.

A tip for measuring golden syrup: place the can of syrup, with the lid off, into the oven as you bring it up to heat. Alternatively, run hot water over the measuring utensil used.

■ **May be frozen.**

2 cups flour
2 tsp baking powder
2 cups thread or flaked coconut
150 g cornflakes
2 cups dried fruit, chopped (e.g. dried apricots, figs, dates, prunes)
1 cup sugar
1 egg
2 tsp vanilla
190 g butter or margarine
¼ cup golden syrup

Preheat the oven to 180°C. Lightly grease or spray a square slice or sponge roll tin. Sift the flour and baking powder into a large bowl. Stir in the thread or flaked coconut along with the cornflakes and the chopped dried fruits.
Whisk the sugar, egg and vanilla together in a bowl.
Melt the butter and golden syrup together, add these to the sugar/egg mixture then add this to the dry ingredients and combine thoroughly.
Transfer the mixture to the prepared tin and press it in evenly and firmly.
Bake at 180°C for 25–30 minutes.
Cool in the tin, then cut into slim fingers.

Persimmon spice cake

Even if you do nothing else with them, persimmons are great peeled and sliced on toast for breakfast with jam and cheese, sliced into raita (yoghurt-based accompaniments to curries) or simply eaten raw, peeled, like an apple. They're also nice roasted with kumara.

This recipe is a quick mix-and-stir recipe based on a favourite apple cake; if possible, use persimmons at their sweetest but while they're still crisp. Enjoy with a cup of coffee or as a casual dessert.

■ **Freezes well.**

500 g persimmons (ripe but not soft)
125 g butter
1 large egg
1 cup sugar
½ cup coconut
1¼ cups plain flour
1 tsp baking soda
1 tsp cinnamon
½ tsp ground nutmeg
½ tsp ground allspice*

Preheat the oven to 180°C. Spray then line the bottom of a 20-cm ring tin with baking paper. Peel the persimmons and slice across the fruit thinly, then into 2-cm pieces. Dice and melt the butter, then blend in the egg with a whisk or fork. Whisk in the sugar and stir in the persimmon, followed by the coconut and the sifted flour, baking soda and spices.
Transfer the cake mixture to the prepared tin and bake at 180°C for 45–50 minutes or until a skewer inserted into the middle of the cake exits cleanly.
Turn out onto a cake rack, remove the baking paper and leave to cool.
Serve at room temperature, dusted with icing sugar and accompanied by crème fraîche, yoghurt or lightly whipped, unsweetened cream.

*Try not to substitute the allspice, as its flavour is unique.

Christmas heaven cake

Christmas fare almost always features dried fruits, nuts and chocolate; all those ingredients most of us love. This cake is not sweet, but is richly endowed with prunes, dried cranberries, plum jam, rum and chunks of chocolate — heavenly. A very good friend made this recipe, in varying sizes, for her daughter's tiered wedding cake, and it was a great success.

50 g glacé cherries, chopped, plus ¼ cup extra
100 g mixed glacé peel
100 g soft prunes, pitted and chopped
100 g dried cranberries
⅔ cup dark rum, brandy or Green Ginger wine
140 g Brazil nuts, chopped
80 g blanched almonds plus ¼ cup extra
130 g hazelnuts
125 g butter, softened
½ cup dark cane sugar
3 eggs
⅔ cup plain flour
1½ cups ground almonds
grated zest of 1 lemon
1 cup plum jam
300 g dark chocolate, chopped

Place the glacé cherries, peel, prunes and cranberries in a large bowl with the liquor for a minimum of 3–4 hours, preferably overnight.
Preheat the oven to 180°C. Lightly grease or spray a 25-cm cake tin and line the bottom with baking paper. (A smaller cake tin will result in a deeper cake and a longer cooking time.)
Chop the Brazil nuts into pieces roughly the size of your small fingernail and set aside. Place the almonds and hazelnuts in a single layer on a baking tray and toast for 7–8 minutes at 180°C, until golden. When cool enough to handle, rub the skins from the hazelnuts and chop both nuts roughly, but not too big. Turn the oven down to 160°C.
Cream the butter and sugar, then add the eggs one at a time. Sift in the flour and combine, using a mixing spoon, then stir in ½ cup of the ground almonds. Mix the lemon zest, the fruit in liquor, and the plum jam together and add to the base mixture along with the chopped nuts, the remaining ground almonds and the chocolate.
Transfer the cake mix to the prepared tin and smooth the top. Stud the top of the cake with the reserved glacé cherries and blanched almonds.
Bake for 1¾–2 hours at 160°C, or until a skewer inserted into the cake exits cleanly and the cake has pulled away from the sides of the tin. This cake cuts more easily if wrapped in cling wrap when cool, and kept refrigerated.

preserves

Plum chutney with sumac & cinnamon 159
Brinjal 160
Spiced banana chutney 161
Smoke & lime feijoa chutney 162
Apricot or persimmon kasundi 163
Sticky figs 164
Everyday zucchini pickle 165
Tamarillo, prune & tamarind chutney 166
Persimmon, tamarind & date chutney 167
Preserved lemons 168
Oscar's favourite Sri Lankan chutney 169
Puliyini (tamarind prune chutney) 170
Caramelised onion confit 171
Quince paste 172

Red capsicum & lime marmalata 173
Kiwifruit marmalade 174
Life's-too-short marmalade 175
Ginger plum conserve 176
Limoncello 177
Rum pot 178
Black raspberry vinegar 179
Harissa 180

Plum chutney with sumac & cinnamon

A twist on an old favourite, this chutney hints of the tropics with undertones of spice and citrus.

3 kg tart red plums
800 g onions, peeled and chopped small
1 cup orange juice
1 cup red wine vinegar
80 g prepared fresh garlic
100 g prepared fresh ginger
3 star anise (optional)
1 stick cinnamon bark
3 Tbsp ground sumac (or zest of 1 lemon)
1 Tbsp ground cinnamon
4 tsp chilli powder
pared rind of 2 lemons (no pith) sliced into thin julienned strips
  or a branch tip of kaffir lime leaves (16–20 leaves)
1¼ kg sugar
4 tsp salt or to taste

Halve the plums, then remove and discard the stones if you wish. Chop roughly. Place all ingredients in a jam pan or large saucepan, bring to simmer point and simmer uncovered for 2 hours or until thick. Remove and discard the kaffir lime branch if using.
Spoon or pour into hot, sterilised screw-top jars and screw on hot, sterilised lids.

Brinjal

In all honesty, this eggplant chutney has taken years to perfect, and recipients of gift jars have been known to resort to embarrassing lengths to extract the recipe, bribery and corruption not excluded! Sweet but piquant, it complements curries, cheeses, pastries and just about anything. Use garlic and ginger from jars unless you're a masochist — it makes no discernible difference to the taste.

■ **Makes about 2½ litres.**

---

2 large eggplants, about 500 g each
4 tsp salt or to taste
1 cup oil
¼ cup mustard seeds (I use yellow)
2 Tbsp fenugreek seeds
2 Tbsp coriander seeds
2 Tbsp cumin seeds
100 g crushed garlic
100 g minced ginger
1 Tbsp chilli powder
3 x 410-g tins peeled tomatoes in juice, chopped
¼ cup tamarind concentrate (see Glossary, page 185)
1 cup malt vinegar
1 kg sugar

Slice the unpeeled eggplant into 5-mm dice. Place in a colander and sprinkle evenly with the salt. Set aside over a sink or bowl to drain for 30 minutes.
Meanwhile, prepare the remaining ingredients.
Heat the oil in a large, heavy-based saucepan or jam pan, over a medium–high heat. Add the mustard seeds and heat until they start to pop. Remove from the heat and stir in the fenugreek, coriander and cumin seeds followed by the garlic, ginger and chilli powder. Return to a lowered heat and cook, stirring, for about 4 minutes. Stir in the salted and drained eggplant without rinsing or patting dry — just shake the colander before adding the eggplant, then sauté for 3–4 minutes.
Stir in the chopped tomatoes with juice, ¼ cup of tamarind concentrate, the vinegar and the sugar.
Simmer the mixture, uncovered, for about 1½ hours, stirring occasionally. Oil should rise to the surface after about an hour, and further cooking produces a medium-thick chutney, reduced to almost half the original volume. Bottle in hot, sterilised jars with screw-top lids in the normal way; i.e. fill clean jars with hot water, drain, place in oven at about 160°C for 10–15 minutes.
Place the jar lids in a saucepan, pour boiling water over and leave for 5 minutes while you fill the jars, drain the water from the lids and screw tightly onto the jars. Don't place hot filled jars on stainless steel — a wooden board is safest.

Spiced banana chutney

Banana is the base ingredient here, balanced by kumara and spiked with fennel, coconut and chilli. This is an unusual chutney but one that is always popular and complements most dishes, from curries to any pastry dish, including samosas.

■ **Makes about 4 x 400-g jars.**

4 small to medium-sized onions
2 cups prepared kumara
⅓ cup oil
1 Tbsp finely chopped or grated fresh ginger
2 tsp whole fennel seeds
1 Tbsp ground cumin
1 Tbsp ground coriander
2 Tbsp turmeric
1 Tbsp chilli powder
3 cups wine or white vinegar
½ cup mixed crystallised peel
2 cups sugar
1 Tbsp salt
½ cup lemon juice
6 ripe bananas, diced
1 cup coconut thread or flakes

Peel and finely chop the onions. Peel the kumara and cut into pieces about the size of a small fingernail and set aside.
Heat the oil in a heavy-based saucepan over a low–medium heat, then stir in the onions, ginger and fennel seeds. Sauté until the onions are soft.
Stir in the kumara, cumin, coriander, turmeric and chilli powder. Cook, stirring, for 2–3 minutes until fragrant.
Stir in the vinegar, peel, sugar, salt and lemon juice and bring to simmer point.
Lastly stir in the diced bananas and the coconut.
Simmer uncovered over a low heat for 40–45 minutes.
Pour into hot, sterilised glass jars. Pour boiling water over metal screw-on lids and leave for 5 minutes. Drain and screw the lids tightly onto the jars.

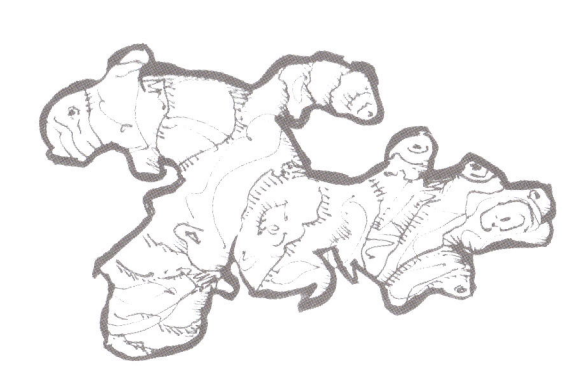

Smoke & lime feijoa chutney

This chutney is really, really good; in fact it's barely possible to make enough batches because friends and neighbours queue up, but hey — there are few things more rewarding than the gift of food.

Smoked paprika and lime engage with the other ingredients here in some mysterious alchemy to produce a complex and totally wonderful flavour. Try it first on a cracker with some vintage Cheddar, and go from there.

Use chillies about 10 cm long — not to be confused with the small 'bird's eye' chillies that have considerably more heat; and for best results don't be tempted to process the feijoas as this 'muddies' the colour of the final product and alters the flavour slightly.

■ Makes 6–8 jars.

---

700 g onions, preferably a mix of red and white, peeled
8 long (about 10 cm) red chillies, seeded and chopped
2 limes, unpeeled, chopped
1 large red capsicum, seeded and diced
200 ml red wine vinegar
300 ml orange juice (no preservatives or sugar)
3 kg feijoas, wiped but not peeled
2 branch tips fresh kaffir lime leaves (about 16–20 whole leaves)*
1 kg white sugar
500 g brown sugar
1 cinnamon stick
1 Tbsp whole coriander seeds
1¼ tsp chilli powder
2 tsp sweet (dulce) Spanish smoked paprika
1 Tbsp salt

*Grow your own kaffir lime tree if at all possible; the leaves are indispensable in Thai cooking. Otherwise, most Asian supply shops now sell fresh leaves, or at least frozen or dried, although of course these are definitely second best. If all else fails, compromise with the thinly peeled rind (zest) of 5 limes or 4 lemons.

Chop the peeled onions roughly and place in a food processor with the chillies and limes. Pulse until chopped small but not puréed.

Place the prepared onions, chillies, limes and capsicum in a large jam pan or saucepan, with the red wine vinegar and the orange juice. Stir to mix and set over a very low heat so the flavours start infusing while you prepare the feijoas.

Top and tail the feijoas but don't peel. Cut them into 1-cm dice (size of your small fingernail), then add to the pan.

Stir in the washed kaffir lime branch tips, and stir in the sugars. Stir in the cinnamon stick, coriander seeds, chilli powder, smoked paprika and salt.

Raise the heat and allow the mixture to come to the boil. Simmer for about 1½ hours or until the mixture has thickened and a small amount on a saucer wrinkles when nudged with a finger (leave to cool for 5 minutes). Discard the kaffir lime leaves and cinnamon stick.

Pour into hot, sterilised jars and seal with hot, sterilised metal screw-on lids.

Apricot or persimmon kasundi

Each summer there is a chance to buy fresh fruit cheaply as 'jam' fruit, and ripe apricots are particularly good in this spicy Fiji/Indian-style sauce. Persimmons also work very well — they should be ripe but not soft.

Using prepared fresh ginger and garlic is much simpler than peeling and mincing your own, and makes no discernible difference to the taste. Fruit kasundi is a chutney/sauce similar to tomato kasundi in style but given a makeover with the use of different spices and fruit instead of tomatoes as the base ingredient.

■ **Serve with rice, lentils, pastry, cheese and curry dishes.**

3 kg ripe apricots, stoned, (or persimmons)*
1 cup oil
2 Tbsp fenugreek seeds
¼ cup mustard seeds, black or yellow
2 tsp fennel seeds
2 Tbsp cumin seeds
200 g fresh ginger, minced
100 g fresh garlic, crushed
2 Tbsp chilli powder
3 Tbsp ground coriander
3 Tbsp salt
550 g sugar
500 ml malt vinegar

*Ripe, red-fleshed plums also work well in this sauce, and can be stoned then puréed as for the persimmons.

Stone the apricots and chop roughly. If using persimmons, peel, chop roughly, then transfer to a food processor and roughly purée in two or three lots — persimmon flesh is not as soft as apricot and will not mush down as easily. Heat the oil in a very large saucepan with a heavy base over medium–high heat. Add the fenugreek and mustard seeds and cook until the mustard seeds begin to pop. Remove from heat at this stage as the oil will be very hot and the mustard seeds will continue to cook.

Stir in the fennel and cumin seeds, the ginger, garlic, chilli powder and coriander all at once. Combine well, return to a lowered heat and cook, stirring, for a couple of minutes. Add the prepared apricots or persimmons and cook, stirring, for a few minutes. Stir in the salt, sugar and malt vinegar. Simmer, uncovered, for about 1 hour or until the mixture thickens.

Pour into hot, sterilised jars with hot, sterilised, metal screw-on lids.

Sticky figs

Serve Sticky Figs as part of an antipasto, or simply with soft cheese such as a Brie or Camembert. There is no need to wait, as they can be served on the day they're made, or sealed to enjoy months later.

Use 'everyday' dried figs or a combination of dried and dessert figs.

Small, attractive jars (125 ml are ideal) filled with home-made sticky figs make great Christmas gifts for the foodies among friends and family.

This quantity makes about 6 x 125-ml jars.

---

500 g dried figs
2 cups red wine
⅓ cup balsamic vinegar
1 cup orange juice
1¼ cups brown sugar
1 cup walnut halves or pieces (or almonds)
1 Tbsp finely chopped fresh rosemary or 1 tsp dried rosemary

Weigh the figs, then slice in half lengthwise. Set aside.
Place the wine, vinegar, orange juice and brown sugar in a large saucepan and bring to simmer point, uncovered. Simmer on low for 5 minutes, then stir in the prepared figs and the nuts. Bring back to simmer point and simmer for 25–30 minutes, uncovered, until the liquid has reduced by about a third and is slightly thickened. Stir occasionally.
Preheat the oven to 140°C. Pour hot water into clean jars, allow to heat through then discard the water and place the jars in the oven to sterilise.
Place metal screw-on lids for the jars in a bowl, and bring sufficient water to the boil to pour over the lids — these need to sterilise in the boiled water for 5 minutes before use.
Place the hot, sterilised jars on a wooden board. Use clean tongs to pack the figs into the jars, then pour over some of the liquid from the saucepan to top up each jar. Drain the lids and screw on firmly.

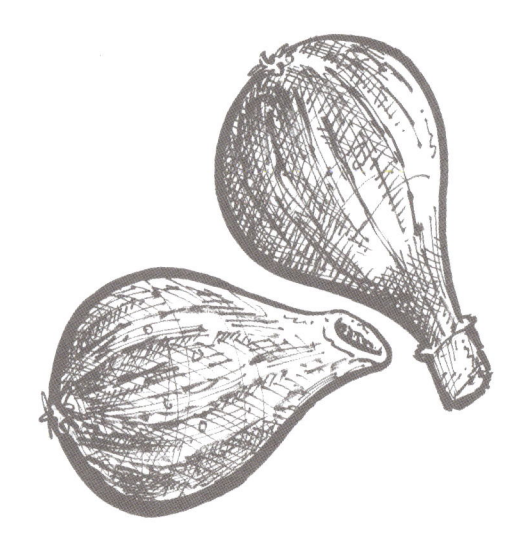

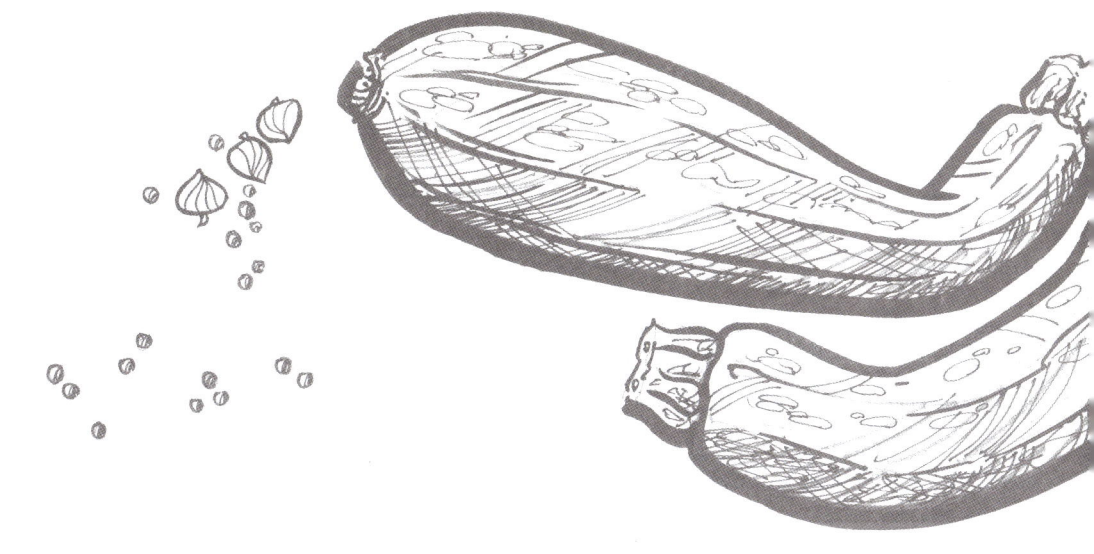

Everyday zucchini pickle

Based on the old 'bread & butter' pickle, this recipe is a great standby as it is uncomplicated, quick to prepare, and can be used to pickle Lebanese cucumbers, gherkins, zucchini or even out-of-control zucchini that have grown into small marrows. Larger zucchini and cucumbers should be seeded.

Although it's often good to preserve when fresh produce is available in bulk, preserving doesn't have to be a huge task, especially if you grow your own and can access produce in smaller amounts over time.

Make these pickles in any quantity, adjusting the other ingredients accordingly from the base recipe.

---

1 kg Lebanese cucumbers or zucchini
4 Tbsp salt
2 tsp yellow mustard seeds
2 tsp black peppercorns
1 tsp turmeric
1 cup sugar
1 cup white vinegar

Wash the cucumbers or zucchini, then slice on a diagonal into 5-mm slices. Place in a non-metallic bowl, toss with the salt, leave for 3 hours and then drain.

Sterilise jars with metal screw-on lids by washing and rinsing, draining, then placing the jars in an oven heated to 150°C for 15 minutes or longer. Transfer to a wooden board (a cold stainless-steel bench top can cause the jars to crack when filled with hot liquid). Pour boiling water over the metal screw-on lids and leave for 5 minutes to sterilise.

Heat the mustard seeds, peppercorns, turmeric, sugar and vinegar together in a large saucepan over a medium heat, stirring. When the mixture simmers, tip in the drained cucumber or zucchini slices and bring back to the boil. When simmer point is reached, simmer for 2 minutes only, then turn the heat off.

Pack the cucumbers/zucchini into the hot, sterilised jars then pour over the sweet vinegar solution, to within 1 cm of the top of each jar.

Screw the hot, sterilised lids on tightly and try to leave for at least a week before tasting.

Tamarillo, prune & tamarind chutney

Who doesn't love tamarillo chutney? This version is particularly good, with tamarind to boost the tamarillo. Serve as an accompaniment for any savoury fritter or pie, or on wholemeal crackers teamed with feta or cottage cheese.

---

2 kg tamarillos
¼ cup oil
2 red onions, peeled and diced small (about 1.5–2 cm)
1½ tsp cumin seeds, lightly crushed
¼ cup peeled and minced fresh ginger*
1½ tsp chilli powder
1 cup balsamic vinegar
½ cup tamarind concentrate (from pulp)**
1 packed cup moist prunes, stoned and diced small
2½ cups brown sugar

Peel the tamarillos by pouring boiling water over them and allowing them to stand for 3 minutes. The skins are then easily slipped off and discarded. Slice off any thick 'pith' from the stem end. Dice the flesh small, about 1.5–2 cm. Set aside.
Heat the oil to a medium heat in a large, heavy-based saucepan. Stir in the prepared onions and sauté until they soften, then stir in the lightly crushed cumin seeds, the ginger and the chilli powder. Sauté for 2–3 minutes, until fragrant.
Stir in the prepared tamarillos, balsamic vinegar, tamarind concentrate, prunes and brown sugar. Bring the mixture to simmer point, stirring. Simmer, uncovered, for about 40 minutes or until thickened. Transfer into sterilised jars and screw on sterilised metal lids.

*Minced ginger from a jar really is quite acceptable and it doesn't detract from the flavour at all — it just makes preparation so much quicker!
** See Glossary, page 185.

Persimmon, tamarind & date chutney

This popular chutney is always in demand, especially when the persimmon season rolls around and fans find they've misplaced the recipe since last season! Team it with cheese, pies, curries, in sandwiches and on crackers.

150 g block tamarind paste
1 cup hot water
2 kg persimmons, peeled and diced small
400 g dates, stoned and chopped small
½ cup cooking oil
2 Tbsp whole fenugreek seeds
2 Tbsp cumin seeds
150 g fresh (or prepared) ginger, peeled and minced
2 tsp chilli powder
3 cups water
1 cup malt vinegar
1 Tbsp salt
750 g brown sugar

Cut and weigh 150 g from a block of tamarind paste — this is far superior to buying tamarind concentrate in a jar. Break up with your fingers into a heat-proof bowl and pour over 1 cup hot water. Soak for 20 minutes. Strain through a sieve, pressing with the back of a spoon to collect as much paste as possible, then scraping the back of the sieve. Discard the seeds with any remaining fibre.

Weigh then peel 2 kg ripe persimmons (not soft). Chop the flesh into small dice about the size of your small fingernail. Stone the dates and chop small, using either a sharp heavy knife or kitchen scissors.

Heat the oil in a heavy-based, large saucepan over a medium heat. Sauté the fenugreek seeds until sizzling, then add the cumin seeds, but don't scorch — have the prepared persimmons, dates, ginger and chilli powder and water ready to add quickly, along with the vinegar, salt and prepared tamarind.

Bring the mix to boiling point then lower the heat and simmer for 30 minutes.

Stir in the brown sugar and simmer for a further 1 hour or until the surface of a teaspoonful on a saucer wrinkles as it cools.

Bottle in hot, sterilised jars with screw-top lids. To sterilise the jars, fill clean jars with hot water, drain, place in oven at about 160°C for 10–15 minutes. Place the lids in a bowl, pour boiling water over the lids, leave for 5 minutes while you fill the jars, drain the water from the lids and screw tightly onto the jars. Don't place hot, filled jars on stainless steel — a wooden board is safest.

Preserved lemons

This recipe is of traditional Moroccan origin, and although variations of it include herbs and/or spices, the method has remained essentially the same for generations.

June to August is the time of year to preserve lemons in the southern hemisphere, especially if you have your own lemon tree, as you need unblemished fruit if at all possible.

Mix finely diced preserved lemon with steamed or sautéed green beans, broad beans or carrots. Whip it into soft butter with finely chopped fresh herbs and use as a topping for steamed asparagus; or make a marinade for olives with fresh herbs and slivers of the preserved lemon rind.

It is important to be scrupulously clean — hands washed, and utensils and jars sterilised to avoid contamination (a dishwasher is a good steriliser). Similarly, when extracting preserved lemons from their jar, ensure that you use a clean, preferably sterilised fork or similar.

Don't use common salt as its flavour is too harsh.

5–6 small to medium-sized lemons, washed
7–8 Tbsp rock salt
juice of 1 large lemon
cold water, preferably filtered or bottled
optional flavourings: 2 dried bay leaves; or whole coriander seeds;
   or dried chillies; or cinnamon stick
¼ cup olive oil

Take a sterilised 500-g glass jar with a sterilised metal screw-on lid. Place 1 tablespoon of the rock salt in the bottom of the jar.
Hold each lemon vertically, stem end up, over a bowl to catch any juice.
With a small, sharp knife, make six or seven vertical incisions running from the stem to within 1 cm of the tip of the lemon. The knife tip should come to the middle of the lemon.
Use your thumb to ease the segments slightly apart, so that the lemon opens like the petals of a flower. Take another tablespoon of the rock salt and pack it between the lemon segments and into the centre of the lemon without breaking it apart. Continue to hold the lemon over the bowl to catch any juice that may escape.
Fold the lemon into a semblance of its former shape and place it in the bottom of the jar. Repeat the process with each lemon, packing them firmly. Don't worry if they squash a bit. Add the bay leaves or other herbs/spices as you go if desired.
Sprinkle 1 tablespoon of the salt over the top of lemons and pour over the reserved juice plus the juice of 1 large lemon.
Fill the jar with cold water, preferably filtered or bottled, leaving a space for the olive oil. Top with the olive oil, which will prevent contact with the air.
The lemons must be completely covered with the liquid.
Screw the top on tightly, and place the jar in a cool, dark place.
Check each day for 3 days as the lemons will soften and deflate slightly as they settle and release some of their juice. Ensure they are still completely submerged — add a

little more oil and/or weight them down if needed (or use pieces of sterilised wooden chopstick or similar to keep them beneath the level of the oil).
Leave for 4–6 weeks. Keep the jar in the refrigerator after opening. These lemons will keep for at least a year in the refrigerator.
Rinse the segments under cold water. Usually only the rind is used for cooking, but the flesh is edible.

Oscar's favourite Sri Lankan chutney

Although this chutney contains garlic, ginger and chilli in not insignificant quantities, it's a certain five-year-old's favourite and at the time of writing he eats it on toast with Cheddar for breakfast, and on crackers with cheese almost every day. It's also particularly good with a slice of dill pickle or even gherkin to complete the combination.

Based on Mrs Fernando's Sri Lankan chutney from *The Vegetarian Adventure*, this version is not quite as sweet and has greater depth of flavour. Use pre-prepared garlic and ginger unless you have extra time on your hands.

2½ kg fresh tomatoes (or tinned, peeled and chopped)
70 g prepared minced garlic
70 g prepared minced ginger
1–1½ Tbsp finely chopped dried chillies, including seeds
2 tsp ground cumin
2 tsp salt or to taste
2 tsp whole cumin seeds
1 cinnamon stick
½ tsp ground cinnamon
½ tsp ground cloves
750 ml malt vinegar
2 kg sugar

Pour boiling water over the tomatoes to cover and leave 3–4 minutes. The skins should then slip off. Chop roughly and transfer them (or the tinned tomatoes with juice if using) to a jam pan or extra large saucepan over a medium heat.
Stir in all the remaining ingredients and bring to simmer point.
Simmer uncovered until the mixture reaches a jam-like consistency (1½ hours approximately), stirring regularly.
Test by placing a few drops on a saucer; cool slightly and nudge with a finger. If it wrinkles, it's done.
Pour into clean, hot, sterilised jars and seal with metal screw-on lids that have had boiling water poured over them and been left for 5 minutes.

Puliyini (tamarind prune chutney)

Puliyini is a wonderful sambal (chutney) to serve with any curry, samosas or pastry; or add a tablespoon or two to soups and stews.

Don't alter the ingredients until you've tried it — the flavour mellows if you can leave it unopened for at least two weeks, resulting in an intriguing balance of hot/sweet/sour. Now that fresh curry leaves are readily available in Indian food shops we have a chance to make use of them. Curry leaves have nothing in common with the spice of the same name; they have a mild citrus flavour.

500 g block tamarind
2 litres hot water
200 g pitted prunes, chopped small
½ cup oil
¼ cup mustard seeds
1 Tbsp fenugreek seeds
2 Tbsp cumin seeds
3 Tbsp chilli flakes
1 cup loosely packed fresh curry leaves*
½ cup peeled and finely minced fresh ginger (or use prepared ginger)
2 Tbsp salt
2 cups jaggery or dark brown sugar

Soak the tamarind in the hot water for 15 minutes, breaking up with your fingers as it loosens. Push through a sieve with a spoon or spatula and discard the seeds and fibre. Set the sieved pulp aside. Chop the prunes small and set aside.

Heat the oil in a large, heavy-based saucepan with the mustard and fenugreek seeds. When the mustard seeds begin to pop, briefly remove from the heat as the oil is very hot at this stage and may 'scorch' the cumin seeds. Stir in the cumin seeds, chilli flakes, fresh curry leaves (stripped from the stalk) and the ginger, then return the saucepan to a moderate heat and cook, stirring, for 3–5 minutes.

Stir in the tamarind/water mixture and the prunes. Simmer, stirring regularly, for 1–1½ hours uncovered, until thickened.

Pour into hot, sterilised jars with metal screw-on lids.

*You can substitute 8 bay leaves and 1 Tbsp lemon zest for curry leaves, but does give a different result.

Caramelised onion confit

As its name suggests, this is sweet but savoury, great with any cheese, egg, pastry or grain dishes. It's also good in filled rolls and sandwiches.

500 g red onions, peeled and sliced fine
4 Tbsp oil
2 tsp mustard seeds
½ tsp cumin seeds
2 large cloves garlic, peeled and sliced thinly
1 tsp freshly ground black pepper
1 Tbsp finely chopped fresh rosemary or 1 tsp dried rosemary
1 cup red wine
½ cup brown sugar
¼ cup balsamic vinegar
1 tsp salt or to taste

Prepare the onions.
Heat the oil in a wide, heavy-based frying pan or saucepan and heat the mustard seeds until they begin to 'pop'. Remove from the heat and stir in the cumin seeds, then add the onions and the garlic. Sauté over a low heat for 10–15 minutes, until the onions are softened and caramelised.
Stir in the pepper, rosemary, wine, sugar, vinegar and salt. Simmer for another 30–40 minutes, or until almost all of the liquid has been absorbed.
Spoon into hot, sterilised jars and screw on hot, sterilised metal screw-on lids.

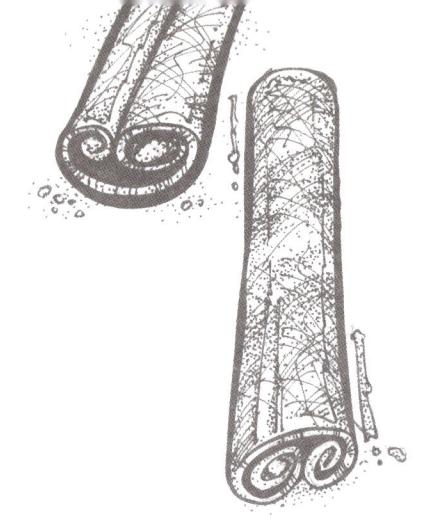

Quince paste

A common perception about the making of quince paste is that it's both an arduous and time-consuming labour of love. If processed in smaller quantities, however, and time-saving equipment such as a microwave is employed, making quince paste is a breeze. Enjoy it on crackers with a soft cheese, such as a Brie or Camembert, or on breakfast breads with soft cheeses and sliced fresh fruits.

The fragrance of quinces ripening is a welcome seasonal treat, and any not needed for cooking look very decorative as well.

---

1 kg ripe quinces
1 cup red wine
2 cinnamon sticks
2¼–2½ cups sugar

Peel, core and cut the quinces into rough chunks. Place in a microwave-proof dish with the wine and cinnamon sticks and cover with cling wrap.
Cook on high for 15 minutes or until very soft.
Remove the cinnamon sticks and set aside. Transfer the fruit and juices to a food processor and purée until very smooth.
In cup measures, transfer the purée to a wide, non-stick frying pan and stir in 1 cup of sugar for every 1 cup of purée. Stir in the cinnamon sticks and heat over a medium heat, stirring constantly, for about 45 minutes or until very thick. Discard the cinnamon sticks. Set aside to cool for 10 minutes while you line 5 or 6 x ½-cup ramekins with cling wrap, leaving enough to drape over the sides. Distribute the paste evenly between them (don't allow the paste to cool too much) and leave to cool completely and set. Fold the cling wrap over the top of the paste and turn out.
Refrigerate until needed.

Red capsicum & lime marmalata

This 'marmalade' is such a gorgeous, eye-catching red that it's almost a surprise to find it tastes as good as it looks. It's a hit as a topping for crackers spread with cream cheese, but use it as you please — there won't be a shortage of ideas once it's tasted.

8 large red capsicums
1 cup orange juice (no preservatives or added sugar)
⅓ cup red wine vinegar
2 Tbsp peeled and minced ginger (or prepared ginger)
3 cups sugar
1 tsp salt or to taste
½–¾ tsp chilli powder
5 bay leaves, preferably fresh
1 branch tip of kaffir lime leaves, 16–20 whole leaves*
thinly pared rind of 2 lemons, finely julienned (sliced)
juice of two lemons

Preheat the oven to 225°C.
Place the capsicums on a baking tray and roast for about 25 minutes or until the skins are blistering and blackened. Remove from the oven and cool until they can be handled (place in a plastic bag if you wish, but this is not necessary). Peel, and discard the core and seeds. Chop finely.
Place all the ingredients into a heavy-based saucepan, bring to simmer point and cook for 30–40 minutes or until the mixture has thickened and is the consistency of jam. Discard the kaffir lime and bay leaves using tongs.
Spoon into hot, sterilised jars and screw on hot, sterilised metal screw-on lids.

*If kaffir lime leaves are not available, use young lime leaves or the pared and finely julienned zest from an extra lime or lemon.

Kiwifruit marmalade

Bumper kiwifruit crops mean that locally grown fruit is very inexpensive, and it's a shame to see this nutritious resource go to waste. Kiwifruit marmalade is quick to make as well as delicious, and either the gold or the green variety of kiwifruit can be used, with slightly different results of course.

Lemons may be substituted for the limes for a mellower but still classy taste treat.

■ **Makes 5–6 jars.**

2 kg gold or green kiwifruit
2 limes or 1 large lemon
1 kg sugar
2 Tbsp peeled and finely chopped ginger

Thinly peel the kiwifruit and cut into small dice, about the size of your small fingernail.
Either thinly peel the limes (or lemon) and slice into very thin strips about 2 cm long, or 'strip' the zest using a zester* and chop roughly. Pare away the pith and discard.
Chop the lime flesh into small dice, as for the kiwifruit.
Place all ingredients in a large, heavy-based saucepan or jam pan and simmer, stirring regularly, for about 45 minutes. Test by placing ½ teaspoon of the marmalade on a saucer to cool then nudging with a finger. If the surface ripples, it is ready to pour into hot, sterilised jars and cover with sterilised metal screw-on lids.

*A zester has a truncated 'blade' with 6 small holes.

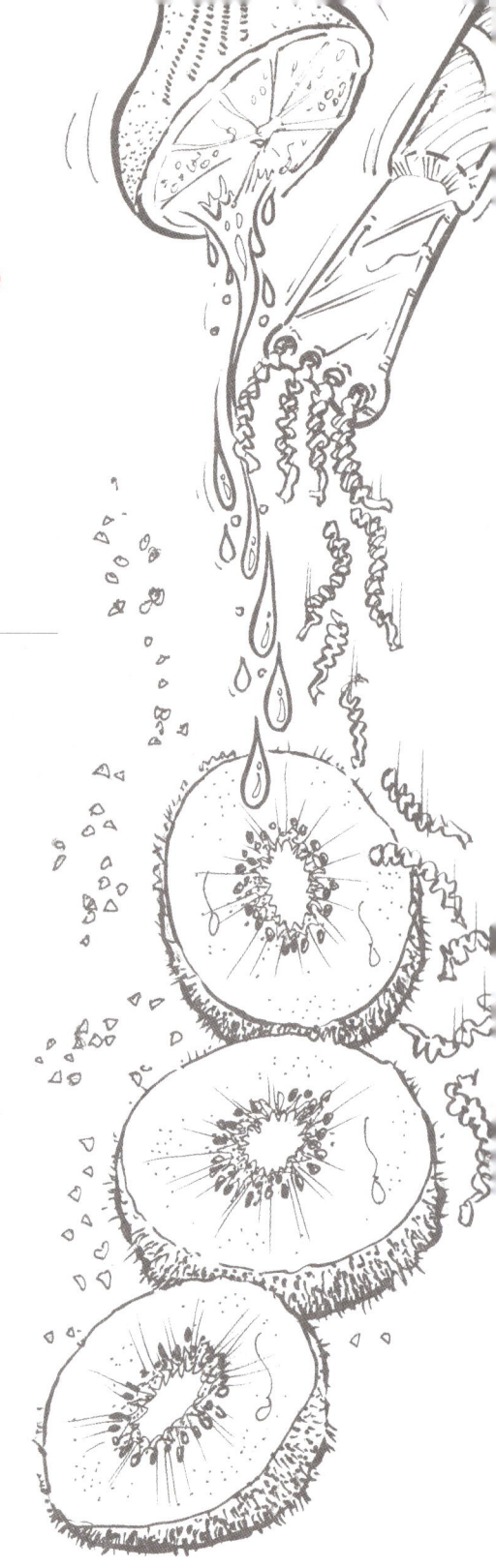

Life's-too-short marmalade

This marmalade is for those who like the best in life. It's a little more time-consuming in terms of yield, but absolutely worth it. The secret is in the method; you simply can't buy marmalade as good as this unless expense doesn't matter. Note: This recipe does not require any added water.

The flavours here are bold and intensely orange, but balanced by the lime to create a particularly delicious spread.

Use all oranges for this marmalade if you prefer, or experiment with other citrus.

■ **Makes 2 x 350-g jars.**

1 kg oranges
250 g limes (3–4, depending on size)
500 g sugar
2 Tbsp peeled and finely chopped fresh ginger (optional)

Using a zester, preferably, or a floating blade peeler, remove the zest from all the fruit, ensuring that none of the pith is attached. Roughly chop the long strips of zest if a zester has been used, or finely slice the peeled zest into lengths, then roughly chop. Transfer to a large saucepan.
With a sharp knife, pare the pith from all the fruit and discard.
Dice the fruit small, about 5 mm, discarding any core or obvious membrane. Try not to lose any juice.
Transfer the diced fruit and juice to the saucepan with the zest, stir in the sugar and ginger, if using, and bring to simmer point.
Simmer, uncovered, for 25–30 minutes, stirring regularly.
Test by placing ½ teaspoon of the marmalade on a saucer to cool, then nudging with a finger. If the surface ripples, it is ready to pour into hot, sterilised jars and cover with sterilised metal screw-on lids.

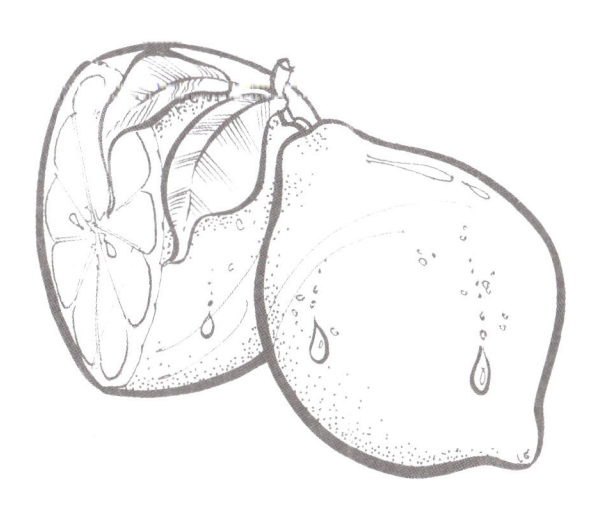

Ginger plum conserve

Simple, simple, simple. Not too sweet, and the ginger enhances the tart fruit flavour to create a perfect spread for eating with cheese and fresh fruit on toast for breakfast!

Most plums can be used successfully for this jam, but those with the best flavour are the old-fashioned heritage plums like Black Doris. (Omega are a good modern alternative to Black Doris.) If you can grow them or if someone offers you some, accept with alacrity and remember that it's not necessary to deal with the fresh fruit immediately. Jams don't suffer in the slightest from being made from frozen fruit.

There is no need to stone plums for jam unless you have a particular aversion to seeing plum stones on your toast — it's much simpler to discard them later.

---

3 kg plums
1½ kg sugar
½ cup minced fresh ginger (bottled is fine)

Depending on the plums, you may need to add ½ cup water to start them cooking, but generally it is possible to place the fresh or frozen plums into a jam pan or similar and cook over low heat, stirring occasionally, until the juices are released. Turn the heat to medium–low and simmer until the plums are soft and beginning to 'pulp', about 30–40 minutes.
Remove the plum stones if you wish to.
Add the sugar and stir in, turning the heat to medium. Cook, stirring regularly, for about 20 minutes or until the surface of a small spoonful cooled on a saucer wrinkles when nudged with a finger.
While the jam is cooking, sterilise jars with screw-on metal lids by washing, then placing on their sides in an oven at 160°C for 15 minutes. Pour boiling water over the lids near the end of cooking time and sit for 5 minutes. Drain.
Fill the hot, sterilised jars with the jam, then screw lids on tightly.

Limoncello

You do need access to quite a few lemons or other citrus to make this liqueur, which can also be served as a sauce for a special ice cream or as a base for summer drinks. Very popular in Italy, it is delicious served ice cold; in fact it's best kept in either the freezer or the refrigerator — the alcohol content ensures it doesn't freeze in the freezer, although it is more viscous than at room temperature — just perfect for a summer sauce.

The recipe follows a method rather than proportions, and is therefore subject to the maker's preference, which in my case is not too sweet — as a sauce, it's likely to be served with a dessert in any case, and liqueurs, in my opinion, shouldn't be camouflaged as syrups.

Use other citrus of choice or availability — oranges, limes, grapefruit — or even a combination of these. It's impossible to go wrong if basic principles are followed and you have a patient disposition (or are so busy that time flies and you're not checking your brew every day).

---

10 lemons
1 litre vodka
1¼ cups sugar
1 cup water

Either thinly peel or, best of all, zest the lemons with a zester. Discard any pith as this can be bitter.
Place the zest in a sterilised glass jar, tip in the vodka and seal it with a tight fitting lid. Shake gently and leave in a cool dark place for about 2 months (or at least 3 weeks).
Stir or shake every now and then.
When the zest has steeped in the vodka for as long as you can wait, place the sugar and water in a saucepan and heat, stirring, until the sugar is completely dissolved. Cool the syrup before adding to the zest/vodka mixture.
Leave to sit for 1–2 weeks, then strain through a sieve or muslin, pressing to extract all the liqueur and citrus oil. Discard the zest and stir the liqueur before pouring into cool, pre-sterilised bottles. Cover with a sterilised, tight-fitting lid and leave for at least 6 days before tasting.
Make twice the quantity once you are more confident and have sufficient lemons, and add a little extra vodka to the finished product if you like more 'fire'.

Rum pot

This recipe is more method than specifics, and is based on a traditional German specialty. A Rum Pot (rumtopf) refers specifically to a lidded ceramic jar used for preserving summer fruits and berries in sugar and liquor — usually white rum, but also vodka or brandy — that is opened with ceremony some six months after, as a mid-winter tradition.

The process is started with the first fruits of summer, and middle and late season fruits, liquor and sugar are added as the season progresses. The result is an adult sauce bursting with the taste and aroma of summer and berry fruits to spoon over ice cream for a simple dessert, or serve as a sauce for dessert soufflés, pies, tarts, fools or trifles. Fresh fruits can of course be served with the rum pot to give it a 'fresh' look and taste.

It is important to have a clean, preferably sterilised container and to work always with clean hands and utensils. The container can be heavy plastic, glass or non-porous pottery, with a close-fitting but not airtight lid. Whatever you use must be wide-mouthed, as the fruit must be kept submerged; use a plate/dish or firm plastic, and place a weight such as a glass on top, under the lid.

The fruit must be ripe but firm, as any overripe or damaged fruit could introduce bacteria into the precious mixture and spoil it.

Fruit with high water content such as watermelon is not suitable. Strawberries are good, though, and raspberries provide great flavour even if they do disintegrate somewhat. Blueberries, cherries, apricots, nectarines, peaches, blackberries and plums are especially good. Although the initial amount of liquor used to start the process may seem a little alarming, this decreases dramatically as more fruits are added. Start with:

700 g prepared fruit
350 g caster sugar
1½ cups vodka, brandy or white rum
OR
1 kg prepared fruit
500 g caster sugar
2 cups liquor

The principle is essentially to prepare the fruit by slicing larger fruits and discarding any pits or stones. In a separate bowl, cover the prepared fruit with half its weight of caster sugar. Leave for 2–3 hours to draw out the juices and start the sugar dissolving. Transfer to a suitable container and weight the fruit down (see above). Cover with a lid and store in a cool place (not a refrigerator). If you are using a plastic or glass container it should also be dark. Very gently stir once a day with a sterilised spoon for the first 3 days to dissolve the sugar.
Wait for 2 weeks before adding the next lot of fruit, sugar, and the alcohol. For every 500 g of prepared fruit added subsequently, add 250 g caster sugar but only ⅓ cup alcohol. The greater volume of alcohol at the beginning of the process is important to ensure success — if any mould develops, the mixture will be spoiled.

Black raspberry vinegar

Raspberry vinegar makes a delicious and versatile dressing/vinaigrette for salads or roast vegetables. It makes a refreshing change from citrus-based dressings and complements almost anything that can be tossed into a salad, including feta, nuts, lentils and dried fruit. Use either frozen or fresh raspberries.

1 kg frozen (or fresh) raspberries
2 cups apple cider vinegar or white/red wine vinegar
½ cup balsamic vinegar
1 cup sugar

Thaw the raspberries (if using frozen) in a wide-mouthed ceramic or glass jar. Mash the raspberries lightly.
Bring the vinegars to simmer point with the sugar, stirring occasionally to ensure the sugar is completely dissolved. Cool before adding to the crushed fruit. Cover tightly and store in a cool dark place for at least 1 and up to 2 weeks. There should be no need to refrigerate unless the weather is very hot. Stir every 2–3 days.
Strain through muslin, preferably, and discard the fruit pulp.
Bring the strained liquid to simmer point and simmer on low for 7–10 minutes.
Store in sterilised bottles capped by sterilised caps or corks. Refrigerate any vinegar not used after 2 months, or earlier if the weather is hot, just to be sure.

Harissa

Harissa is a hot chilli/red capsicum paste used in North African cooking. The paste doesn't need to be so hot it burns a hole in your throat; use large Chinese dried chillies, which are readily available and considerably milder than their smaller-sized cousins. The paste can be added to vinaigrettes, soups, casseroles, stews or dips. It will last for several weeks in the refrigerator and excess can be frozen — thus it is not strictly a preserve.

40 g large dried chillies (8–9 cm long)
1 tsp cumin seeds, toasted
2 cloves garlic, peeled and chopped
½ tsp salt or to taste
60 g roasted and peeled red capsicum*
50 ml olive oil

Chop the chillies roughly — instead of using a knife, try using sharp kitchen scissors. Place the chopped chillies in a bowl or jug and cover with warm water. Include the seeds, but use only half of them if you prefer a milder mix. Although
these large chillies are not nearly as fiery as the smaller variety, they do of course have some 'bite'.
Toast the cumin seeds in a dry frying pan, taking care not to scorch them. Cool, then grind in a mortar and pestle or crush finely with a knife.
Drain the chillies, reserving 50 ml of the soaking water. Process the drained chillies, the reserved soaking water and the garlic in a food processor until smooth.
Add the cumin seeds, salt and drained, roasted red capsicum and process again.
Slowly pour in the oil while the motor is running, and blend until smooth.
Transfer to a jar and store in the refrigerator.

*Roasted and peeled red capsicums are available in jars from supermarkets if you don't have time to prepare your own.

glossary

CHESTNUTS can be boiled, steamed or roasted but need to be peeled to remove the outer shell and the pellicle, or inner skin, which is bitter tasting.

A chestnut cutter is recommended to prepare the chestnuts for cooking, as it very easily cuts through the shell and pellicle, around the circumference of the raw nut, so that the two halves simply lift off. This leaves the raw meat whole and ready for any remaining pellicle to be shaved or snipped off. Boil or steam shelled nuts for 10 minutes or toast at 180°C for 10 minutes.

If a specialised cutter is not available, however, use garden secateurs to pierce the shell, or a sharp knife to cut a cross in the bottom of the chestnuts.

If cooking unshelled, either cover with water and simmer, covered, for about 15 minutes, covered or steam in a collapsible basket in a saucepan, covered, in about 2 cm water, also for about 15 minutes. Don't cook too many at a time as they are much easier to peel while still hot — keep them hot and cook in batches if necessary. A rubber glove on your left hand could be useful for holding the hot nuts while using a small sharp knife to peel with the other; or toast unshelled chestnuts at 180°C for 15–20 minutes before peeling.

FLORENCE FENNEL (bulb) can be quite easily grown from seed and is a useful and versatile vegetable, with a distinctive but very pleasant anise flavour. Florence fennel is an annual, unlike the common perennial that most people are familiar with (which is also very useful for its leaves, especially in salads); it's shorter, and is quite distinctive as its stem swells as it grows to form a 'bulb'. All parts of the plant can be eaten — the stems can be chopped and added to salads, as can the leaves — but the bulb is the prize.

Fennel bulbs can be harvested and eaten at all stages of their growth. Baby fennel bulbs are, like most 'baby' vegetables, tender, sweet, and delicious, especially if they are sautéed or roasted. One favourite combination is baby Florence fennel and baby beetroot, tossed with a little oil and seasoning and roasted together — the flavours complement each other perfectly.

HORSERADISH is a member of the mustard family, which explains why it is 'hot' — quite a different heat from chilli, though it contains similarly addictive qualities and is helpful for clearing the sinuses. Ground or grated horseradish is commonly mixed with vinegar to dilute its heat and produce various condiments, which may also contain spices or salt, sugar, cream or oil. The most common horseradish is a white root that is easy to cultivate and fast-growing.

KECAP MANIS is a thick, sweet soy sauce with a unique flavour. It is readily available from Asian supply stores.

LENTILS are inexpensive and quick-cooking; a pulse that contain high levels of protein and when eaten with grains provide a complete protein. They are available in many colours and forms — with or without skins, whole or split, and slightly different cooking times.

French green lentils or especially Puy lentils are highly regarded as they hold their shape better than most other varieties and have a less 'earthy' taste.

Puy lentils are arguably the crème de la crème of lentils, and also the most expensive, but are nevertheless a French green lentil — they come from a specific area in France: Auvergne.

ORANGE-BLOSSOM WATER is an extract from orange flowers that imparts the flavour of orange blossom but not citrus. Used extensively throughout the Middle East to enhance cooked fruits and fruit salads, as well as such dishes as lamb, chicken and rice dishes (just a few drops are sufficient).

PAPRIKA/SPANISH SMOKED PAPRIKA is a relatively benign spice or seasoning, an import known more for its colour than its flavour, whereas sweet (dulce) Spanish smoked paprika has a much deeper and definitively smoky flavour.

The name is protected by law in Spain, and it is an essential ingredient in many Mediterranean dishes. It is made from red capsicums of exceptional quality from a region in the southwest that enjoys a particularly favourable climate. The capsicums are picked at optimal ripeness and then infused with the smoke of smouldering oak logs to intensify their flavour while preserving their vibrant red colour. They are then ground repeatedly between stones until the powder is fine and has a unique silky texture.

Three different capsicums are used to produce this distinctive pepper spice — sweet, bittersweet and hot (picante). All are used to different effect, but if you just want to try one to start with, the dulce (sweet) is probably the one to buy.

POLENTA — it is fantastically satisfying to take a common, so-called 'peasant' food and transform it into something delicious. Polenta is a coarse-ground cornmeal, known as grits in the southern United States, where it is most often served as a kind of porridge; but it is also a staple of Italian cooking, where it is more imaginatively treated. Polenta is versatile, nutritious and inexpensive. Use either the regular or the instant polenta.

POTATOES contain only about 100 calories each but have excellent Vitamin C content, potassium, and of course fibre and carbohydrates.

There is some confusion about the terminology to describe which potatoes are suitable for which cooking purposes.

Floury — excellent for mashing, roasting, making chips or baking in their skins. They are also good in soups for thickening, as they tend to fall apart when boiled — they don't hold their shape as waxy potatoes do. When roasted or fried, as in chips, they cook with a crisp outer skin and a soft fluffy inside. Agria are a current favourite, with a hint of nuttiness in the flavour, smooth texture and golden flesh.

Waxy — ideal for boiling and holding their shape, but not for mashing (these are the ones that can turn to glue). Waxy potatoes are ideal for using in potato salads, or for scalloped potato dishes.

You can buy varieties described as all-purpose potatoes — but as the attributes of floury versus waxy are at completely different ends of the spectrum of cooking needs, this term is somewhat baffling — unless, of course, texture is of little importance to the dish.

PULSES (dried legumes) are cheap, versatile, sustaining and nutritious. They have a high protein content, especially when eaten with grains. They also contain carbohydrates and fibre, but are low in fat, and are important sources of some 'B' vitamins.

Pulses are available tinned, but these seem outrageously expensive compared to buying in bulk and cooking them yourself. You don't need a pressure cooker, but if you're likely to forget to soak them overnight, a pressure cooker certainly makes life a lot simpler, as there's no need to soak, and cooking time is usually more than halved. Cook in 3–4 times water to beans. Don't add salt until after pulses are cooked, as this can toughen the skins.

If cooking in a slow cooker, pulses must be soaked overnight and boiled for 10 minutes, as slow cooking does not reach the temperatures required to destroy some toxins. Cook more than you need at one time, as all pulses freeze well and defrost quickly. Pinto beans are not quite so 'earthy' as kidney beans, but either can be used in dishes such as chilli beans, refried beans or fritters for tasty, nutritious and inexpensive meals that can be prepared very quickly. Baby lima beans are great for adding to stews and soups, and of course we need chickpeas for making falafel, hummus and various salads as well as curry dishes, etc.

	Soak/Boil	*Pressure Cook*
Chickpeas	*2½ hours*	*30 minutes*
Pinto beans	*1½ hours*	*30 minutes*
Lima beans	*1 hour*	*25 minutes*
Kidney beans	*1¼ hours*	*25 minutes*
Split peas	*30 minutes*	*10–12 minutes*
Soya beans	*3 hours*	*50–55 minutes*

QUINOA is not strictly a grain, as it isn't a grass, but it has higher protein content than grains such as wheat and rice, and is more balanced in terms of nutrients. It is also gluten-free.

It makes a nice alternative to rice or couscous as it is distinctively different from either of these, with a light fluffy texture when cooked and a mild, faintly nutty flavour. Cook it as you would rice, in a two to one ratio of water to quinoa; in a saucepan on the stove, in a rice cooker or as you would a pilaf. When cooked, the germ separates from the seed so that it looks like a tiny curl and should have a slight bite to it, like al dente pasta. In its dried form it makes a high protein breakfast, served as you would cornflakes.

ROCKET is a wonderfully versatile herb and one of the easiest to grow throughout the year. Variously known as rucola, arugula and roquette, it is a member of the mustard family and has a distinctive peppery/nutty flavour. It is regarded as a 'bitter' green, which means, really, that it has a bit of an attitude in terms of taste; unique and even faintly addictive.

The most common form of rocket is the annual variety, which has leaves shaped rather like an oak leaf, whereas the perennial variety has an attractive, serrated leaf, is darker in colour and is more pungent in taste. The annual variety makes a delicious salad in its own right, but the perennial variety is most often combined with other greens because of its more robust flavour; the young leaves, though, are quite mild.

Both varieties are used primarily as a salad green, but they can also be added to hot dishes such as soups, sauces and pastas. When rocket is heated it loses most of its pungency, leaving a more subtle but still unique flavour.

SPICE MIX, RAS EL HANOUT — there's no one recipe for Ras el Hanout; it has been freely interpreted for generations, and apart from the fact that it almost always contains nutmeg, cinnamon and cloves, cumin and coriander, the number and quantities of ingredients vary wildly. In addition, whole spices are sometimes used and even roasted separately before grinding. In this very good, but simpler, version ground spices are used:

1 tsp nutmeg
½ tsp ground cloves
2 tsp turmeric
2 tsp cinnamon
1 Tbsp ground coriander
1 Tbsp ground cumin
2 tsp ground ginger
2 Tbsp paprika
½–1 tsp chilli powder
1 tsp whole fennel seeds, ground
1 tsp freshly ground black pepper

Combine thoroughly and keep in an airtight jar, in a cool dark place.

SZECHUAN PEPPERCORNS are not related to peppercorns at all, but are dried berries from a member of the citrus family, the prickly ash. The most prized part of the dried berry for culinary purposes is the husk, rather than the small black seeds inside. The husks are most commonly used lightly toasted and ground, as they can be unpleasantly grainy. Toast in a dry pan over medium heat until the colour darkens and their wonderful lemon fragrance is released. Grind thoroughly with a mortar and pestle. Szechuan peppercorns are not spicy or hot in themselves, but enhance the flavours of ginger, garlic, chilli etc.

STERILISING jars and lids for preserves such as chutneys, pickles and jams is simple but essential: fill clean jars with hot water, drain, place in oven at about 160°C for 10–15 minutes. Pour boiling water over the jar lids in a bowl, leave for 5 minutes while you fill the jars, drain the water from the lids and screw tightly onto jars. Don't place hot filled jars on stainless steel — a wooden board is safest.

SUMAC is a spice made from the berries of the Mediterranean sumac bush. The spice has a rich red/brown colour and a refreshing fruity tart flavour reminiscent of, but not as overpowering as, lemon, and is sometimes used on the table instead of salt.

TAHINI (sesame seed paste) is essential in many Middle-Eastern dishes and can be a healthy alternative to magarine spreads.

TAMARIND is a very important food ingredient of African origin but now commonly used throughout Asia, Latin America and the Pacific. Tamarind has a tart fruit flavour and is often used instead of lemon as a souring agent.

To make tamarind concentrate from block pulp:

Take 125 g from a block of tamarind pulp, available from any Asian food store. Break it up and soak in 1 cup of hot water for 15 minutes, breaking it up further as it soaks. Push it through a sieve and discard any leftover fibre and seeds. Measure the amount required and freeze the excess for future use.

An acceptable substitute to making your own concentrate is tamarind paste, available from Asian outlets (especially the Pantainorasingh brand).

WILD RICE is related to 'true' rice but is more grass-like. Most of the world's wild rice grows in water around the Great Lakes region of North America and is harvested by hand, mostly by the Ojibwe First Nations people. It has a pleasant chewy texture, a nutty flavour and cooks much more quickly than commercially produced wild rice grown in paddy fields, which is harder and denser.

VIETNAMESE MINT is really a Vietnamese coriander and is also known as laksa herb or laksa leaves. It has a definitive hot mint flavour and is indispensable to Vietnamese, Thai, Malaysian and Singaporean food. The leaves are delicious chopped on top of any noodle soup (including laksa) or any stir-fried meat or vegetable dish.

WASABI is also known as 'Japanese horseradish' and is a member of a plant family that includes both mustard and horseradish. Much of the wasabi paste sold in the West is in fact a mixture of horseradish, mustard and food colouring, rather than a paste made from the wasabi root itself, which is more expensive and has a much shorter shelf life.

index

Aïoli 44
Al fresco potato salad 117
apples
    Apple & cranberry custard pie 139
    Feijoa (or apple) coconut cake 123
    Tart Madeleine 137
    Tirami trifle (apple juice) 128
    Zucchini salad 115
apricots
    Apricot or persimmon kasundi 163
    Chewy chocolate chunk cookies 154
    Festive Moroccan couscous 111
artichokes
    Artichoke gratin 101
    Jerusalem artichoke soup 40
    Pizza 78
    Warm spinach & artichoke dip 8
arugula: *see* rocket
asparagus
    Asparagus combo 56
    Asparagus flan with cashew nut pastry 54
    Asparagus salad with lime, ginger, soy & sesame 95
    Tunis roast vegetables with chickpeas 90
aubergine: *see* eggplant
avocado
    Avocado hummus & jalapeno dip 9
    Black bean salsa/dip 13
    Green pea guacamole 22
    Spanish black bean soup 36

basil
    Asparagus flan with cashew nut pastry 54
    Briam 52
    Chickpea, zucchini & herb fritters 89
    Fast-lane lasagne 58
    Green sauce 43
    Herb mayo 46
    Layered eggplant Napoli 64
    Lentils 'n' thyme 96
    Mediterranean pasta salad 63
    Mexican chowder 33
    Mexican pumpkin pie 73
    Mushroom tapenade pasta with scorched cherry tomatoes 68
    Roast capsicum & tomato dip 25
    Stuffed red capsicums 60
    Summer picnic pie 80
    Tofu, lemon & herb lasagne 66
    Tomato pasta sauce 48
beans: dried (pulses) 183
    Beans & feta fritters 93
    Black bean salsa/dip 13
    Mexican mole 74
    Mexican pumpkin pie 73
    Smokin' beans 72
    Spanish black bean soup 36
    White bean pâté with smoked paprika & garlic topping 16
beans: green
    Asparagus (or bean) combo 56
    Mediterranean fava bean salad with sumac, mint & eggplant 110

    Quinoa salad with broad beans, mandarins, mint & sesame 98
    Sesame noodles with seared tofu 83
    Szechuan 'clay pot' casserole 82
    Tuscan broad beans 118
beetroot
    Beetroot & fennel pesto 15
    Borscht with kumara & fennel 37
    Brazen beetroot soup 35
    Fresh beetroot relish 27
    Glazed beetroot salad 112
berries: dried
    Apple & cranberry custard pie 139
    Christmas heaven cake 157
    Festive Moroccan couscous 111
    Kiwi cassata 141
berries: fresh
    Berry cups 142
    Black raspberry vinegar 179
    Blackberry pie 143
    Raspberry sorbet 132
    Rhubarb & raspberry muffins 148
    Rhubarb & strawberry pie 140
    Rum pot 178
Bev's feijoas in pink wine syrup 135
biscuits/cookies
    Brownie biscuits 152
    Chewy chocolate chunk cookies 154
    Spiced gingernuts 153
Black bean salsa/dip 13
Black raspberry vinaigrette 43
Black raspberry vinegar 179
Blackberry pie 143
Borscht with kumara & fennel 37
Brazen beetroot soup 35
bread
    Herb foccacia 145
    Wild rice & pumpkin seed bread 147
Briam 52
Brinjal 160
Brown & wild rice with roast lemon 116
Brown rice & seaweed salad 102
Brownie biscuits 152
brûlée: Citrus crème brûlée 121
Burghul, couscous or quinoa tabouleh 98

Café gingerbread 146
cakes
    Chocolate feijoa cake 129
    Christmas heaven cake 157
    Feijoa (or apple) coconut cake 123
    Kingston cake with grilled mandarins 130
    Sachertorte 138
    Venus cake 133
capsicums (peppers)
    Al fresco potato salad 117
    Briam 52
    Capsicum pizza base sauce 78
    Corn & coriander fritters 92
    Harissa 180
    Malai kofta 86
    Mexican chowder 33

Mexican mole 74
Party muffins 22
Piperade 108
Pizza 78
Red capsicum & lime marmalata 173
Rice paper salad rolls with satay dipping sauce 20
Roast capsicum & almond sauce 50
Roast capsicum & tomato dip 25
Sesame noodles with seared tofu 83
Smoke & lime feijoa chutney 162
Smokin' beans 72
Spanish black bean soup 36
Stuffed red capsicums 60
Summer picnic pie 80
Tunis roast vegetables with chickpeas 90
Tuscan tart 81
Caramelised balsamic vinegar 45
Caramelised onion confit 171
Caramelised shallot tarte tatin 69
Caramelised tomatoes 112
Cardrona chew 155
carrot
    Sahara carrot sauté 97
    Venus cake 133
Cauliflower & almond curry 88
Cheese & olive sticks 19
cheeses
    blue vein
        Pasta with spinach, cherry tomatoes
           & creamy blue sauce 70
        Pizza (cheese topping) 79
    Camembert
        Whole mushrooms en croûte 67
    Cheddar
        Artichoke gratin 101
        Cheese & olive sticks 19
        Chickpea, zucchini & herb fritters 89
        Corn & coriander fritters 92
        Crisped polenta 65
        Light wholemeal shortcrust pastry 150
        Mexican pumpkin pie 73
        Party muffins 22
        Polenta primo 71
        Tofu, lemon & herb lasagne 66
        Warm spinach & artichoke dip 8
    cottage
        Diva chocolate cheesecake
           with chocolate sauce 124
        Fast-lane lasagne 58
        Layered eggplant Napoli 64
        Malai kofta 86
        Mexican pumpkin pie 73
        Stuffed red capsicums 60
        Tofu, lemon & herb lasagne 66
    cream
        Diva chocolate cheesecake
           with chocolate sauce 124
        Mexican chowder 33
        Mushroom crème soup 30
        Stuffed red capsicums 60
        Tirami trifle 128
        Warm spinach & artichoke dip 8

feta
    Bean & feta fritters 93
    Fast-lane lasagne 58
    Feta & Rosemary baked figs 23
    Layered eggplant Napoli 64
    Mediterranean pasta salad 63
    Party muffins 22
    Pizza (cheese topping) 79
    Roast kumara, nut & feta salad
        with raspberry vinaigrette 105
    Stuffed red capsicums 60
    Summer picnic pie 80
    Tofu, lemon & herb lasagne 66
    Tuscan tart 81
haloumi
    Herbed haloumi 23
    Mediterranean pasta salad 63
mozzarella
    Fast-lane lasagne 58
    Layered eggplant Napoli 64
    Mushroom galette 57
    Polenta primo 71
    Tofu, lemon & herb lasagne 66
    Warm spinach & artichoke dip 8
Parmesan
    Asparagus flan with cashew nut pastry 54
    Crisped polenta 65
    Fast-lane lasagne 58
    Layered eggplant Napoli 64
    Pasta with spinach, cherry tomatoes
        & creamy blue sauce 70
    Rocket pesto 17
    Tofu, lemon & herb lasagne 66
    Whole mushroom en croûte 67
ricotta
    Fast-lane lasagne 58
    Stuffed red capsicums 60
yoghurt
    Garlic & dill labna 24
    Labna (yoghurt cheese) 24
cheesecake: Diva chocolate cheesecake
    with chocolate sauce 124
Chermoula 46
cherries
    Roast cherries with rum 122
    Rum pot 178
chestnuts, preparation & cooking of 181
    Pumpkin & chestnut soup 38
Chewy chocolate chunk cookies 154
chickpeas (garbanzo beans), cooking 183
    Avocado hummus & jalapeno dip 9
    Chickpea, zucchini & herb fritters 89
    Falafel 77
    Madras chickpeas, eggplant & spinach 85
    Tunis roast vegetables with chickpeas 90
chillies: Harissa 180
chocolate
    Chewy chocolate chunk cookies 154
    Chocolate feijoa cake 129
    Christmas heaven cake 157
    Diva chocolate cheesecake with chocolate sauce 124
    Kiwi cassata 141

    Mexican mole 74
    Sachertorte 138
    Whisky & chocolate ice cream 127
Christmas heaven cake 157
chutneys/preserves
    Brinjal (chutney) 160
    Caramelised onion confit 171
    Oscar's favourite Sri Lankan chutney 169
    Persimmon, tamarind & date chutney 167
    Plum chutney with sumac & cinnamon 159
    Puliyini (tamarind prune chutney) 170
    Smoke & lime feijoa chutney 162
    Spiced banana chutney 161
    Tamarillo, prune & tamarind chutney 166
Citrus crème brûlée 121
Cocktail mushrooms 21
coriander (cilantro)
    Al fresco potato salad 117
    Black bean salsa dip 13
    Chermoula 46
    Chickpea, zucchini & herb fritters 92
    Coriander, mint & cashew pesto 14
    Corn & coriander fritters 92
    Rice paper salad rolls with satay dipping sauce 20
    Roast capsicum & tomato dip 25
    Tamarind mint sambal 48
    Tomatillo salsa dip 10
    Yoghurt sauce/dressing 49
corn
    Corn & coriander fritters 92
    Mexican chowder 33
courgettes: *see* zucchini
couscous
    Burghul, couscous or quinoa tabouleh 98
    Festive Moroccan couscous 111
Creamed parsnip & leek with toasted cumin seeds 109
Crisped polenta 65
curries
    Cauliflower & almond curry 88
    Curried okra 106
    Madras chickpeas, eggplant & spinach 85
    Malai kofta 86
    Saag 84
    Thai pumpkin soup 29

dates: Persimmon, tamarind & date chutney 167
Dhal (yellow split pea) 119
dips & salsas
    Avocado hummus & jalapeno dip 9
    Black bean salsa/dip 13
    Last-minute tomato salsa/dip 12
    Melitzanosalata: Greek eggplant dip 11
    Roast capsicum & tomato dip 25
    Tomatillo salsa/dip 10
dressings: *see also* vinaigrettes
    Aïoli 44
    Chermoula 46
    Green sauce 43
    Herb mayo 46
    Paul's tropical dressing 49
    Summer mayo 45
    Yoghurt sauce/dressing 49

eggplant
    Briam 52
    Brinjal (chutney) 160
    Eggplant salad with yoghurt mint dressing 100
    Layered eggplant Napoli 64
    Madras chickpeas, eggplant & spinach 85
    Mediterranean fava bean salad
        with sumac, mint & eggplant 110
    Melitzanosalata: Greek eggplant dip 11
    Mexican mole 74
    Moroccan spice & honey eggplant 114
    Roast eggplant & pomegranate
        with tzatziki-style dressing 104
    Spanish black bean soup 36
    Summer picnic pie 80
    Szechuan 'clay pot' casserole 82
    Tunis roast vegetables with chickpeas 90
Everyday zucchini pickle 165

Falafel 77
Fast-lane lasagne 58
feijoas
    Bev's feijoas in pink wine syrup 135
    Chocolate feijoa cake 129
    Feijoa (or apple) coconut cake 123
    Rhubarb & feijoa pie 126
    Smoke & lime feijoa chutney 162
fennel
    Apricot or persimmon kasundi 163
    Beetroot & fennel pesto 15
    Borscht with kumara & fennel 37
    Briam 52
    Florence fennel & pea salad 103
    Mango, fennel & watercress salad 100
    Rock melon or mango salad with Asian dressing 107
Feta & rosemary baked figs 23
Festive Moroccan couscous 111
figs
    Feta & rosemary baked figs 23
    Fig & nut meringue torte 131
    Sticky figs 164
flans: *see also* pies, tarts & galette
    Asparagus flan with cashew nut pastry 54
    Pear & lemon flan 122
Florence fennel & pea salad 103
Fresh beetroot relish 27
fritters
    Bean & feta fritters 93
    Chickpea, zucchini & herb fritters 89
    Corn & coriander fritters 92
    Kumara fritters with toasted cumin 91

galette: Mushroom galette 57
garlic
    Garlic & dill labna 24
    White bean pâté
        with smoked paprika & garlic topping 16
    Roast eggplant & pomegranate
        with tzatziki-style dressing 104
Ginger plum conserve 176
Glazed beetroot salad 112
Green pea guacamole 22

Green sauce 43
Grilled mandarins 131
Gula melaka 136

Harissa 180
Herb foccacia 145
Herb mayo 46
Herbed haloumi 23
Home-made vegetable stock 29

ice cream
    Basic ice cream with five flavours 127
    Kiwi cassata 141

Jerusalem artichokes
    Artichoke gratin 101
    Jerusalem artichoke soup 40

kaffir limes
    Smoke & lime feijoa chutney 162
    Red capsicum & lime marmalata 173
kasundi: Apricot or persimmon kasundi 163
Kingston cake with grilled mandarins 130
Kiwi cassata 141
Kiwifruit marmalade 174
kumara
    Borscht with kumara & fennel 37
    Kumara fritters with toasted cumin 91
    Mexican chowder 33
    Mushroom crème soup 30
    Roast kumara, nut & feta salad
        with raspberry vinaigrette 105
    Spiced banana chutney 161
    Tunis roast vegetables with chickpeas 90

Labna (yoghurt cheese) 24
    Garlic & dill labna 24
Last-minute tomato salsa/dip 12
Layered eggplant Napoli 64
leeks
    Creamed parsnip & leek with toasted cumin seeds 109
    Leek 'n' lentil soup 32
    Jerusalem artichoke soup 40
    Tofu, lemon & herb lasagne 66
lemons
    Brown & wild rice with roast lemon 116
    Chermoula 46
    Citrus crème brûlée 121
    Limoncello 177
    Pear & lemon flan 122
    Preserved lemons 168
    Tart Madeleine 137
    Tofu, lemon & herb lasagne 66
lentils 181–182
    Leek 'n' lentil soup 32
    Lentil, caper & olive salad 95
    Lentils 'n' thyme 96
    Mediterranean fava bean salad
        with sumac, mint & eggplant 110
    Pumpkin & lentil soup 41
    Tomato tamarind dhal soup 34
Life's-too-short marmalade 175

Light wholemeal shortcrust pastry 150
limes: *see also* kaffir limes
    Asparagus salad with lime, ginger, soy & sesame 95
    Citrus crème brûlée 121
    Kiwifruit marmalade 174
    Mango, fennel & watercress salad 100
    Tuscan broad beans 118
Limoncello 177

Macerated tamarillos 132
Madras chickpeas, eggplant & spinach 85
Malai kofta 86
mandarins
    Grilled mandarins 131
    Kingston cake with grilled mandarins 130
    Quinoa salad with broad beans, mandarins,
        mint & sesame 98
    Sweet clementines 135
mango
    Mango, fennel & watercress salad 100
    Rock melon or mango salad
        with Asian dressing 107
marmalade
    Kiwifruit marmalade 174
    Life's-too-short marmalade 175
    Red capsicum & lime marmalata 173
    Tart Madeleine 137
Mediterranean fava bean salad
    with sumac, mint & eggplant 110
Mediterranean pasta salad 63
Melitzanosalata: Greek eggplant dip 11
Mexican chowder 33
Mexican mole 74
Mexican pumpkin pie 73
mint
    Burghul, couscous or quinoa tabouleh 98
    Chermoula 46
    Coriander, mint & cashew pesto 14
    Eggplant salad with yoghurt mint dressing 100
    Fresh beetroot relish 27
    Malai kofta (sauce) 87
    Mediterranean fava bean salad
        with sumac, mint & eggplant 110
    Mint & almond pesto 12
    Quinoa salad with broad beans, mandarins,
        mint & sesame 98
    Tamarind mint sambal 48
Moroccan spice & honey eggplant 114
Moroccan tomato soup with Ras el Hanout 31
muffins
    Party muffins 22
    Rhubarb & raspberry muffins 148
mushrooms
    Cocktail mushrooms 21
    Fast-lane lasagne 58
    Mediterranean pasta salad 63
    Mushroom crème soup 30
    Mushroom galette 57
    Mushroom risotto 76
    Mushroom tapenade pasta
        with scorched cherry tomatoes 68
    Orzo, mushroom & thyme 62

Szechuan 'clay pot' casserole 82
Whole mushrooms en croûte 67

okra: Curried okra 106
olives
    Cheese & olive sticks 19
    Lentil, caper & olive salad 95
    Mushroom tapenade pasta
        with scorched cherry tomatoes 68
    Olive & prune tapenade 14
    Tuscan tart 81
onions: Caramelised onion confit 171
oranges
    Kingston cake with grilled mandarins 130
    Life's-too-short marmalade 175
    Venus cake 133
Oscar's favourite Sri Lankan chutney 169
Orzo, mushroom & thyme 62

pannacotta: Orange blossom pannacotta with sweet clementines 134
parsnip
    Creamed parsnip & leek
        with toasted cumin seeds 109
    Jerusalem artichoke soup 40
    Parsnip soup with saffron & spice 39
pasta
    Asparagus combo 56
    Fast-lane lasagne 58
    Mediterranean pasta salad 63
    Mushroom tapenade pasta
        with scorched cherry tomatoes 68
    Orzo, mushroom & thyme 62
    Pasta with spinach, cherry tomatoes &
        creamy blue sauce 70
    Sesame noodles with seared tofu 83
    Tofu, lemon & herb lasagne 66
pastry: *see also* flans, pies, tarts & galette
    Cashew nut pastry 150
    Light wholemeal shortcrust pastry with semolina 150
    Sweet shortcrust pastry with semolina 152
    Tuscan pastry 151
    Whole mushrooms en croûte 67
    Yoghurt pastry 151
Party muffins 22
Paul's tropical dressing 49
peanuts
    Real peanut butter 26
    Satay sauce 47
Pear & lemon flan 122
peas
    Brown rice & seaweed salad 102
    Florence fennel & pea salad 103
    Green pea guacamole 22
persimmon
    Apricot or persimmon kasundi 163
    Persimmon spice cake 156
    Persimmon, tamarind & date chutney 167
pesto
    Beetroot & fennel pesto 15
    Coriander, mint & cashew pesto 14
    Mint & almond pesto 12

    Rocket pesto 17
pickle: Everyday zucchini pickle 165
pies: *see also* tarts, flans & galette
    Apple & cranberry custard pie 139
    Blackberry pie 143
    Mexican pumpkin pie 73
    Rhubarb & feijoa pie 126
    Rhubarb & strawberry pie 140
    Summer picnic pie 80
    Whole mushrooms en croûte 67
Piperade 108
Pizza 78
plums
    Ginger plum conserve 176
    Plum chutney with sumac & cinnamon 159
    Rum pot 178
polenta 182; *see also* cornmeal (fine polenta)
    Crisped polenta 65
    Polenta primo 71
pomegranate: Roast eggplant & pomegranate with tzatziki-style dressing 104
pomegranate molasses
    Café gingerbread 146
    Moroccan spice & honey eggplant 114
    Roast pumpkin with pomegranate molasses 115
Portuguese custard tarts 149
potatoes 182
    Al fresco potato salad 117
    Asparagus combo 56
    Briam 52
    Cauliflower & almond curry 88
    Mexican chowder 33
    Spicy wedges 113
Preserved lemons 168
prunes
    Christmas heaven cake 157
    Olive & prune tapenade 14
    Puliyini (tamarind prune chutney) 170
    Tamarillo, prune & tamarind chutney 166
Puliyini (tamarind prune chutney) 170
pulses 183; *see also* beans & lentils
pumpkin
    Mexican pumpkin pie 73
    Pumpkin & chestnut soup 38
    Pumpkin & lentil soup 41
    Roast pumpkin with pomegranate molasses 115
    Thai pumpkin soup 29
pumpkin seeds
    Brown & wild rice with roast lemon 116
    Brown rice & seaweed salad 102
    Roast pepitas 18
    Wild rice & pumpkin seed bread 147

Quince paste 172
quinoa 183
    Burghul, couscous or quinoa tabouleh 98
    Quinoa salad with broad beans, mandarins, mint & sesame 98

Ras el Hanout 184
raspberries
    Berry cups 142

Black raspberry vinaigrette 43
Black raspberry vinegar 179
Raspberry sorbet 132
Rhubarb & raspberry muffins 148
Roast kumara, nut & feta salad
   with raspberry vinaigrette 105
Rum pot 178
Real peanut butter 26
Red capsicum & lime marmalata 173
relish: Fresh beetroot relish 27
rhubarb
   Rhubarb & feijoa pie 126
   Rhubarb & raspberry muffins 148
   Rhubarb & strawberry pie 140
rice: wild rice 185
   Brown rice & seaweed salad 102
   Brown & wild rice with roast lemon 116
   Mushroom risotto 76
   Wild rice & pumpkin seed bread 147
Rice paper salad rolls with satay dipping sauce 20
Roast capsicum & almond sauce 50
Roast capsicum & tomato dip 25
Roast capsicum soup 42
Roast cherries with rum 122
Roast eggplant & pomegranate
   with tzatziki-style dressing 104
Roast kumara, nut & feta salad
   with raspberry vinaigrette 105
Roast pepitas 18
Roast pumpkin with pomegranate molasses 115
Rock melon or mango salad with Asian dressing 107
rocket (roquette) 183
   Florence fennel & pea salad 103
   Mexican pumpkin pie 73
   Pizza (toppings) 79
   Roast kumara, nut & feta salad
      with raspberry vinaigrette 105
   Rock melon or mango salad
      with Asian dressing 107
   Rocket pesto 17
   Tuscan tart (topping) 81
Rum pot 178

Saag 84
Sachertorte 138
saffron
   Crisped polenta 65
   Festive Moroccan couscous 111
   Parsnip soup with saffron & spice 39
Sahara carrot sauté 97
salads
   Al fresco potato salad 117
   Asparagus salad with lime, ginger, soy & sesame 95
   Brown & wild rice with roast lemon 116
   Brown rice & seaweed salad 102
   Burghul, couscous or quinoa tabouleh 98
   Eggplant salad with yoghurt mint dressing 100
   Florence fennel & pea salad 103
   Glazed beetroot salad 112
   Lentil, caper & olive salad 95
   Lentils 'n' thyme 96
   Mango, fennel & watercress salad 100
   Mediterranean fava bean salad
      with sumac, mint & eggplant 110
   Quinoa salad with broad beans, mandarin,
      mint & sesame 98
   Roast eggplant & pomegranate
      with tzatziki-style dressing 104
   Roast kumara, nut & feta salad
      with raspberry vinaigrette 105
   Rock melon or mango salad with Asian dressing 107
   Zucchini salad 115
salsas: *see* dips
sambal: *see also* chutneys & relish
   Tamarind mint sambal 48
Satay sauce 47
sauces
   Chocolate sauce 124
   Citrus sauce 133
   Green sauce 43
   Roast capsicum & almond sauce 50
   Satay sauce 47
   Tomato pasta sauce 48
   Yoghurt sauce/dressing 49
seaweed (nori): Brown rice & seaweed salad 102
sesame oil & seeds *see also* tahini
   Asparagus salad with lime, ginger, soy & sesame 95
   Brown rice & seaweed salad 102
   Sesame noodles with seared tofu 83
   Quinoa salad with broad beans, mandarins,
      mint & sesame 98
Smoke & lime feijoa chutney 162
Smokin' beans 72
sorbet: Raspberry sorbet 132
soups
   Borscht with kumara & fennel 37
   Brazen beetroot soup 35
   Home-made vegetable stock 29
   Jerusalem artichoke soup 40
   Leek 'n' lentil soup 32
   Mexican chowder 33
   Moroccan tomato soup with Ras el Hanout 31
   Mushroom crème soup 30
   Parsnip soup with saffron & spice 39
   Pumpkin & chestnut soup 38
   Pumpkin & lentil soup 41
   Roast capsicum soup 42
   Spanish black bean soup 36
   Thai pumpkin soup 29
   Tomato tamarind dhal soup 34
   Spanish black bean soup 36
Spiced banana chutney 161
Spiced gingernuts 153
Spicy wedges 113
spinach
   Fast-lane lasagne 58
   Madras chickpeas, eggplant & spinach 85
   Malai kofta 86
   Pasta with spinach, cherry tomatoes & creamy
      blue sauce 70
   Pizza (topping) 79
   Saag 84
   Stuffed red capsicums 60
   Tofu, lemon & herb lasagne 66

Warm spinach & artichoke dip 8
Sticky figs 164
strawberries
    Rhubarb & strawberry pie 140
    Rum pot 178
sterilising jars (for preserves) 184
stock: Home-made vegetable stock 29
Stuffed red capsicums 60
sumac 184
    Chickpea, zucchini & herb fritters 89
    Herbed haloumi 23
    Mediterranean fava bean salad 110
    Plum chutney with sumac & cinnamon 159
Summer mayo 45
Summer picnic pie 80
Sweet clementines 135
sweet potato: *see* kumara
Sweet shortcrust pastry with semolina 152
Szechuan 'clay pot' casserole 82
Szechuan peppercorns 184

tabouleh: Burghul, couscous or quinoa tabouleh 98
tahini (sesame paste) 185
    Avocado hummus & jalapeno dip 9
    Melitzanosalata: Greek eggplant dip 11
    White bean pâté with smoked paprika
      & garlic topping 16
tamarillos
    Macerated tamarillos 132
    Tamarillo, prune & tamarind chutney 166
tamarind 185
    Brinjal (chutney) 160
    Persimmon, tamarind & date chutney 167
    Puliyini (tamarind prune chutney) 170
    Satay sauce 47
    Tamarillo, prune & tamarind chutney 166
    Tamarind mint sambal 48
    Tomato tamarind dhal soup 34
tarts: *see also* flans, pies & galette
    Caramelised shallot tarte tatin 69
    Portuguese custard tarts 149
    Tart Madeleine 137
    Tuscan tart 81
Thai pumpkin soup 29
trifle: Tirami trifle 128
tofu
    Saag (spinach curry) 84
    Sesame noodles with seared tofu 83
    Szechuan 'clay pot' casserole 82
    Tofu, lemon & herb lasagne 66
Tomatillo salsa/dip 10
tomatoes
    Black bean salsa dip 13
    Brazen beetroot soup 35
    Briam 52
    Brinjal 160
    Caramelised tomatoes 112
    Last-minute tomato salsa/dip 12
    Madras chickpeas, eggplant & spinach 85
    Mexican mole 74
    Moroccan tomato soup with Ras el Hanout 31
    Mushroom galette 57

    Mushroom tapenade pasta
      with scorched cherry tomatoes 68
    Pasta with spinach, cherry tomatoes &
      creamy blue sauce 70
    Roast capsicum & almond sauce 50
    Roast capsicum & tomato dip 25
    Roast capsicum soup 42
    Smokin' beans 72
    Spanish black bean soup 36
    Tomato tamarind dhal soup 34
Tunis roast vegetables with chickpeas 90
Tuscan broad beans 118
Tuscan pastry 151
Tuscan tart 81

Vegetable stock, home-made 29
Venus cake 133
Vietnamese mint 185
vinegar
    Black raspberry vinegar 179
    Caramelised balsamic vinegar 45
vinaigrette
    Black raspberry vinaigrette 43
    Honey cider vinaigrette 44

walnuts
    Apple & cranberry custard pie 139
    Pasta with spinach, cherry tomatoes
      & creamy blue sauce 70
    Roast kumara, nut & feta salad
      with raspberry vinaigrette 105
    Sachertorte 138
    Sticky figs 164
Warm spinach & artichoke dip 8
wasabi 185
wedges: Spicy wedges 113
White bean pâté with smoked paprika
    & garlic topping 16
Whole mushrooms en croûte 67
wild rice 185; *see also* rice
Wild rice & pumpkin seeds bread 147

yoghurt
    Labna (yoghurt cheese) 24
    Orange blossom pannacotta
      with sweet clementines 134
    Tzatziki-style dressing 104
    Yoghurt mint dressing 101
    Yoghurt pastry 151
    Yoghurt sauce/dressing 49

zucchini
    Asparagus flan with cashew nut pastry 54
    Briam 52
    Chickpea, zucchini & herb fritters 89
    Everyday zucchini pickle 165
    Fast-lane lasagne 58
    Party muffins 22
    Pizza topping 79
    Sesame noodles with seared tofu 83
    Summer picnic pie 80
    Zucchini salad 115